THE OKINAWA PROBLEM

THE
OKINAWA
PROBLEM

A chapter in Japan-U.S. relations

AKIO WATANABE

Lecturer in History
University of Hong Kong

MELBOURNE UNIVERSITY PRESS

First published 1970

Printed in Australia by
Wilke and Company Limited, Clayton, Victoria 3168, for
Melbourne University Press, Carlton, Victoria 3053
Great Britain and Europe: ISBS Inc., London
USA and Canada: ISBS Inc., Zion, Illinois 60099

Registered in Australia for transmission by post as a book

ISBN 0 522 84000 0
Dewey Decimal Classification No. 952.81

To the memory of my father,

Masao Watanabe

Preface

The Okinawa problem is a matter of concern to many who are seriously interested in contemporary Japan. It has received little publicity outside Japan, although a great deal has already been written on it in Japanese. Indeed, as the chapter on the Japanese press in this book suggests, Okinawa has been occupying public attention in Japan for many years. Most of the literature on Okinawa is, however, polemical rather than analytical, journalistic rather than academic. As a result, there is a lack of detached or comprehensive treatments of the subject. In fact, hardly any analytical study has been made on one particular aspect of the problem—the formation of Japanese attitudes towards Okinawa and their bearing on relations between the United States and Japan.

This book has been designed to make a contribution to the study of international conflicts. The Okinawa problem is not a major conflict likely to lead to armed hostilities between the states. It has never assumed a particularly serious character. Neither side of the dispute has ever thought of recourse to arms. It is rather a sort of intra-alliance conflict which can, unless skilfully handled, create serious obstacles to lasting collaboration between the states in alliance. It is in this fashion that Okinawa poses problems to political leaders of the countries concerned and to students of international politics.

It is not hard to delineate the problem in terms of the international factors affecting it. The number of entities involved is very limited: Japan, the United States and Okinawa. In spite of the efforts of some elements to 'internationalize' the issue, the United States and Japan have been successful in limiting the problem to themselves alone. Outsiders—national or international—can intervene only indirectly, by attempting to influence 'insiders' in their relations with each other. Thus the matter depends almost entirely on the development of relations between the two allies, which in its turn depends upon various forces at work in Japan and the United States on the relationship existing between their countries. In this sense it may be said that the Okinawa problem, rather than being a conflict between the Japanese and the United States governments, is actually a conflict between the Japanese and the United States governments on the one hand and those who are critical in one way or another of their alliance (or of the place given to Okinawa therein) on the other.

Theoretically, such criticism can come from either direction, that is either from within Japan (including Okinawa) or from within the United States. In fact, however, a solution of the Okinawa problem was demanded primarily and overwhelmingly by anti-alliance forces in Japan and, of course, in Okinawa. This fact, among others, compelled the author to give attention, rather one-sidedly, to the Japanese side.

The book consists of two parts. Part One is composed of a chapter outlining the historical relations between Japan and Okinawa and of four chapters describing the sequence of important events over the past twenty-five years. Efforts were made to relate the development of the Okinawa problem to that of the overall relationship between the United States and Japan.

The next six chapters (comprising Part Two) are devoted to a cross-sectional analysis of various forces at work in Japan. Attitudes of government departments, the parliament, political parties, pressure groups and the press are analysed in detail. In all, they are intended to be an anatomy of contemporary Japanese politics as related to a particular issue. The Conclusion is an attempt to deduce some lessons by comparing the Okinawa problem with another conflict of a similar type—that between France and Germany over the Saar after World War II.

This study was originally written in 1966 as a thesis to fulfil the requirements of the degree of Doctor of Philosophy at the Department of International Relations, School of Pacific Studies, Institute of Advanced Studies, in the Australian National University. It has subsequently been revised so that more recent data may be included, and an introductory chapter has been added to provide the historical background. The basic structure of the original thesis remains, however, unchanged.

My primary thanks go to my supervisor, Mr D. G. S. Sissons, for his constant encouragement and constructive criticism. I am also

Preface

indebted to Dr G. Modelski who shared the supervision of the thesis especially in its initial stage, and to Dr J. A. A. Stockwin who has always been helpful to me both in academic and personal matters since the beginning of our friendship which started in Tokyo in the spring of 1962.

The collection of material for this study was greatly facilitated by a number of people who were kind enough to spare me their time and supply information. Although I shall refrain from making a long list of their names hereunder, I should like to express my sincere gratitude for their kindness.

I am further indebted to the *Okinawa Shiryō Sentā,* Tokyo, and the University of Ryukyus, the Library of the Legislative Assembly of the Government of the Ryukyu Islands and the Naha Public Library where I found much useful material on the subject. The Prime Minister's Office of the Japanese Government, the *Nampō Dōhō Engokai,* and the United States Civil Administration of the Ryukyu Islands (USCAR) were also generous in providing me with materials. The Australian National University kindly granted the necessary expenses for my visit to Okinawa in March 1963. My second visit to Okinawa in the summer of 1968 was subsidized by the Centre of Asian Studies in the University of Hong Kong.

Some Okinawan scholars greatly helped me either through their writings in various journals or by personal correspondence. Among them are Professor Higa Mikio and Professor Miyasato Seigen in the University of the Ryukyus. Professor H. Passin at the Columbia University read my original MS. and made many useful suggestions. Mrs Joan McGee and Mrs Janet Bennett kindly helped me in removing the Japanese flavour from my English style. I received assistance from Dr T. G. McGee of the Department of Geography at the University of Hong Kong in preparing maps.

Had it not been for the assistance of these and others, I should not have been able to complete this book. It goes without saying, however, that the responsibility for any deficiency rests entirely upon me.

A.W.

Hong Kong January 1970

Since the MS. was finished there have been some new developments concerning Okinawa. The term of the U.S.-Japan Security Treaty expired in June 1970. The Japanese government decided, as was expected, on its continuation. Despite some street demonstrations, mainly by radical student groups, the protests against the Treaty were not comparable to those of 1960. It would be too hasty, however, to think that the Treaty has become a dead issue. Problems of the Treaty, including Okinawa's connection with it, may well become an important political question in Japan in the near future.

Another development which deserves mention here is the first election for Okinawan representatives in the Japanese Diet. A Bill was passed on 24 April 1970 by the Diet to permit the Okinawans to elect five representatives for the Lower House and two for the Upper House. The results of the elections (conducted on 8 November 1970) were: in the Lower House, the Liberal Democrats won two seats and 43.6 per cent of the total vote, and the Opposition groups won three seats and 46.3 per cent of the vote (the latter included OPP's candidate, Senaga Kamejirō, who gained the second-largest vote); the two seats for the Upper House were won by Kiyammu Shinei, chairman of the Council for the Return of Okinawa Prefecture to the Fatherland, who was supported by the three Opposition parties, and a Liberal Democratic candidate (they gained 49.8 per cent and 45.4 per cent of the vote respectively).

By the time this book is published, some of its account will inevitably have become out of date. It is, however, the author's belief that the book, as an historical study of American-Japanese relations, assists the understanding of the Okinawa problem in a proper historical perspective.

December 1970   A.W.

Author's Note

Japanese personal names are written in the original order, i.e. with the surname first and the given name second (e.g. Yoshida Shigeru).

Names of bodies, official or non-official, are used in the original form, accompanied on their first appearance in the text by their English translation: e.g. the Prime Minister's Office *(Sōrifu)* and the Okinawan Federation *(Okinawajin Remmei)*. The original spelling of American institutions is always maintained, for example Department of Defense.

Japanese geographical names are given in their original form except in quotations from English. Thus, for example, Chishima, Karafuto, Ogasawara are used instead of the Kuriles, Sakhalin, the Bonins. 'The Ryukyu Islands' (or 'the Ryukyus') and 'Okinawa' are used in this book interchangeably although in a strict sense the former is used to designate the whole islands of the archipelago while the latter refers to the main island in it.

In citing Japanese material, original titles are romanized without an English translation. Distinction should be made, for instance, between the *Okinawa Taimusu* (in Japanese) and the *Okinawa Times* (in English).

Length marks (⁻) are omitted when referring to very common proper nouns, such as Tokyo, Osaka.

Contents

Abbreviations

ACLU	American Civil Liberties Union
DSP	Democratic Socialist Party *(Minshu Shakaitō)*
GHQ	General Headquarters of the Allied Forces in Tokyo
GRI	Government of the Ryukyu Islands *(Ryūkyū Seifu)*
JCLU	Japan Civil Liberties Union
JCP	Japan Communist Party *(Nihon Kyōsantō)*
JSP	Japan Socialist Party *(Nihon Shakaitō)*
LDP	Liberal Democratic Party *(Jiyū Minshutō)*
OLDP	Okinawa Liberal Democratic Party *(Okinawa Jiyū Minshutō)*
OPP	Okinawa People's Party *(Okinawa Jimmintō)*
OSMP	Okinawa Socialist Masses Party *(Okinawa Shakai Taishūtō)*
OSP	Okinawa Socialist Party *(Okinawa Shakaitō)*
SCAP	Supreme Command for Allied Powers
USCAR	United States Civil Administration of the Ryukyu Islands

Glossary

Chifuren (Zenkoku Chiiki Fujindantai Renraku Kyōgikai)
Federation of Regional Women's Societies
Chishima
Kurile Islands
Fukkikyō (Okinawa-Ken Sokoku Fukki Kyōgikai)
Council for the Return of Okinawa Prefecture to the Fatherland
Gaimushō
Ministry of Foreign Affairs of the Japanese government
Guntō (lit. archipelago)
Administrative units set up by the American authorities in the
Ryukyus in the post-war period. The whole area of the American-
held Ryukyus was divided for that purpose into four groups (i.e.
Amami-Oshima, Okinawa, Miyako and Yaeyama), each of which
was called *guntō* (e.g. Okinawa *Guntō*)
Hōmushō
Ministry of Judicial Affairs of the Japanese government
Hōkoku Okinawa Kyōkai
Patriotic Okinawan Society
Jichishō
Ministry of Local Government of the Japanese government
Karafuto
Sakhalin
Kiseikai (Okinawashotō Nihon Fukki Kiseikai)
Association for the Realization of the Return of the Okinawa
Islands to Japan
Kōmeitō
Clean Government Party
(a political party affiliated with the Buddhist society, *Sōka
Gakkai*)

Minren (Minshushugi Yōgo Renraku Kyōgikai)
  Council for Vindication of Democracy
Nampō Dōhō Engokai
  Association for Relief of our Compatriots in the Southern Areas
Nampō Renraku Jimukyoku
  Liaison Bureau for the Southern Areas in the Prime Minister's
  Office
Nanren (Naha Nihon Seifu Nampō Renraku Jimusho)
  Liaison Office of the Japanese government at Naha
Nihon Bengoshi Rengōkai
  Japan Bar Association
Nihon Jiyū Jinken Kyōkai
  Japan Civil Liberties Union
Nisseikyō (Nihon Seinendan Kyōgikai)
  Japan Council of Youth Organizations
Ogasawara
  Bonin Islands
Okinawa Henkan Kokuminundō Kyogikai
  Council for the National Movement for the Return of Okinawa
Okinawa Henkan Yōkyū Kokuminundō Jikkō Iinkai
  Organizing Committee for the National Movement Demanding
  the Return of Okinawa
Okinawa Henkan Sokushin Iinkai
  Committee for Promoting the Return of Okinawa
Okinawa Kaihō Dōmei
  League for the Liberation of Okinawa
Okinawa Kaihō Sokuku Fukki Sokushin Kondankai
  Association for the Promotion of Okinawa's Liberation and its
  Return to the Fatherland
Okinawa Kenjinkai
  Society of People from Okinawa Prefecture
Okinawa Kyōkai
  Okinawan Association
Okinawa Mondai Kakuryō Kyōgikai
  Committee of Ministers concerned with Okinawa Problems
Okinawa Mondai Kondankai
  Discussion Group on the Okinawa Problem
Okinawa Nihon Fukki Sokushin Kiseikai
  Association for the Promotion of the Return of Okinawa to
  Japan
Okinawa Nihon Fukki Sokushin Seinen Dōshikai
  Junior League for the Return of Okinawa to Japan

Okinawa Ogasawara Henkan Dōmei
League for the Return of Okinawa and Ogasawara
Okinawa o Kataru Kai
Discussion Society on Okinawa
Okinawa Shiryō Sentā
Okinawa Data Centre
Okinawa Sokoku Fukki Sokushin Kyōgikai
Council for the Promotion of the Return of Okinawa to the Fatherland
Okinawa Tochimondai Kaiketsu Sokushin Kyōgikai
Council for the Promotion of the Solution of the Land Problem in Okinawa
Okinawajin Remmei
Okinawan Federation
Okinawa-Ren (Okinawa Mondai Kaiketsu Kokuminundō Renraku Kaigi)
Liaison Conference for the National Movement for the Solution of the Okinawa Problem
later renamed *(Okinawa Henkan Yōkyū Kokuminundō Renraku Kaigi)*
Liaison Conference for the National Movement Demanding the Return of Okinawa
Okinawashotō Sokoku Fukki Kiseikai
Council for the Return of the Okinawa Islands to the Fatherland
Ōkurashō
Ministry of Finance of the Japanese government
Senkyo Seido Shingikai
Election System Inquiry Commission
Shigakuren (Zenkoku Shiritsu Daigaku Gakusei Jichikai Rengōkai)
National Federation of Private Universities' Student Unions
Sōhyō (Nihon Rōdō Kumiai Sōhyōgikai)
General Council of Japanese Labour Unions
Sōrifu
Prime Minister's Office of the Japanese government
Tokuren (Tokubetsu Chiiki Renraku Jimukyoku)
Liaison Bureau for the Special Districts in the Prime Minister's Office
Zengakuren (Zennihon Gakusei Jichikai Sōrengō)
All Japan Federation of Student Autonomous Associations

PART ONE

1

Historical Background

The most fundamental reason for the whole argument for the return of Okinawa to Japan—the central theme with which this book will be concerned—is the concept that Okinawa is an integral part of Japan; that is to say, the people in Okinawa are historically, ethnically and culturally a part of the Japanese nation. Public opinion polls conducted in 1967 almost simultaneously in Japan and Okinawa by the *Asahi Shimbun*, the nation's leading newspaper publisher, revealed that 85 per cent of both samples favoured the return of Okinawa to Japan.[1] A majority of them gave as reasons for their preference what may be termed nationalistic feelings such as (of the Okinawan sample) 'we are Japanese' (21 per cent); 'Japan is our fatherland' (20 per cent); 'We dislike alien rule' (7 per cent); 'It is the national aspiration to fulfil the reversion' (4 per cent); and (of the Japanese sample) 'Okinawa is historically Japanese territory' (47 per cent); 'The Okinawan people are Japanese' (11 per cent); and 'the national aspiration' (8 per cent).

Although it is possible to discern delicate shades of opinion between Japanese and Okinawans as well as among the different political groups within Japan or Okinawa, one will miss the crucial point if one does not understand the consensus existing among the overwhelming majority of the Japanese and Okinawan people regarding their national identity.

There seems, however, a fairly widespread misunderstanding about the ethnic and cultural affinity between the Japanese and the Okinawans. Some facts of Okinawan history are indeed liable to cause such misunderstanding. The recent linguistic studies show that Ryukyuan and Japanese are cognate languages which were separated from each other probably some time between 1,450 and 1,700 years ago.[2] Anthropologists, ethnologists and archaeologists have also provided evidence in support of the theory of the common ethnic origin of these two groups.[3] It seems safe, therefore, to say that the Ryukyuan people are a variant of the mainstream of Japanese culture which began to take its own course of development at a certain stage of the historical evolution of the Japanese people.

Much of the early history of the Okinawan people remains, however, unknown. Scattered, fragmentary and often ambiguous accounts in ancient annals of China and Japan tell us only little about it. More valuable sources of Okinawan history before the thirteenth century are to be found in 'unwritten' forms, such as folklore, architectural styles, the use of some extinct expressions of ancient Japanese in today's Okinawan dialect, and among others, the *omoro*, a collection of ancient songs and prayers which had been transmitted orally from generation to generation and was first recorded in *hiragana* (a Japanese syllabary) in the sixteenth century. Evidence in these forms shows that there was a certain degree of cultural contact between Okinawa and Japan in these early centuries. Although these waves of culture influencing Okinawa from the Japanese mainland exerted considerable influence on Okinawan society, it continued to enjoy for many centuries an autonomy in political affairs. This fact, together with the Chinese influence in medieval times, contributed toward making things Okinawan somewhat different from things Japanese.

It may seem surprising, in view of the geographical proximity of the Chinese continent, that the Ryukyu Islands did remain for many centuries outside Chinese influence both culturally and politically. This is perhaps because China was not a maritime power.[4] It was only in the latter half of the fourteenth century that China under the reign of Ming succeeded in establishing a lasting contact with the Ryukyus in the form of tributary relations. It was also the time when the political unification of the Ryukyu Islands was in progress, which culminated in the formation of the Ryukyu Kingdom in 1429. Its king obtained investiture from the Chinese Emperor and his domain covered the area roughly comparable to today's Ryukyus including the Amami-Ōshima group. Throughout its life the Ryukyu Kingdom remained one of the most 'faithful' tributary states, sending regular and frequent tribute-bearing missions to the Chinese court. The period from the mid-fifteenth to the sixteenth century was the 'golden era' of the island kingdom, which enjoyed a prosperous economy thanks to a profitable tribute trade. Ryukyuan junks were seen sailing to and fro between Foochow and various trading ports in South China and Southeast Asia.[5]

Trade existed also between the Ryukyus and Japan, but it constituted only part of the whole system of tributary relations with China as its centre. Naturally China had a stronger pull than Japan in every aspect of the Ryukyuan life in this period. At the request of the king of the Ryukyus, the Ming Emperor sent several families from Fukien Province to help the Ryukyuans in dealing with clerical, commercial, and nautical work related to the tributary trade— the most important function of the Ryukyuan court. Descendants of these families formed a small colony and remained in the service of the court from generation to generation. Although they were gradually assimilated into the Okinawan community by intermarriage, they enjoyed high prestige in the cultural and political life of the Okinawan society and high-ranking officials of the Ryukyuan court

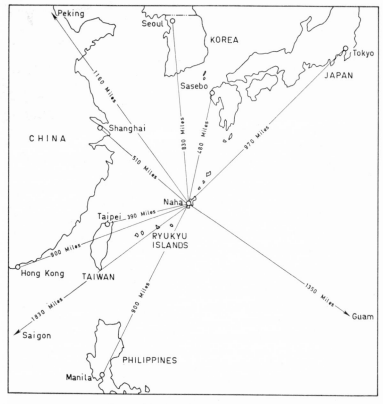

Geopolitical position of Okinawa

were sometimes appointed from among men of Chinese origin. Thus Chinese culture and institutions were implanted in Okinawa.

Despite the permeation of Chinese methods and customs among the court aristocrats and literati immediately dependent on the court, the basic character of Okinawan society remained Japanese. When Ryukyuan trading activities changed from multilateral trade throughout Southeast Asia to intermediary trade between China and Japan, and Japan emerged re-unified in the last quarter of the sixteenth century, the Ryukyus again came under Japanese influence. This trend resulted in the subjugation of the Ryukyus by the Shimazu house, *daimyō* of Satsuma (the feudal domain in the southern part of Kyūshū), in 1609.[6]

Thereafter the Ryukyus came under the political supervision of the Shimazu house although they were permitted, on the surface, to maintain the status of an autonomous kingdom. Shimazu's policy can be explained mainly by its desire to use the Ryukyu Kingdom as an intermediary through which the Shimazu could gain profit from China trade without violating the law of national seclusion. In other words, the Ryukyus were useful for the Shimazu as a loophole in Tokugawa's seclusion policy. The lord of Satsuma was also pleased with the idea of having a 'foreign' king as his subordinate for prestige purposes. For these reasons the Shimazu did not promote 'Japanization' of the Ryukyus but instead preserved the exotic appearance of the island kingdom. Consequently the Ryukyus continued to be a tributary state of China on the one hand and a *de facto* dependency of Japan (or of the Shimazu house) on the other. This arrangement was also in the interest of the Ryukyuan king and his court nobility who could enjoy a certain degree of autonomy. Nor was it officially questioned by the Chinese court which did not appear to care very much about the internal condition of the small kingdom so long as it continued to exercise due courtesy towards the Celestial Empire.

This ambiguous status of the Ryukyus (which is usually referred to as 'dual subordination') remained unquestioned until well into the nineteenth century when the Western peoples began to frequent the east Asian waters.[7] The political status of the Ryukyus appeared odd to the eyes of the Westerners who had been accustomed to the modern concept of territorial states. They wanted to know whether the Ryukyus were really an independent kingdom or belonged to either China or Japan. This was a problem of practical significance especially to those Westerners who had an eye on these islands as a possible commercial and naval outpost. That is why Commodore

Perry showed great interest in the Ryukyus and took great pains to discover the exact situation of the islands' political status during his historic expeditions to Japan in 1853–4.[8] Perry's enthusiasm failed to arouse favourable response from the higher authorities in Washington, and once the great purpose of opening up Japan was successfully fulfilled, the Western interest in the Ryukyu Islands diminished.

Becoming aware of Japan's shaky position on the Ryukyus in the light of modern international law, leaders of Meiji Japan initiated a policy of integrating the Ryukyus into the Japanese body politic both in name and reality with the result that the kingdom was formally abolished in 1879. It was reorganized as the Okinawa Prefecture whose governor was, like other prefectural governors, appointed by and accountable to the central government in Tokyo. This entailed, of course, the abolition of the time-honoured practice of sending tribute from the Ryukyus to China.

While the Western powers did not question these measures taken by the Japanese government with regard to the Ryukyus, China protested against them. Some of the Okinawan aristocrats were extremely reluctant to accept the decision of the Tokyo government to abolish their king and even went to present their case before the foreign diplomatic representatives in Tokyo. A secret mission was also sent to Peking to ask for Chinese help to stop the Japanese action. Fearing undesirable effects on other neighbouring states, especially Korea, the Chinese government decided to take issue on the Ryukyuan question.

The Japanese government took the view that Japan's sovereignty over the Ryukyus was an established fact, and that China had recognized this by admitting in the Peking agreement of October 1874 that Japan's expedition to Taiwan to punish its natives who had murdered shipwrecked Ryukyuan fishermen was a 'just and rightful proceeding to protect her own subjects'.[9] From that point of view the Japanese government would not heed the Chinese protest. At this stage of the dispute, the former United States President, General Ulysses Grant, happened to visit Peking and Tokyo while on a trip around the world. When asked for advice about the Ryukyu controversy by both the Chinese and Japanese governments the retired American President suggested that the two governments seek an amicable settlement on this question by direct negotiations. Consequently, the representatives of the two governments met in Peking in 1880 and reached an agreement by which the two island groups near to Taiwan (i.e. Miyako and Yaeyama groups) were to go to China and the remaining Ryukyus, including the main island of Okinawa, to Japan.

This arrangement was displeasing to more uncompromising politicians in the Chinese court, and under their influence the Chinese government refused to sign the agreement. Thus the negotiations came to nothing.[10]

After that the Japanese government did not show any interest in Chinese proposals to revive the issue until the Japanese victory over China in the 1894–5 war made the Ryukyu controversy recede into the background. The matter was, however, to be long remembered by the Chinese as an early instance of national disgrace inflicted on their country by Japanese expansionists.[11]

The Sino-Japanese war of 1894–5 had tremendous impact on the political life of the Ryukyuan people. After the abolition of the king-dom in 1879, some members of the former ruling class of Okinawa would not submit to Japanese rule. Those who intended to restore the kingdom looked to China for help, and fierce factional strife arose between pro-Chinese and pro-Japanese groups. China's defeat in the war crushed the former group's hope that the mighty Chinese fleet would come to rescue the Ryukyus.[12]

The war also brought about a marked change in Japanese policy towards Okinawa. Before the war the Japanese government had been careful not to take radical steps to reform Okinawan life, fearing that such steps might worsen the already troublesome situation by upsetting the vested interests of the influential members of the Okinawan society. With the decline of the conservative pro-Chinese elements after the war, the government accelerated its policy of 'assimilating' Okinawa.

Okinawa was, however, much behind in introducing such important policies as the land tax reform (which was carried out from 1873–81 in Japan proper and from 1899–1903 in Okinawa), the national conscription law (1873 in Japan; 1896 in Okinawa) and the election law for the House of Representatives (1890 in Japan; 1912 in Okinawa). Okinawa lagged behind also in other aspects of modernization. Take for instance the spread of education. The number of students attending government universities and other institutions of higher education in 1932 was, on the national average, 10.8 per 10,000 persons while the comparable figure for Okinawa was only 1.8; similarly the numbers of middle-school students were 106.9 (national) and 56.8 (Okinawa) respectively. The sole exception was found in normal schools, where the national average was 5.9 while the Okinawan figure was 8.2.[13]

This can be interpreted as the result of the practical exclusion of the Okinawans from influential posts in all areas of Okinawan life except education. The domination of the Okinawan society by mainland Japanese *(naichijin)* could be seen not only in political but also in civic life, including commercial activities in which Kagoshima and Osaka merchants excelled. So much so that a pre-war Okinawan writer said that such a complete lack of local influence could not be imagined in any place but a colony.[14]

The lot of most of those Okinawans who sought jobs in mainland Japan was also a hard one. Even though they were treated as technically equal with other Japanese citizens, they were more often than not regarded as somewhat inferior in everyday life.[15] The narrow opportunities for success within the country drove quite a few Okinawans abroad, especially to Hawaii, the Philippines and South America.[16]

Their long isolation from the mainstream of national evolution; the hesitation or ambivalence they showed towards the national cause at the critical stage of modern nation-building of Japan; the tardy development of Okinawa's modern society, partly because of a late start but more because of the Japanese government's unsympathetic and short-sighted policy; the domination of the local scene by prejudiced officials and relentless merchants from the mainland; and the humiliation and hardship that the Okinawan people had to suffer in various phases of social life in Japan—all these factors contributed to the formation of what may be termed the 'inferiority complex' of the Okinawan people. However it was not expressed, with a few exceptions, in the form of open revolt or of a secessionist movement. Their feeling towards Japan could perhaps best be explained in terms of their quest for thorough identification or complete equality with their fellow citizens in the Japanese body politic. In other words, to the Okinawans, it was not a matter of course to be Japanese. Unlike the ordinary Japanese, the Okinawans had to *become* Japanese. This was a grim task to fulfil in such a highly homogeneous society as Japan, because it was a problem essentially alien to the ordinary Japanese who tended to be intolerant of insufficient conformity.

The desire of the Okinawan people to narrow the existing psychological gap with the rest of the Japanese (such desire was, for the reasons mentioned above, almost one-sided in pre-war Japan) could drive them to an extreme form of devotion to their country. The best example of this is provided by a pathetic episode of the war which was made widely known through a popular film *Himeyuri no*

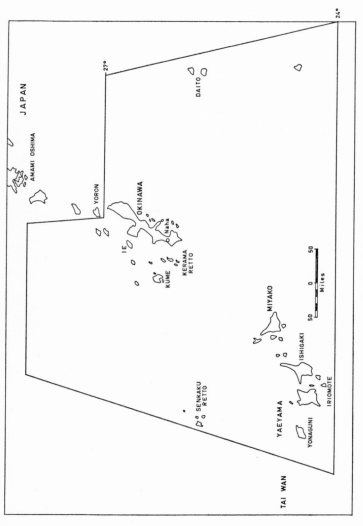

Ryukyu Islands

tō (The Monument for the Little Lily Corps) after the war. This was the story about a volunteer nurse corps composed of Okinawan girls of middle- or high-school age. They never abandoned their difficult duties and finally, being driven into the farthest corner of the island, committed group suicide in front of the enemy. This was a typical example but only one among many other similar stories.[17]

Some years ago, a prominent Japanese critic, Ōya Sōichi, during his visit to Okinawa, critically referred to the behaviour of the Okinawan people during the war, describing it as an exhibition of 'a domestic-animal-like devotion', meaning 'servile'. Probably it was Mr Ōya's intention to caution the audience against an uncritical acceptance of any political creed. Whatever his real intention may have been, his rather blunt remarks offended the Okinawan audience.[18]

Summing up, the more the Okinawan people felt the existence of a certain psychological difference between themselves and the *naichijin,* the keener their desire for oneness. The social-psychologist would call this a 'marginal nationalism', other examples of which can be found in the Saar, Alsace-Lorraine, Schleswig and so on.[19]

The post-war experiences added some further factors to the already complicated problem of Okinawan self-consciousness. The sudden collapse of Japanese power, the almost complete breakdown of all sorts of communication between the island and the rest of the country, and the liberal and paternalistic tone of American administration all seemed to encourage the idea of a new, independent Okinawa. When the United States military government first permitted the Okinawans to form the Central Okinawa Administration under a locally nominated 'governor' in April 1946, the *Uruma Shimpō,* the only existing local newspaper, described Okinawa as a 'victim of the evil Japanese militarism' and praised the Americans for having 'liberated our Okinawa upon the principle of world peace'. Shima Kiyoshi, the publisher of *Uruma Shimpō* and later Democratic Socialist member of the House of Councillors in the Japanese Diet, in a signed article which appeared in the same issue of that paper, went so far as to say that the pre-war Japanese rule of Okinawa had been nothing but 'a colonial and bureaucratic-type administration', whereas the Americans were treating the Okinawans as if they were not American enemies, and even gave them the freedom to choose their own governor.[20] The 'governor' was in fact appointed by the military government after he was nominated by a group of eighty-six representatives which included mayors and members of the Advisory Council. This was an advisory body established under the direction of the American military government immediately after the war and which was now transformed into the new Central Okinawa Administration. At any rate, it seems that the Okinawans regarded this 'election' as the first step towards a genuine self-government of Okinawa.

The Okinawan 'governor', Shikiya Kōshin, told visiting American reporters that a majority of the Okinawan people desired to build a peaceful state under the protection of the United States, although he mentioned the existence of a small minority which seemed in favour of the return to Japan.[21]

It is hard to evaluate the extent to which these opinions represented the real feeling of the Okinawan people and the extent to which they reflected the supposed wish of the Americans. It is certain, however, that no influential Okinawans voiced an articulate opinion in favour of return to Japan during the first years of American occupation. The two main issues of public attention in Okinawa during this period were the popular election of the governor and the shortage of food. Not Japan but America seemed to be the answer to both of these questions. Thus political leaders in Okinawa were talking of introducing a free government under the guidance of the United States, while the ordinary Okinawans found relief from hunger, thanks to the American military provisions.

As the time for peace with Japan appeared to be approaching in late 1949 and early 1950, more articulate opinion began to be heard from Okinawa with regard to its future relations with Japan. The earliest editorials on this subject in the Okinawan press appeared in November 1949. The *Okinawa Taimusu* (15 November 1949) urged the public to give serious attention to the Allied move for peace with Japan, without clarifying their own preference. The *Uruma Shimpō* (29 November 1949) cautioned its readers against wishful thinking, pointing out that it was not likely that the United States would give up Okinawa for another decade or more. This fact, in their opinion, ruled out the possibility of Okinawan independence in the near future. The same editorial also warned that the Okinawans should not take seriously the Japanese claim to Okinawa because Japan no longer had a serious interest in Okinawa, since its significance as a stepping stone for their southward expansion had been lost. Neither of these two major Okinawan newspapers argued for return to Japan throughout the following year. Nor did this subject offer an important campaigning issue in the elections in September 1950 for Governor and Assemblymen of the newly instituted Okinawa *Guntō* government.[22]

The earliest sign of the 'reversion movement' appeared in mid-1951 when an Association for the Promotion of the Return of Okinawa to Japan and its youth organization, a Junior League for the Return of Okinawa to Japan, were formed in order to campaign for signatures to a petition. The recently elected Okinawan Governor, Taira Tatsuo, and his party, Okinawa Socialist Masses Party, supported this campaign. Some 199,000 signatures thus collected (which represented 72.1 per cent of the whole electorate of Okinawa *Guntō*), together with appeals from the Governor and the Okinawan Assembly, were forwarded to the American and Japanese delegates to the San Francisco Peace Conference.[23]

The conversion of the Okinawan thinking on this subject was, however, neither sudden nor complete. Two political parties, the Socialist Party (which is different from the present Socialist Party in Okinawa) and the Democratic Alliance, which jointly supported the unsuccessful candidate in the gubernatorial election of 1950, had been advocating respectively union with the United States and independence. Although the former was practically a 'one-man party' and never gained popular support, the latter merged into a Republican Party which formed a small but stubborn minority in the Okinawan Assembly. In mid-March 1951 when the majority in the Assembly proposed a resolution in favour of the return to Japan, Republican Party members made strenuous but vain efforts to obstruct its passage.[24]

The Okinawan press was also not yet unanimous. While the *Okinawa Taimusu* gradually emerged from a non-committal attitude to open support for the reversion cause, the *Uruma Shimpō* continued to counsel the public to be realistic about the best possible way to meet the needs of the Okinawan society.[25] Denouncing its opponents' argument as being based merely upon sentimental grounds, the *Shimpō* raised the question: which was more important, sentimental affiliation with Japan or practical necessity for continued American assistance to achieve the economic rehabilitation of Okinawa? They also reminded the public of the past Japanese administration which treated Okinawa as 'a colony like Korea', and concluded 'Either politically or economically, it is not unreasonable to believe that the United States will be able to give us more than Japan will be'. Refuting these arguments, the *Taimusu* emphasized the common racial, cultural and historical background of Okinawa and Japan. What was more, they argued, post-war Japan was no longer a militaristic and authoritarian country. As for the vital problem of economics, they warned against a hasty conclusion that Japan would be unable and unwilling to give economic assistance to Okinawa, while admitting that American assistance had made a great contribution to the reconstruction of the Okinawan economy. What mattered, the *Taimusu* concluded, was the spirit of self-reliance, both politically and economically; and the best possible method of realizing this purpose would be to live with Japan.

The following months witnessed the gradual strengthening of the pro-reversion camp and the decline of its opponents, resulting in the dissolution in February 1952 of the Republican Party which had been advocating Ryukyuan independence.[26] This trend was also reflected in the results of the first election for the Ryukyuan Legislature which was held that April. The two parties which appeared in favour of the reversion movement, the Socialist Masses Party and the People's Party, obtained ten seats and one seat respectively while the Socialists (in favour of American trusteeship) got none; the remaining seven seats were distributed among independent candidates.[27] A new Ryukyu Democratic Party was established soon afterwards with the American-appointed Chief Executive, Higa Shūhei, as its President; it absorbed some elements of the Socialist Masses Party as well as former Republican Party members and formed the majority in the Legislature. This new Party pledged in its first platform 'the early realization of reversion to the motherland' within the framework of 'positive co-operation with American policies'.[28] This did not mean a complete disappearance from the Party in particular and from the Okinawan society at large of a few who preferred Ryukyuan independence or who were against a premature return to Japan.[29] Nevertheless, public opinion was increasingly on the side of reversion.

It should be mentioned here, however, that those who advocated the return of Okinawa to Japan did not intend to oppose the use of the island by the United States Forces. But they could not see why the United States needed to retain *de facto* sovereignty over Okinawa in order to secure her rights to use military installations there, if she could obtain similar privileges in Japan proper under the provisions of the then proposed U.S.-Japan Security Treaty. And, as Governor Taira put it, they did not see why it would be anti-American to advocate their island's return to Japan which itself was now taking a pro-American policy.[30]

Another point which deserves mention is that behind all Okinawan opinions, either for or against the return to Japan, lay deep-rooted discontent with the Japanese government's forgetfulness of the fate of Okinawa. Apart from the remote past, its failure to protect Okinawa from the American invasion and the neglect of its duty to assist the Okinawan people in their efforts to recover from the war-time devastation appeared to be sufficient evidence of its usual indifference to the lot of the Okinawan people. In anticipation of the Japanese peace, they were all afraid that the political status of Okinawa might be decided regardless of Okinawan wishes. That is to say, some were afraid that the Ryukyus might be returned to Japanese administration despite their wish for independence; others were afraid that they might be left uncared-for by the Japanese government despite their wish for reversion. The fact that the San Francisco Peace Treaty provided for continued American rule of Okinawa was only to 'prove' the latter's view and consequently to deepen discontent, and even resentment, towards the Japanese government for its forgetfulness.

With this historical and psychological background, it is small wonder that a long delay, such as the Okinawan people were to see in the following years, in the restoration of their island to Japan's sovereignty is regarded by them as resulting mostly from lack of sincere efforts on the part of their 'home' government to take heed of Okinawan opinion.[31] In other words, America's refusal to restore Okinawa to full Japanese sovereignty intensified the Okinawan grudge against the Japanese government, because in the eyes of the Okinawans it showed that the Japanese government placed diplomatic considerations for the United States above its duty to take care of its own people. Or has the government refused equal treatment of Okinawa simply because it does not regard the Okinawan people as Japanese despite its assertion to the contrary? Unless the Japanese government proves otherwise not by words but by deeds, the Okinawan people will never be satisfied.

Various events that followed the ones described have added some other factors: the inevitable conflict between the Okinawans' desire for political and civil freedom and the military considerations of the United States; an increasing anxiety about their personal security in the midst of the huge American military base complex equipped with such highly sophisticated 'weapons' as IRBMs, B-52s and even lethal gas; various social and personal inconveniences from their prolonged separation from Japan; a growing expectation of better living and working conditions in proportion to

15

the economic improvement of Japan; and so forth. These converge to form today's Okinawan opinion for 'equalization' *(ittaika)* or 'the same and equal treatment' *(hondonami)* of Japan and Okinawa. As the foregoing account shows, however, the Okinawan quest for an equal status within the Japanese body politic has deep roots in history.

2

Genesis: from Surrender to the Peace Treaty (1945–52)

The most important decision affecting the present status of Okinawa was the conclusion of the Peace Treaty with Japan (signed in September 1951, effective in April 1952). Article 3 of the Treaty reads:

> Japan will concur in any proposal of the United States to the United Nations to place under its trusteeship system, with the United States as the sole administering authority, Nansei Shotō south of 29 degrees north latitude (including the Ryukyu Islands and the Daitō Islands), Nampō Shotō south of Sōfu Gan (including the Bonin Islands, Rosario Island and the Volcano Islands) and Parece Vela and Marcus Island. Pending the making of such a proposal and affirmative action thereon, the United States will have the right to exercise all and any powers of administration, legislation and jurisdiction over the territory and inhabitants of these islands, including their territorial waters.[1]

The rights given to Japan under the provision of this article are generally referred to as 'residual sovereignty' since that is the term used at the San Francisco Peace Conference by John Foster Dulles, the chief architect of the Treaty, although the expression is not used in the text of the Treaty.[2]

Both Dulles's expression 'residual sovereignty' and the peculiar way of providing for Okinawa in the Treaty gave the impression that the future status of Okinawa awaited further negotiations. This gave rise to an optimistic expectation among the Japanese people of a rapid improvement of the state of affairs concerning Okinawa in accordance with the future betterment of U.S.-Japan relations.

It caused, on the other hand, considerable anxiety in Japan over the American position on Okinawa. At any rate the decision made on Okinawa at San Francisco in 1951 constituted not the end but the starting point of the Okinawa disagreement between Japan and the United States.

The present chapter will attempt to shed light on some problems relating to this decision by reconstructing the main events which led to it. This is made difficult by a dearth of primary sources, especially concerning the diplomatic processes. With this in view, however, the following account sets forth the essential factors which produced the Okinawa decision in 1951.

Needless to say, the Okinawa question originated directly from Japan's defeat in World War II. Disposition of Okinawa was one of the topics discussed by war-time leaders in relation to the 'Pacific problem'.

At Cairo in late 1943, President Franklin D. Roosevelt raised the Okinawa question before Generalissimo Chiang Kai-shek, asking more than once during the conversation whether China had any claims on the island. In replying to this, Chiang stated that China would agree to joint occupation of the Ryukyu Islands by China and the United States and, eventually, joint administration by the two countries under the trusteeship of an international organization.[3] After having discussions with Joseph Stalin at Teheran, Roosevelt reported to the Pacific War Council that Stalin was familiar with the history of the Ryukyu Islands and that he was in complete agreement that they belonged to China and should be returned to her.[4]

No further record has been found of reference to the future status of Okinawa at any other conferences of war-time Allied leaders. Neither was there any specific mention of the island either in the Cairo or Potsdam Declarations or in the secret agreement at Yalta. All this indicates that the Allied Powers did not come to a final conclusion regarding the future status of Okinawa, although they were sympathetic to the Chinese interests in the Ryukyus on historical grounds.

The immediate course of action was determined by military rather than political considerations. With the short (by present standards) range of naval and air striking forces, the United States had recourse to a strategy of 'island hopping', by which the front line could gradually be pushed forward closer to the ultimate goal —the Japanese mainland. Okinawa was chosen as the last stepping stone for that purpose. It fell into the hands of the American forces after three months of fierce fighting which claimed the lives of 12,500 Americans and 110,000 Japanese.[5] The Americans constructed base-facilities for B-29 operations on the island of Okinawa and another base for Very Long Range fighter escorts on Iejima, a tiny island adjacent to Okinawa. It was not until the last night of the war, however, that Okinawa-based B-29s carried out their first (and last) offensive mission against the Japanese homeland.[6]

The very fact that the Americans captured Okinawa and other islands of the Ryukyus during the war added some new factors to the subsequent development of their attitude towards the islands.

In the first place, it contributed to the formation, or strengthening, of the opinion among the military planners (particularly of the Navy) that the United States should take outright possession of the outlying Japanese islands (including the Ryukyus) together with her former mandated territories in the Pacific as part of a far-flung network of 'strategic strong points' of the United States. The great loss of life which occurred in seizing the islands, the large amount spent on developing base facilities and the belief that the inhabitants desired to live under the American flag were advanced as justification for this action.[7]

The military demands for complete American sovereignty over the ex-Japanese mandated islands clashed with the position taken by the State Department that such an action would be incompatible with the principle of non-territorial aggrandizement that the Allied Powers solemnly declared in war-time documents. The latter contended that an exclusive American trusteeship would adequately protect American interests in these islands. A compromise was reached between the two views by creating a peculiar institution of 'strategic trusteeship' for the former Japanese mandated territories.[8]

A similar conflict of opinion existed between the American military authorities who wanted to see the Ryukyu Islands placed under, if not full American sovereignty, at least a trusteeship with the United States as the sole administering power, and those who did not see why other members of the United Nations, especially China, should be excluded from the machinery of administration in Okinawa.[9]

The Okinawa question could be further complicated by the problem of Chishima. Some Congressmen suggested that Chishima might be placed under a joint trusteeship of the United Nations if any of the Pacific islands conquered by the United States—especially Okinawa—were to be treated in a similar way.[10] (The public was not informed at that time of the secret agreement reached at Yalta between Roosevelt and Stalin in which the former promised to support the Soviet Union's claim to Chishima and the southern half of Karafuto at a future peace conference.)

The American negotiators chose to seek Soviet support for the American proposal to the United Nations Security Council for placing the ex-Japanese mandated islands under an exclusive American trusteeship. In exchange they reaffirmed the promise made by Roosevelt at Yalta concerning Chishima. It was decided that disposition of Okinawa should be postponed until a formal peace treaty.[11]

Another factor underlying the Americans' attitude towards Okinawa even up to the present time has its root in their experience of manipulating the Okinawans during and after the campaign. For purposes of psychological warfare, the Americans treated the Okinawans as being people of a different stock and culture from the Japanese, who had economically and politically exploited them.[12] Although so far there is no evidence that the Americans made systematic efforts to elevate this policy of differentiation between the Okinawans and the Japanese into the more sophisticated policy of encouraging political independence of Okinawa from an 'imperial' Japan, this line of thinking had unmistakable effects upon the American policy towards Okinawa after the war.[13]

By right of conquest and in accordance with the terms of surrender of the Japanese Forces in the Ryukyus,[14] the power of control over the former Japanese islands south of 30° N. latitude (which include Okinawa and Amami-Ōshima) was assumed by the United States Forces. There was an initial short period of division of labour between the Navy (to which the administration of the Okinawa Group or Okinawa *Guntō* was assigned) and the Army (which controlled the other three groups of Miyako, Yaeyama and Amami). Then the task of administering the whole area was assigned to the U.S. Navy and subsequently transferred to the U.S. Army.[15]

An important result of the policy of American military authorities is that a clear differentiation was made between Japan proper and the Ryukyu Islands with the dividing line set at latitude 30° N. This was formally established by a SCAP (Supreme Command for Allied Powers) directive in January 1946.[16] Although it was explained that this step was taken purely for administrative convenience and that it was not to be interpreted as an indication of Allied policy relating to the ultimate disposition of the islands,[17] it entailed a few consequences of significant practical import. First, Okinawa was placed under the sole control of the United States, whereas the rest of Japan was, at least in a formal sense, under Allied control. This meant that in Okinawa the United States was not responsible to the Allied machinery of Japanese occupation such as the Far Eastern Commission or the Allied Council for Japan.[18] Secondly, while the occupation policy was conducted through the Japanese government on the mainland, Okinawa was controlled directly and exclusively by the American military government. All kinds of communication between Okinawa and the rest of Japan were cut off or strictly controlled by the United States.[19] In short, Okinawa was treated for every purpose as if it were a foreign country like Korea or Taiwan.[20] All this contributed to the exclusive influence of the United States in Okinawa and to the resulting post-war developments between Okinawa and the Japanese homeland.

The fundamental pattern of international relations in the Far East in which the Okinawa problem was placed remained unchanged until 1949. While the Allied hostility towards Japan still lingered, the new and growing cleavage among the Allied Powers was already big enough to defy all efforts to agree on an early conclusion of a peace treaty with Japan. The advent of a Communist regime in Peking and the outbreak of the Korean war, however, changed the whole situation drastically. Accordingly, Japan's international status shifted from that of chief enemy of the world at large to that of a prospective ally for the West led by the United States. This situation required the United States to make a fresh approach to the problem of Okinawa, too.

There were various possibilities for the status of Okinawa in the early post-war period: outright annexation by the United States, exclusive American trusteeship, some kind of international control with China as one of the important participants to independence. Only the plan for placing Okinawa under a trusteeship with the United States as the sole administering authority survived the tremendous transformation of the Far Eastern political scene. In his famous speech on American policy for Asia in January 1950, Secretary of State Dean Acheson disclosed America's intention to propose sole U.S. trusteeship for Okinawa which he regarded as an important link in America's defence line along the periphery of the Asian continent.[21]

With the new strategic plan for Asia, the United States began to make fresh efforts to consolidate her military position on Okinawa. As early as mid-1949 the American military authorities, apparently anticipating a Communist victory in China and the momentous changes such a victory would entail, succeeded in gaining from Congress an appropriation of $U.S.50 million to build permanent military installations on Okinawa.[22] The construction work actually began in early 1950 with the participation of some Japanese contractors. From 1949 to 1951 top-level American military leaders visited Okinawa frequently. One of their purposes was to assess the importance of Okinawan bases in relation to the possible change of status of American forces stationed on the Japanese mainland with the conclusion of a peace treaty. In spite of division of opinion about the place of Japanese bases in the post-treaty American strategy in the Far East, they all agreed that Okinawan bases were very important.[23]

Measures were also taken in this period to reorganize the governmental structure of Okinawa. Under a directive of General Douglas MacArthur in late 1950, a United States Civil Administration of the Ryukyu Islands (USCAR) was created, with the Commander-in-Chief of the Far East (located in Tokyo) as Governor of the Ryukyu Islands. Day-to-day operation of the administration was discharged by the Commanding General of the Ryukyu Command (RYCOM) who held the additional post of Deputy Governor; he was assisted by a newly created Civil Administrator who was also appointed from among Army officers with the rank of general.

Besides these American-held offices an indigenous Provisional Central Government of the Ryukyu Islands was brought into being on 1 April 1951. Exactly one year later this was developed into a Government of the Ryukyu Islands (GRI) headed by a Chief Executive who was appointed by the Americans from among local leaders. Its legislative branch consisted of thirty-one locally elected members.[24]

It was with this background that Dulles, who was appointed adviser to the Secretary of State in April 1950, undertook the task of drafting and negotiating a peace treaty with Japan. The information at our disposal is not enough to compare the provisions for Okinawa in the various peace drafts prepared by State Department officials since the end of the war. It is known, however, that in Dulles's first memorandum on Japan (written on 6 June 1950) Japan was required to accept any decision of the United Nations which extended the trusteeship system to all or part of the Ryukyu and Bonin Islands.[25] In a document (called the Seven-Point Memorandum) which Dulles prepared after his first visit to Tokyo, Japan was required, however, to 'agree to United Nations trusteeship, with the United States as administering authority, of the Ryukyu and

Bonin Islands.'[26] In making this modification, Dulles was probably influenced by the opinion of the military leaders whose inspection tour to Japan and Korea coincided with that of his own in mid-1950.

The attitudes of the Japanese to the Treaty were no less important than those of the Allies, even though Japan was not a participant in the treaty-making in the ordinary sense.[27] Thus Dulles visited Tokyo again in January 1951 with the Seven-Point Memorandum.

In the early post-war period, the Japanese said little (responsible or irresponsible) on the problem of Okinawa.[28] The first public statement by Japanese leaders on this problem was made by Foreign Minister Ashida Hitoshi (of the Katayama coalition Cabinet of the Socialist and Democratic Parties) who told a meeting of the foreign press club that the Japanese people doubted whether the territorial provisions in the Potsdam Declaration applied to Okinawa and part of Chishima (perhaps referring to the Chishima Islands south of Kunashiri); he added that although Okinawa was of no economic importance to Japan national sentiment made her seek the return of the island.[29] This statement only caused adverse reactions from abroad as well as from the leftist groups at home. For example, a spokesman for the British Foreign Office stated that the British government regarded the Yalta Agreement as a final decision which would not need to be confirmed by a formal peace treaty.[30] A United Press dispatch from Washington reported the view of the U.S. authorities that there would be no objections to the Soviet claim to the southern half of Karafuto and Chishima as well as to the American control of Okinawa and other Japanese outlying islands.[31] A strong objection was raised also by the Shanghai Municipal Assembly which passed a resolution against Japanese control of Okinawa.[32] In such circumstances, *Gaimushō* experts had little hope of recovering Chishima and Okinawa.[33]

The situation had changed, however, by the time of Dulles's second visit to Tokyo in early 1951. Now Japan could expect her opinion to be heard on matters such as Okinawa. In the period from late 1950 to early 1951, quite a few politicians openly expressed in the Diet their desire for the return of Okinawa, Ogasawara and Chishima. This feeling was most articulately expressed by nationalist-oriented conservative politicians (particularly in the Democratic Party), who were echoed by the Socialists and, to a lesser extent, by some members of the Liberal (Government) Party. In spite of remarkable silence in the Japanese press on the matter, this seemed to be the prevailing feeling among all sections of Japanese society, with the seemingly strange exception of the Communists.[34] It is important to note that Japanese opinion on the Okinawa problem at this point was a naive and spontaneous expression of national aspirations rather than anti-American or anti-military base feelings.

A note submitted by the Japanese government to Dulles on 30 January 1951 stated in relation to Okinawa: (1) it would be most desirable for the United States to refrain from carrying out the trusteeship proposal for Okinawa and Ogasawara for the sake of an enduring friendship between the United States and Japan; (2) Japan would be prepared to offer these islands for America's free use for military purposes in full appreciation of her interests in them; (3) in case, however, the islands were brought into trusteeship, Japan would hope to become a joint trustee for them. She also would want it expressed that the islands would be eventually returned to Japan whenever the military necessity for keeping them under such a system ceased to exist.[35]

One of the *Gaimushō* officials who helped the Prime Minister, Yoshida Shigeru, in these negotiations has said that Dulles looked unmistakably displeased when the Japanese views were expressed, refusing to conduct any further discussions about this topic during the conference at the time.[36]

It seems, however, that Dulles was impressed by the opinion expressed by the Japanese government which was also that of almost all leading figures whom he met to discuss the problem of a peace treaty during his stay in Tokyo at this time. Consequently he realized that the matter needed reconsideration.[37]

The result of Dulles's re-examination of the Okinawa clause was embodied in an American draft which was completed in March 1951. It was shown, first of all, to Yoshida when Dulles flew to Tokyo in April 1951. Putting aside minor differences in style, the provision for Okinawa therein was almost identical with the relevant part of the final Treaty. A new aspect in it was that, while the Seven-Point Memorandum simply envisaged an exclusive American trusteeship, the March draft included an additional provision that the United States would have the right to exercise all power over Okinawa until a proposal for such a system of trusteeship was actually made and carried into effect. It was also significant, the negotiators thought, that the draft did not specifically provide for detachment of Okinawa and Ogasawara from Japanese sovereignty. These facts gave the Japanese negotiators the hope that the United States would not dare to implement the trusteeship clause for the islands and that they would be eventually returned to Japan.[38]

This point in the American version survived the subsequent adjustments with the British delegate who originally required Japan to renounce sovereignty over these islands.[39] A draft Japanese Peace Treaty, which came out of the Anglo-American agreement and which was to be incorporated in the final Treaty after only minor verbal modifications, was officially made public on 12 July 1951.[40]

Public response to the Okinawa clause in the disclosed draft treaty was very unfavourable, particularly so in Amami-Ōshima where disappointed people went on hunger strikes.

Japanese leaders were anxious to get the United States' permission to explain to the general public in a more express way the purpose of the provision of Article 3, believing that the obscurity of the clause was to some extent responsible for the adverse public response.[41] A high-ranking official (who was believed to be Iguchi Sadao, Permanent Undersecretary for Foreign Affairs and a right-hand man of Yoshida) disclosed the government view that the prospective treaty would not require Japan to renounce her sovereignty in Okinawa and Ogasawara and therefore sovereignty in these islands would remain with Japan, even if they should be placed under a U.N. trusteeship for a certain period of time. This was, he added, one of the positive results of their negotiations with Dulles.[42] He also told the press that the Japanese government had reason to expect that a trusteeship agreement for the islands, if any, would be one with a specified term after the expiration of which they should be restored to full Japanese sovereignty. He also revealed that the government was negotiating with the United States to prevent the erection of tariff barriers between these island areas and the Japanese homeland.[43]

It is not known whether these statements were made with the prior understanding of the United States.[44] They were, however, endorsed to a large extent by Prime Minister Yoshida. He pointed out in his explanatory speech before the Diet that the Treaty simply provided that Japan would concur in any proposal of the United States to the United Nations for placing these islands under American trusteeship. He emphasized the fact that the Treaty was so flexible on this matter that there was much room left to hope that reasonable arrangements would be worked out in regard to the civil status of the inhabitants and their trade and communications with the Japanese homeland.[45]

Through these statements the Japanese government tried to clarify two points: the significance of the fact that the Treaty did not require Japan to renounce her sovereignty in Okinawa and Ogasawara; the reasonable assumption that Japan would have some voice in arranging the socio-economic relations of these islands with the Japanese mainland. The first of these two points was endorsed by Dulles at San Francisco in September 1951, where he said that Article 3 of the Treaty would permit Japan to retain residual sovereignty, while making it possible for the islands to be brought into a trusteeship system with the United States as administering authority. The British delegate (Kenneth Younger) also confirmed this, saying that 'the treaty does not remove these [i.e. Okinawa and Ogasawara] from Japanese sovereignty'.[46]

Regarding the second point, Japanese leaders apparently expected that, in spite of the treaty provision which granted the United States the right to do so, she would not need to exercise 'all and any powers of administration, legislation and jurisdiction over the territory and inhabitants of these islands', and she would allow Japan to maintain quasi-domestic relations with them, especially in regard to the inhabitants' civil status (nationality), trade and communications, education and so forth. While the need for the manipulation of public opinion made them present a hopeful picture on this matter, the Japanese leaders themselves seemed to be quite optimistic at this moment. It may be said this expectation was to some extent at least based on reality, because the American position still remained fluid and flexible on this matter. Dulles revealed, for example, in reply to a question in Congress before which the treaty was placed for ratification, that 'there had been no final crystallization of thought within the United States Government as to how to exercise the rights and privileges given us by Article 3', adding that a decision on this point would have to be made in the light of various factors, 'sentimental and historical' as well as 'strategic'. At the same time he even suggested the possibility of not applying for trusteeship, pointing out the fact that the United States was not obliged to do so by the Treaty.[47]

Before concluding the present chapter, it might be appropriate to see briefly what place had been given to Okinawa in various plans of post-Peace Treaty security arrangements with Japan. Okinawa had been invariably regarded as one of the places where the United

States should maintain its forces for some time, while there had been considerable variation and vacillation in the American thinking about the wisdom of holding bases in Japan after the conclusion of a peace treaty.

In the early post-war period, when the idea of making the Japanese homeland open to American bases had not yet crystallized, there nevertheless seemed no doubts even among those who were favourably inclined towards a 'neutral' Japan that American bases in Okinawa should be retained. These people, as represented by General MacArthur, regarded it as necessary and wise to maintain American forces in Okinawa and some other outlying Japanese islands. The alternative would be a more costly (in a political sense) policy of continuing American occupation of Japan, either to keep vigilance over post-Treaty Japan to prevent any chauvinistic attempt to remilitarize, or to guarantee a disarmed Japan against armed attack from outside.[48]

It seemed that the Japanese leaders would accept a scheme under which American forces stationed in Okinawa and some other outlying islands would guarantee Japan's security. In September 1947 Ashida, Foreign Minister of the Katayama Cabinet, put forward a proposal for the post-Peace Treaty security system for Japan on the basis of a unilateral agreement with the United States. This formed a departure from the earlier idea of a collective guarantee of Japan's security by the principal Allied Powers or the United Nations as a whole; as such, it can be regarded as an embryo of the U.S.-Japan Security Treaty (signed in September 1951 alongside the Peace Treaty) which was eventually instituted. But there was an important difference between Ashida's plan and those in later periods. Under his plan, the United States would keep its forces *close to Japan but not in Japan* and would move them only in case of emergency to bases in Japan maintained by the Japanese for that purpose;[49] the treaty which was subsequently concluded allowed the U.S. forces to be stationed all the time *in and about Japan* (Article 1) (my italics). It is not known what area was actually meant by 'close to Japan', but quite likely Ashida was thinking of a guarantee of Japan's security by American forces stationed, among other areas, in Okinawa and Ogasawara.

When both Japanese and American leaders decided to take a different course of action and to conclude a kind of base rights agreement, thereby granting the United States the right to dispose various facilities on Japanese soil for military purposes, some might well have thought that the relative importance of Okinawa in the

American strategy in the Far East had somewhat declined and, accordingly, that the Americans might loosen their control of Okinawa.[50] But reality failed to meet their expectation, and Japanese negotiators had to realize how firm the American military's stand on Okinawa was.

In spite of the fact that the United States obtained free access to Japanese bases by the newly established treaty, Okinawa was given special significance for various reasons. It is a well-known fact that Okinawa was an important air-base during the Korean war. It is not clear, however, whether it was indispensable for the American military operations in that war. At any rate it seems difficult to contend that the Korean war was the reason for the American decision to retain Okinawa under American rule. A more plausible reason was a still strong concern, particularly among some British Commonwealth countries in the Pacific, over the revival of Japanese militarism. A typical expression of this anxiety was made by some Australian politicians who were concerned 'in establishing such a system of security as would prevent for all time a resurgence of Japanese aggression', and regarded Japan's 'geographical disarmament through the loss of potential springboards for aggression against her neighbours' as the most important single factor of such a system of security against Japan.[51] Another and perhaps more important reason, although not openly stated, was that the United States wanted to hold on to Okinawa, so to speak, as an insurance in case the bases in Japan were lost. In other words, because Japan's future course was unpredictable, they thought, the United States would have to secure special privileges in Okinawa so that the American position there would not be subject to any future change in Japanese politics and Japan's relations with the United States.[52]

Evidence shows, however, that Dulles was not quite clear about the place to be given to Okinawa in relation to the U.S.-Japan Security Treaty. One high-ranking *Gaimushō* official, who was engaged in the treaty negotiation, revealed that the original draft of the security treaty proposed by Dulles read in relevant part 'such disposition [i.e. the disposition to give the United States the right to station its armed forces in and about Japan] *would be designed solely for the defence of Japan against armed attack from without'*. In the course of the negotiations Dulles proposed to change this to *'would be designed to contribute to the security of Japan against armed attack from without'*, to allow the United States to use its forces in Japan for the defence of, say, Okinawa. Further modification of the phrasing of Article 1 into what became the final text ('Such forces may be utilized to contribute to the maintenance of international peace and security in the Far East and to the security of Japan against armed attack from outside . . .) was proposed by the United States in the last stage of the negotiations; the reason given for this change was that, under its former wording, the Treaty might be interpreted so that it would not automatically allow the United States to use military forces in and about Japan in case of hostilities like another Korean war.

This story tells what place the United States planners tried to give to Japan in the complex of three 'treaty areas' in the Far East which were militarily inseparable but legally distinguished. These were (1) Japan proper; (2) the 'Japan Area' comprising Japan proper and the area in her vicinity (the latter meant, Japanese negotiators understood, Okinawa and other areas which were placed under American control by the provision of Article 3 of the Japanese Peace Treaty); and (3) the wide concept of the 'Far East' to whose security the United States committed herself by a series of bilateral security arrangements with various countries.

Apart from the controversial concept of the 'Far East', it is worth while noting here that, as the frequent reference to 'in and about Japan' in the Treaty suggests, Okinawa was given a peculiar, and somewhat ambiguous, place in the U.S.-Japan Security Treaty. The question remains, for example, whether the United States needed agreements with Japan about the use of its forces in Okinawa in accordance with Article 1 of the Security Treaty (whereby Japan granted the United States the right to dispose its forces in and *about* Japan) or Article 3 (which provided that the conditions governing the disposition of such forces should be determined by administrative agreements between the two governments). This question was not actually raised either by America or Japan and Okinawa has been always beyond Japan's reach.[53]

In short, throughout the discussion about the post-Peace Treaty security problem of Japan, it seemed a foregone conclusion that the United States should retain Okinawa under a special legal framework irrespective of Japan's place in the alliance system. As we have already seen, the 'residual sovereignty' provision was Dulles's solution to this necessity.

The greatest peculiarity of Article 3 of the Japanese Peace Treaty was that it made no concrete decision on the status of Okinawa but postponed it to an undetermined date. It did not give any indication of when a final decision should be made and in what way the transitory situation should be resolved. This indecisiveness and obscurity was the result of the desire of the leaders on both sides to avoid conflict on two factors: the wish of the American military for a free use of the islands, and the national aspirations of the Japanese people for restoring and retaining political, economic and sentimental identification of Okinawa with the Japanese community.

What were the gains and losses of both sides from the compromise reached? From the American side, this compromise was diplomatically necessary to win the favour of a country which they now sought as an ally in their struggle against the Communist bloc. They secured the substance only at the expense of the shadow. They maintained the vested rights derived from the conquest, although these rights suffered from a somewhat shaky legal framework for a lengthy period of occupation.[54]

For Japan it was a gain, too, because she prevented a definite decision from being made under international circumstances which were not yet favourable enough for her. The fact still remained, however, that the Japanese leaders sacrificed the welfare of the people in Okinawa (who were claiming to be compatriots of the Japanese people) to the nation's early and perhaps rather easy re-entry into international society.

On the whole, the equilibrium of the two factors in the making of the arrangement concerning Okinawa at San Francisco was much in America's favour. It was to be subject, of necessity, to the subsequent shift of Japan's position in relation to the world at large and especially to the United States. In this sense the Okinawa decision in 1951 formed not the end but the beginning of the Okinawa problem.

3

Evolution: from the Peace Treaty to Land Settlement (1952–8)

At the time of the conclusion of the Japanese Peace Treaty, there were two possible courses for the future development of the Okinawa problem. The first possibility was that there would be a favourable change in the status of Okinawa when the overall relations between Japan and the United States were further improved. Recovery of Japan's economic strength and the consequent increase of her military contribution to the Western alliance would enable her to negotiate over Okinawa with the United States on more favourable terms. Only time would help the two countries to work out a solution acceptable to them both.

The other possibility was that improvement of Japan's status in relation to the United States would not necessarily facilitate a solution of the Okinawa problem. On the contrary, the American military might adhere more and more stubbornly to the *status quo* on Okinawa as Japan gained more voice in the operation of the U.S.-Japan alliance system.

As mentioned in the previous chapter, Japanese leaders were thinking largely in terms of the first course while many Americans were envisaging the second.

For the first few months after the conclusion of the Japanese Peace Treaty, events seemed to favour the first view. In this period the American authorities appeared ready to take a very lenient attitude towards Japan's special relations with Okinawa. On the occasion of the inauguration of the Government of the Ryukyu Islands (GRI), which took place shortly before the Peace Treaty came into force, General M. B. Ridgway, the then Governor of the Ryukyu Islands, gave an outline of post-Treaty policy in Okinawa

31

in his message. It included the following points: (1) the Ryukyu Islands would be politically separate from Japan for a certain period of time under the provisions of the Peace Treaty. This would not, however, sever the time-honoured cultural and economic ties between the Ryukyus and Japan; (2) relations between them would be restricted only as was necessary for military security; (3) the United States would remove unnecessary restrictions on travel, communication and trade between the Ryukyus and Japan; and (4) cultural, educational and economic ties of the Ryukyus with Japan which had been interrupted by the last war should be restored.[1]

A similar liberal tone was recognized in the American policy concerning 'self-government' of Okinawa. The Civil Administrator of the Ryukyu Islands emphasized in his speech made on the same occasion that the U.S. policy in Okinawa would aim at the establishment of a freely elected government based on democratic principles because, he pointed out, no matter how excellent its achievement might be, a government run by an appointed official would not match a popular government from the viewpoint of welfare for the people. He referred more specifically to the newly established Ryukyuan Legislature as an important step in that direction and said that the goal would be achieved by another step, namely, a popular election for the head of the executive branch of the GRI.[2]

On the diplomatic level, negotiations for the 'Note Concerning Trade and Financial Arrangements between [Japanese] Mainland and Nansei Shotō' (July 1952) was a test of the American policy dealing with the mutual relations between the Ryukyus and Japan. The matter was originated by GRI officials in charge of trade and industry with the intention of establishing special (i.e. quasi-domestic) relations between Japan and Okinawa in the fields of trade and financial arrangements, so that Okinawa would be treated more favourably than other countries in customs duties, quota of imported goods and so on. Although, strictly speaking, GRI was not empowered to conduct diplomatic negotiations with any countries, including Japan, the American authorities consented that the parties to the negotiations for this particular matter should be the Japanese government and the GRI. Thus for the first time since the war an official contact was made between the Ryukyus and Japan. The negotiators signed an agreement in Tokyo on 10 July 1952. Drafters of this document carefully avoided the use of words which might imply that the relations between the two signatories were the same as the relations between foreign states, because they were afraid that a third country might take advantage of this to ask for a most-favoured nation treatment.

Although the Americans accepted GRI's explanation on these points, they raised some difficulties about the formality of the document, insisting that signatures of Japanese officials of permanent undersecretary rank and of a GRI official with a corresponding status would be insufficient to effect the agreement. The Japanese and Okinawans contended that signatures of upper-level officials would not be necessary because the document concerned only semi-domestic relations. Consequently the note came into effect on 1 October signed by the Deputy Governor of the Ryukyu Islands only and without any signature of higher authorities on the Japanese side.[3]

Although it is not quite clear whether the Americans accepted the Japanese (and Okinawan) contention about the 'quasi-domestic' status of Okinawa, the conclusion of this and other 'agreements' of similar sort in fact granted Okinawa special privileges in relation with Japan.[4]

Regarding the long-term policy of the United States towards the islands specified in Article 3 of the Japanese Peace Treaty, two views were held in the American government. This was illustrated by the difference in opinion concerning the Ogasawara islands between the State and the Defense Department. Some seven thousand former inhabitants, who had been evacuated by the Japanese Navy during the war, were now longing to return to their home. The State Department officials in charge of Japanese affairs were sympathetic to their cause, but the Defense Department experts took a firm stand. When Robert Murphy, the first American Ambassador to Japan after the war, showed enthusiasm for a solution of this problem, Admiral Arthur W. Radford, Commander-in-Chief of the Pacific, went to Tokyo to persuade him not to relinquish Ogasawara, emphasizing its strategic value to the U.S. Navy. The Admiral succeeded in his mission and as a consequence the Japanese demand was turned down.[5]

There was some evidence that a similar discussion about Okinawa was going on in U.S. government circles, particularly regarding a possible return of the Amami group of the Ryukyu Islands to Japan.[6] Murphy was quoted by *Gaimushō* officials as having revealed his sympathy on this subject, although this was repudiated shortly afterwards by a State Department spokesman.[7]

The American intention to return the Amami to Japan was

announced officially in August 1953 by Secretary of State Dulles who was visiting Tokyo for the purpose of persuading the Japanese government to accelerate its defence build-up. This promise was realized by the conclusion of the 'Agreement between Japan and the United States of America concerning the Amami Islands' (signed at Tokyo on 24 December 1953; effective 25 December 1953).[8] Although the return of the islands was generally welcomed by the public, the suddenness of the United States' decision made some people wonder what its real intention was. For example, it was suggested in the Diet debate that the Japanese government might have made important concessions on the status of the remaining Ryukyu Islands in exchange for the return of the Amami islands. In replying to this question, Okazaki Katsuo, Minister of Foreign Affairs, said that the Americans had proposed, in a note attached to the agreement, to confirm the American rights to retain the remaining Ryukyus until conditions of an endurable peace and security were established in the Far East; he revealed that the Japanese negotiators had opposed this. Consequently, the United States withdrew the proposal and instead issued a unilateral statement declaring its position.[9]

With the conclusion of the Amami Agreement, the Okinawa problem entered the second phase which was characterized by the United States' tougher policy. The first sign of this was Dulles's statement on the occasion of the signing of that agreement, which said in part:

> The United States Government believes that it is essential . . . that the United States continue to exercise its present powers and rights in the remaining Ryukyu Islands and in the other islands specified in Article 3 of the peace treaty so long as conditions of threat and tension exist in the Far East . . . [10]

The course set out in Dulles's statement was reaffirmed in President Dwight D. Eisenhower's State of the Union message to Congress in January 1954, which stated: 'We shall maintain indefinitely our bases in Okinawa.' This position was to be confirmed repeatedly by the U.S. authorities on various occasions.

The main purpose of these statements by top American leaders was to make clear to the Japanese and Okinawans that they would not make any further concessions regarding Okinawa in the foreseeable future. By so doing, they hoped to dismiss any doubts about the continued American military presence in the island. Behind the Americans' firm stand on Okinawa lay their belief in the increased importance of the Okinawan base in the new American defence policy in Asia. Writing about this time, Secretary of State Dulles said:

> On December 26, 1953, President Eisenhower made an important statement which clearly reflected our present policy as applied to Asia. He announced a progressive reduction of United States ground forces in Korea. However, he went on to point out that United States military forces in the Far East will now feature 'highly mobile naval, air and amphibious units;' and he added that in this way, despite some withdrawal of land forces, the United States will have a capacity to oppose aggression 'with even greater effect than before.' In the same month the United States reaffirmed its intent to maintain in Okinawa the rights made available to us by the Japanese Peace Treaty. *This location is needed to ensure striking power to implement the collective security concept* [my italics].[11]

In other words, Dulles's concept of collective security in the Western Pacific depended partly on the effective use of Okinawa by the United States. Thus 1954 saw many indications that the United States was strengthening its control over Okinawa.

First an open attack was made against the local movement for reunion with Japan. Elaborating the purport of the presidential message of January 1954, General David A. D. Ogden, Deputy Governor of the Ryukyu Islands, issued a statement in which he warned all persons and groups who had been engaged in the movement that they desist from activities organized for that purpose, describing it as 'a mere waste of labour'. He also emphasized the special character of the Okinawan bases as distinguished from those on the Japanese mainland, pointing out that it was impossible in Okinawa, as it was not in Japan, to separate civil administration from military control.[12] The warning was directed in particular to the Council for the Return of the Okinawa Islands to the Fatherland *(Okinawashotō Sokokufukki Kiseikai)* and to its most active member, the Okinawa Teachers' Association. Consequently, Yara Chōbyō, the chairman of the Council who was also the president of the OTA, was forced to resign from the chairmanship of the Council.[13]

Secondly, the United States now showed a marked reservation about the question of self-rule for Okinawa, especially the popular election of the Chief Executive of the GRI. The American authorities virtually withdrew their promise to grant the Okinawan people the right to elect their own leader by popular vote. The Ryukyuan

Legislature had passed an Act providing for procedures for the election of the Chief Executive. The U.S. Civil Administration of the Ryukyu Islands (USCAR) issued an Ordinance suspending implementation of this Act, pending its decision.[14] This step could not, however, prevent Okinawan legislators from making further efforts. In the first half of 1954 they carried a resolution calling for an early conduct of an election for a Chief Executive. USCAR flatly refused this demand, declaring that such an action of the legislators was *ultra vires*. So long as there was a threat of 'communist aggression' in Okinawa, USCAR stated, not all the political freedoms which the Okinawan people wanted could be realized.[15]

Third and most important, there was the ambitious but perhaps ill-conceived programme of the United States on the matter of military land acquisition in Okinawa. It caused serious friction between the United States and the local population. The importance and complexity of the land question justifies its description in some detail.[16]

Originally, the United States acquired Okinawan land as an act of war, with no compensation to the landowners. The legal ground for that action was provided, the Americans maintained, by the 'Regulations Respecting the Laws and Customs of War on Land' attached to the Hague Convention no. 4, of 18 October 1907 (Section III, Article 52). The situation remained unchanged until 28 April 1952 when the Japanese Peace Treaty came into force. In this way some 42,000 acres of Okinawan land were requisitioned for the United States Forces.[17]

In the meantime there was a growing demand among the dispossessed landowners for compensation for their land. The United States disclaimed any legal responsibility for making compensation for the use of Okinawan land before the Japanese Peace Treaty came into force on the ground that in that treaty Japan waived all claims of that kind. The U.S. Army, however, thought it necessary for political reasons to satisfy the Okinawan landowners. Thus the United States decided to make rental payments retrospectively to 1 July 1950, but to retain the use of such lands under a twenty-years' lease with this date as the starting point.

This programme was strongly resisted by the interested landowners who were dissatisfied both with the idea of a long-term lease and with the amount to be paid. Originally, the annual rental for each individual tract was determined at 6 per cent of the fee value of land as of 1 July 1950. Since most landowners failed to make a contract on such terms, the U.S. Army re-appraised the value of the military land in Okinawa as of 28 April 1952 so that the amount of annual rental was to be computed at 6 per cent of the estimated market value. Since, however, land was rarely sold in Okinawa, it was difficult to estimate the market value of land. The re-appraisal often had to be made, therefore, on the basis of the declared value of the land as registered for tax purposes. This meant that the land values were underestimated because the registered values did not represent fairly the actual worth of land. The American efforts to obtain leases from Okinawan landowners based on the new appraisals were again unsuccessful. In the face of such difficulties, the U.S. military had to resort to coercive measures in some cases, in order to implement its land acquisition programme as it wished.[18] This in turn not only intensified the objections of the interested landowners but also caused resentment amongst the Okinawan public at large.

The United States tried to solve this difficulty by introducing lump-sum payments in lieu of the existing annual rental system. This method would, they thought, not only help them to get rid of frictions about annual rentals once and for all but also permit the dispossessed landowners to resettle elsewhere in the islands.[19]

When this policy was announced, however, the Okinawan reaction turned out to be contrary to American expectations. Virtually all political parties and the land representative body were against it. On 30 April 1954, the Ryukyuan Legislature adopted a resolution which set out 'four principles' for an acceptable settlement of the land problem. They were: (1) the United States should renounce the purchase of land or permanent use thereof and a lump-sum payment of rentals; (2) just and complete compensation should be made annually for the land currently in use; (3) indemnity should be paid promptly for all damage caused by the U.S. Forces; and (4) no further acquisition of land should be made, and the land which was not urgently needed by the United States government should be restored promptly.[20]

These Okinawan viewpoints were presented by a delegation headed by Higa Shūhei, Chief Executive of the GRI, before the U.S. House Armed Services Committee in June 1955. After hearing the appeal from the Okinawan delegation, the Committee sent a special subcommittee led by Congressman Melvin Price to inspect the problem on the spot, and deferred a final decision pending its report.[21] The Price Subcommittee submitted a recommendation which on the whole favoured the policy of acquiring the 'fee title' to the lands by the payment of lump sums, although it admitted that

37

the method of determining the amount of compensation under the existing scheme was inadequate and unrealistic.[22]

Once the Price Subcommittee Report was made public, it aroused active opposition not only in Okinawa itself but also in Japan. Objections centred on the doubt whether, if this policy was successfully carried out, the landowners concerned would lose all title to their lands, which meant in effect establishment of a U.S. sovereign area in Japanese territory. In spite of repetitive explanations by United States officials that legal title would rest with the former landowners even if the new land policy came into effect, they could not dispel the serious doubt in the minds of the general public. Thus the Okinawa problem, which had hitherto attracted little notice from the outside world, came to the fore as a matter of national concern for Japan.

The Japanese government could have taken advantage of this situation to resume diplomatic negotiations with the United States on the Okinawa problem after a long stalemate which had lasted since the latter part of Yoshida's premiership. The Hatoyama Cabinet failed to do that mainly because it was preoccupied with the problem of restoring diplomatic relations with the Soviet Union. It was Kishi Nobusuke who succeeded Hatoyama Ichirō (after a short-lived Ishibashi Cabinet) and undertook this task. He raised the matter at his talks with President Eisenhower in June 1957. Although he got no substantial concessions from the President, Kishi expressed the strong desire of the Japanese people for a return of administrative power over Okinawa and Ogasawara to Japan. The relevant part of the joint communiqué of President Eisenhower and Prime Minister Kishi on 21 June 1957 read as follows:

> The Prime Minister emphasized the strong desire of the Japanese people for the return of administrative control over the Ryukyu and Bonin Islands to Japan. The President reaffirmed the United States position that Japan possesses residual sovereignty over these islands. He pointed out, however, that so long as the conditions of threat and tension exist in the Far East the United States will find it necessary to continue the present status. He stated that the United States will continue its policy of improving the welfare and well-being of the inhabitants of the islands and of promoting their economic and cultural advancement.[23]

The Japanese government was now finally in a position to make diplomatic negotiations with the United States concerning Okinawa.

It is important that the main theme of the Kishi-Eisenhower joint communiqué of June 1957 was a review of security arrangements between the two countries in the light of a new stage of U.S.-Japan relations and that the question of Okinawa was discussed also in this connection. As for the larger problem of the U.S.-Japan alliance system, the communiqué suggested a basic line for future discussions by confirming the U.S. decision to withdraw from Japan substantial numbers of its forces, including all ground combat troops, within the coming year. This, however, implied that additional weight would be attached to Okinawa in American strategy in Asia. Less reliance of the United States on foreign (in this case Japanese) bases would entail its heavier dependence on 'sovereign' (i.e. Okinawan) bases. In fact, it seems that this was the premise on which the United States decided to withdraw its combat forces from Japan.

Various efforts by the United States to consolidate its military position on Okinawa during this period substantiate this conjecture. For example, parts of the Third Marine Division (roughly three-quarters of the whole division) which had been stationed in Japan were moved to Okinawa. This was obviously part of the whole programme of reorganization of the American forces in the Pacific because of the withdrawal from Japan. In line with the current emphasis on the tactical use of nuclear weapons for limited war, the United States decided to arm Okinawa with Nike Hawks.[24]

In order to retain Okinawan bases for a long period, the United States found it necessary to reshape its policy to Okinawa in certain points. Regarding the constitutional question, some amendments were made by Executive Order no. 10713, Providing for Administration of the Ryukyu Islands (5 June 1957).[25] It was provided therein that a new office of High Commissioner of the Ryukyu Islands should be created in place of Deputy Governor. A High Commissioner was to be appointed by the Secretary of Defense (and therefore accountable to him) unlike the Deputy Governor who was appointed by the Governor, namely the Commander-in-Chief of the Far East Command. However, like his predecessors, the High Commissioner was to be appointed from among Army officers on active duty. Thus the administration of Okinawa was brought under direct supervision of the Washington government.

The Executive Order also provided that a Chief Executive of the GRI should be appointed by the High Commissioner 'after consultation with representatives of the legislative body', while under the old regulations he had been appointed simply by the Deputy

Governor. In a sense this can be regarded as an amendment in the interests of the Okinawan people. One must not, however, overlook the fact that the popular election of the head of the government disappeared completely from the new regulation; it was not even an ultimate goal of constitutional development in Okinawa.

More important, however, the United States finally decided the land issue. In April 1958 General James E. Moore, the High Commissioner, revealed in his statement to the Ryukyuan Legislature that a new land policy was under study in Washington.[26] Secretary of State Dulles confirmed this, saying that 'the present policy did not seem to win complete favour among the Okinawans'.[27] After Ryukyu-American negotiations in Washington and at Naha, an agreement was finally reached on a new programme. The United States renounced its former policy of acquiring land through 'determinable estate' and, instead, was to have either an indefinite leasehold or a five-year leasehold, subject to the option of the landowner in question. A concession was also made with regard to the land rental rate so that it would approximately double that under the former system.[28] The United States thus finally removed the source of greatest friction over its policies in Okinawa.

The settlement of the land problem in Okinawa marked the end of an era in the post-Treaty development of the Okinawa problem.[29] The decisive factor in this period was the growing friction between the United States and the local population of Okinawa chiefly because of the mismanagement of the land question by the United States.

This period was characterized, except initially, by the United States' tough policy on Okinawa. The liberal tone which tinged the American attitudes in the beginning almost entirely disappeared with the conclusion of the Amami Agreement. The statement of Secretary of State Dulles on Okinawa on that occasion confirmed the American position that it would remain in Okinawa semi-permanently. This enabled the U.S. Army in Okinawa to work out a long-term programme. The military land acquisition programme was a basic part of the whole plan. The Americans' insensitivity to local sentiment on this matter produced tension with the Okinawan people. This, together with the United States' reversal of its attitude towards the movements for self-rule and for the return of Okinawa to Japan, led to the charge that it was practising colonial rule in Okinawa. The advent of Senaga Kamejirō, leader of the leftist Okinawa People's Party, as mayor of Naha (capital of Okinawa) in December 1956 and the pressure applied by the American authorities in Okinawa to make him resign certainly seriously damaged the United States' public image as a democratic country.[30]

In the diplomatic field, a marked feature of this period was the Japanese government's inactivity. But the crisis of land settlement in Okinawa brought the Okinawa problem to public attention in Japan. The post-Treaty resurgence of Japanese nationalism partly helped the growth of public concern about Okinawa at this time. The Okinawan people now finally escaped from a sense of isolation.

The United States found itself in an awkward situation after this development. If, as the Price Report pointed out, the lack of militant nationalism in Okinawa justified the U.S. policy of maintaining Okinawan bases for a long while, the emotional involvement of the Japanese people in the Okinawa problem greatly reduced the merit of this arrangement. This meant that public opinion in Japan now became a factor which the United States could not ignore in dealing with the Okinawa problem. Although the Japanese government could only render indirect and moral support on the land controversy, it was almost inevitable that public opinion would push it towards more positive efforts which would produce a solution. The next chapter will deal with the Okinawa problem as a diplomatic question between the United States and Japan.

4

Towards U.S. – Japan Partnership (1958–65)

The advent of the Kishi administration in 1957 introduced a new factor in the post-Treaty U.S.-Japanese relations. Although its fundamental orientation was a pro-Western alliance, the new leaders were receptive to the current feeling of national self-assertion. In this regard, the Kishi government followed the policy of the Hatoyama government. But while Hatoyama had tried to express national feeling by restoring diplomatic relations with the Soviet Union, Kishi attempted to do so by improving Japan's relations with the United States. It was the aim of his visit to Washington in mid-1957, to use Kishi's own words, 'to put Japan on an equal footing with the United States and, by so doing, to make the relationship between the two countries that of a genuine partnership'. He believed that various problems pending between the two countries, Okinawa being one of them, should be dealt with by this principle.[1]

What then was the Kishi administration's approach to the Okinawa problem in particular? The Kishi government showed that it regarded it as part of the broader question of revision of the U.S.-Japan Security Treaty. As early as August 1957, Fujiyama Aiichirō, Foreign Minister of the Kishi Cabinet, was asked about the *modus operandi* of a newly established U.S.-Japan Committee on Security Problems which was one of the results of the Kishi-Eisenhower conference. He told the press conference that he did not see any reason to avoid discussion about Okinawa and Ogasawara in the committee because, he said, the problem of these islands was, after all, connected with the problem of security arrangements between the United States and Japan.[2] Actually, however, the committee did not discuss the Okinawa problem. Neither did it work out any programme for revising the Security Treaty.[3]

It was in the Dulles-Fujiyama talks in September of the following year that the United States agreed to the Japanese proposal to start negotiations with a view to revising the Security Treaty.[4] It was reported that the Kishi government intended to include Okinawa and Ogasawara in the defence area which would be covered by a new security treaty with the United States. There were two justifications for this proposal. Firstly, from a diplomatic viewpoint, if Japan wanted to have a mutual defence type treaty she would have to offer an obligation of joint defence in those areas which were under American administration, if not in the American territory itself. Secondly, for domestic considerations, such a proposal would provide the government with a political weapon to embarrass the Opposition: if the Opposition consented, it would be a significant departure from their sacred policy of non-participation in military conflicts outside Japan; if they opposed it, they would be accused of preoccupation with Japan's safety at the expense of their compatriots in Okinawa.[5]

The Kishi government had to, however, withdraw this proposal because of severe criticism at home.

In the meantime, the Japanese government had been trying to obtain an understanding from the United States government about increased economic assistance to Okinawa. In this field, too, the Dulles-Fujiyama talks of September 1958 marked the first step towards a co-operative relationship between the United States and Japan. On that occasion,

> Foreign Minister Fujiyama welcomed the current discussions taking place between the United States authorities and Ryukyuan representatives looking towards a satisfactory resolution of the land problem. Secretary Dulles expressed his understanding of this Japanese interest in the Ryukyus and it was agreed that on Ryukyuan matters the two governments would continue to exchange views through diplomatic channels.[6]

Although this joint statement did not specify the aspects on which the two governments would exchange their views with respect to the Ryukyus, it was clear from Fujiyama's explanation before the Japanese Diet that the discussion would be conducted with a view to 'increasing economic assistance for the promotion of the welfare of the Okinawan people'.[7] In the subsequent negotiations the United States agreed to accept Japan's offer of some 23.6 million yen for technical assistance in Okinawa for the Japanese fiscal year of 1959.[8] Although the Japanese government had been appro-

43

priating money for economic assistance to Okinawa since Japan regained her independence in 1952, the case in 1959 set a new precedent because assistance was rendered on an explicit agreement with the United States (see Table 1).

Table 1

RECAPITULATION OF JAPANESE APPROPRIATED FUNDS FOR OKINAWA
(in thousands of yen)

Fiscal year	Economic assistance	Administration*	Annuities, pensions, etc.	Total
1952	2,160	11,456	—	13,616
1953	5,874	90,900	48,471	145,245
1954	7,722	60,785	532,779	601,286
1955	10,259	29,730	978,139	1,018,128
1956	1,145,788†	74,070	2,141,360	3,361,218
1957	19,977	74,576	2,674,010	2,768,563
1958	33,576	77,342	2,656,496	2,767,414
1959	104,993	50,643	3,007,799	3,163,435
1960	81,095	57,702	3,687,960	3,826,757
1961	511,824	67,749	3,881,654	4,461,277
1962	1,012,831	61,271	2,741,455	3,815,557
1963	1,830,671	152,860	3,070,203	5,053,734
1964	1,864,358	131,578	3,030,277	5,026,213
1965	2,861,630	123,189	2,320,533	5,305,352
1966	5,800,971	142,629		
1967	10,352,768			
1968	15,377,176			
1969	22,749,023			
1970	35,016,885			

SOURCE: Sōrifu, *Okinawa sankō shiryō* (mimeo, January 1966), pp. 456-7; Ōkurashō Zaisei Chōsakai, *Kuni no yosan*.
*Expenditures for various Japanese governmental agencies in charge of Okinawan affairs in Tokyo and at Naha.
†The special expenditure in the name of *mimaikin* (i.e. solatium) that amounted to 1,128,170,000 yen (the greatest part of which was paid to the Okinawan landowners for the damage caused by the American forces before the Peace Treaty) accounts for the unusual increase for 1956.

This trend continued in the following year. A new feature in the 1960 programme was the 'Iriomote development plan'. It was a programme to promote agricultural, forestry and other industrial developments in the island of Iriomote, which was the second-largest island in the Ryukyus next to the main island of Okinawa, but which had remained at a very low stage of development. The American authorities in the Ryukyus responded with considerable enthusiasm to the Japanese government's proposal that the two countries should make collective efforts to explore the island's potential. As a result of this, several survey teams were sent, separately and jointly, to Iriomote in 1960–1. 'The Iriomote development plan' received much publicity in the Okinawan and Japanese press and was spoken of as a symbol of U.S.-Japanese collaboration over Okinawa.[9]

It is desirable to turn our attention for a while to Okinawa itself. In August 1958 when the final settlement of the land problem became merely a matter of time, the United States authorities in Okinawa announced important economic policies. In the first place, it was decided that U.S. dollars would be adopted as the sole legal tender in Okinawa in place of the existing Okinawan yen. (One Okinawan yen, which was usually called 'B yen', was roughly equivalent to three Japanese yen.) In connection with this, they introduced successive new measures: they established a free trade area at Naha port and amended the regulations governing foreign capital so as to attract more foreign investment into Okinawa.[10] These steps were obviously taken to make Okinawa economically viable and thereby secure continued control of the island by the United States. In spite of considerable hostility at the outset against such measures,[11] these economic policies, together with a timely inflow of money from the United States and Japan, created a seemingly prosperous economy in Okinawa within a few years.[12]

Backed by this success in the economic field, the United States also restored political stability in Okinawa. A conspicuous sign of this success was a sweeping victory for the Conservatives in the 1960 elections for the Legislature; they won twenty-two out of the total twenty-nine seats; previously they had had fourteen. The United States authorities welcomed this 'healthy showing' of Okinawan politics.[13]

An important characteristic of the new leadership in Okinawa, generally known as the Ōta regime, was its pro-American and at the same time pro-Japanese orientation. Ōta Seisaku, leader of the newly united Okinawa Liberal Democratic Party (OLDP), advocated that the U.S., Japan and Ryukyu jointly promote the welfare of the inhabitants of Okinawa. In more concrete terms, he proposed a tripartite commission for the economic and social advancement of Okinawa financed by both the American and Japanese governments. This policy, he argued, would prevent anti-American elements from exploiting the Okinawa problem in their own interests and would assist the ultimate return of the island to Japan in a practical and orderly way. He described this policy as a 'step-by-step return to Japan' *(tsumikasane fukki).*[14]

Collaboration was, however, only one aspect of the policy of U.S.-Japan partnership on Okinawa; competition was another. Not

The Okinawa Problem

only pecuniary matters but also psychological factors became involved in this competition. Although it was only at a later stage of the development of this policy that its competitive aspect imposed some diplomatic problems for the two countries, there were already some signs of rivalry at this stage. For example, one of the most important purposes behind the legislation of the Price Act[15] in the U.S. Congress was to give the Ryukyuan man-in-the-street a

> sense of belonging which he does not now have, a feeling that the United States is interested in his welfare and well-being and that the people of the United States are willing to pledge continuation of that interest as long as the present arrangement of control exists.[16]

It can be said that the purpose of the Price Act was to present American 'economic aid' to Okinawa more tangibly and impressively to the Okinawan public.

The problem involved here was the reconciliation of the different purposes of the United States and Japan in their policy of co-operation. The Americans wanted to show their intention to remain in the Ryukyus for a long time 'by demonstrations of brotherly assistance';[17] the Japanese wanted to increase their say in the civil administration in Okinawa and, if fortunate, recover the island to their full sovereignty by increasing their country's economic contributions. Most of the Ikeda Cabinet's diplomatic efforts on Okinawa were to be centred on this problem.

In June 1960 the controversial new U.S.-Japan Security Treaty was finally ratified by the Diet despite the Opposition's boycott and frequent street demonstrations by the indignant public. President Eisenhower's visit to Tokyo, which was intended to be the highlight of the new era of U.S.-Japanese relations, had to be cancelled, although the President made a brief visit to Okinawa on 19 June. Kishi resigned and Ikeda Hayato took office in July. In Washington, too, the new leadership under President John F. Kennedy was organized in January 1961 after eight years of Republican rule. In February of the same year, General Paul W. Caraway succeeded General Donald P. Booth as the new High Commissioner for Okinawa. What were the effects of these changes of three leading figures on the Okinawa problem?

Unlike his predecessor, Ikeda took little interest in the military aspects of U.S.-Japanese relations, but rather concerned himself with strengthening Japan's economic power. Japan's economic contribution to development programmes in Okinawa fitted in well with the general pattern of his political method.[18] Japanese political and business leaders showed great sympathy toward Ōta, when the Okinawan leader visited Tokyo in July-August 1960 to appeal to the Japanese government to increase its financial assistance to Okinawa. The Japanese press also gave considerable publicity to the idea of a 'new U.S.-Japan-Ryukyu partnership' advocated by Ōta.[19]. As a result, the Japanese government decided to increase six-fold its economic aid for 1961 to the Ryukyus (see Table 1).

The advent of the Kennedy administration was also welcomed by those who were in favour of progressive U.S.-Japanese co-operation over Okinawa, because it was free, they thought, from what had been said and done about Okinawa in the past by its Republican predecessor.[20]

Small wonder, therefore, that many people had great expectations of a Kennedy-Ikeda conference. In anticipation of Ikeda's visit to Washington there was a rush of petitions and demands from various individuals, groups and political parties in Japan and in Okinawa. The various demands they presented can be summarized in four points: (1) return of the political control over Okinawa to Japan as soon as possible; (2) enlargement of the political rights of the people of Okinawa; (3) increase of Japan's economic assistance to Okinawa and (4) a clearer understanding in the United States of Japan's part in the continued development of the economy and social welfare of the Okinawan people, and in particular the creation of an inter-governmental committee to facilitate such co-operation.

There were some indications, however, that the American military authorities were anxious about the tendency towards an increasing Japanese involvement in Okinawa. Various statements and actions made or taken by officials of USCAR in the first few months of 1961 can be interpreted as expressing this feeling. A high-ranking USCAR official showed reluctance at the Ryukyuans' request for the right to have their own representatives in the Japanese Diet. He also stated rather outspokenly that a U.S.-Japan-Ryukyuan commission to promote the economic advancement of Okinawa would be of no use.[21] The High Commissioner showed no interest in the Okinawan pleas for the extension of their own government's authority but hinted instead that he might tighten his control over it.[22] It was also announced that the scheme to send Japanese school teachers, intended to improve education in Okinawa, should be cancelled for 1961, the third year of an annual programme which had started in 1959.[23] In his address to the

Legislature in May 1961, Chief Executive Ōta failed to say even a word about the much publicized plan of a U.S.-Japan-Ryukyu commission.[24] This attitude may have been influenced by the luke-warm response from USCAR officials.

All this happened during the few months after the appointment of the new High Commissioner Caraway and, therefore, was generally attributed to his own personality. At the same time, how-ever, it might have been reflection of the views prevailing among the Defense Department officials at that time. These views were expressed, for example, in a statement that the Defense Department had made public in reply to questions by a Japanese news agency, the *Kyōdō*. It was revealed in this statement that no consideration was being given to a change of policy to allow the Okinawan people to hoist the Japanese flag for public purposes; they also said that they saw no necessity to delegate administrative functions con-cerning Okinawan education to the Japanese government because it was a common practice, they maintained, both in the United States and in Japan, for local authorities to assume responsibilities for such matters.[25]

These attitudes were obviously related to the conviction, strengthened by the current military and political situations in the Far East (e.g. the Laotian crisis in 1961–2), that Okinawa was and would continue to be America's single most important military base in that part of the world. As a high-ranking Defense Department official stated in testimony to Congress,

> If circumstances were to force our military planners to select the base complex in the Far East which the United States should maintain, I am confident that they would unanimously name the Ryukyus without a moment's hesitation or regard for the colour of their uniform; for the Ryukyus, particularly Okinawa, con-stitute a major U.S. military complex in the Western Pacific.[26]

A special commission of the Department of Defense studied a plan of the Kennedy administration for reorganizing the global network of American military bases. It took the view that, irrespective of the necessary closing of some of those bases, the complete military installations on Okinawa should be maintained without any change for a long period in view of current and long-term military require-ments of the United States.[27] It should be pointed out here that it had been decided in the previous year to build launching sites for Mace B intermediate range ballistic missiles (IRBMs) on Okin-awa.[28]

It was under these circumstances that the Kennedy-Ikeda conference was held in June 1961 in Washington. The Okinawa problem was among the most important subjects in their talks.[29] The
relevant passage of their joint communiqué read as follows:

> The President and the Prime Minister exchanged views on
> matters relating to the Ryukyu and Bonin Islands, which are
> under United States administration but in which Japan retains
> residual sovereignty. The President affirmed that the United
> States would make further efforts to enhance the welfare and
> well-being of the inhabitants of the Ryukyus and welcomed
> Japanese co-operation in these efforts; the Prime Minister
> affirmed that Japan would continue to co-operate with the
> United States to this end.[30]

The characteristic feature of the Kennedy-Ikeda communiqué on
Okinawa was that they affirmed co-operative efforts to enhance the
economic and social conditions of the Okinawan people. Another
product of the Kennedy-Ikeda talks was (although it was not
expressed in the communiqué) the approval by the United States of
the right of the Okinawan people to hoist the Japanese flag on all
Okinawan public holidays.[31]

These were interpreted as a victory for the advocates of U.S.-
Japan-Ryukyu partnership in Okinawa. In fact, the Kennedy
administration displayed considerable enthusiasm for a reshaping
of Okinawa policy. Shortly after the Kennedy-Ikeda conference,
the President appointed a special survey team headed by Dr Carl
Kaysen (Deputy Special Assistant to the President for National
Security Affairs) to investigate current conditions in Okinawa and
to determine what steps should be taken to improve American
policies and programmes in force there.[32] One of the most important recommendations made by the Kaysen team, which visited
Okinawa in October 1961, was the urgent need to increase American economic assistance to Okinawa and, for that purpose, to raise
the annual limitation of $6 million set out in the Price Act to $25
million. Attorney-General Robert F. Kennedy, who visited Japan
in early 1962, was also greatly impressed with the widespread wish
of the Japanese people for the return of Okinawa to Japanese
administration.[33] All this formed the background of Kennedy's
statement on Okinawa made in March 1962 and of a new Executive Order (no. 11010) amending Executive Order no. 10713
(which was originally issued by Eisenhower in June 1957).[34]

Compared to the stereotyped language in various policy statements on the Okinawa problem in the Eisenhower period, Kennedy's statement had a new outlook on the matter. 'I recognize', Kennedy said, 'the Ryukyus to be a part of the Japanese homeland and look forward to the day when the security interests of the Free World will permit their restoration to full Japanese sovereignty'. An American leader had never before made clear in such unmistakable terms that the return of Okinawa to Japan would be a final settlement of the Okinawa problem, although Kennedy failed to specify the date for such a return.

The immediate problem before the United States policy makers was, to quote again from his statement, how to reconcile 'the military imperative for continued United States administration with the desires of the Ryukyuan people to assert their identity as Japanese and obtain the economic and social welfare benefits available in Japan, and to have a greater voice in the management of their own affairs'.

In more concrete terms, there were three problems which Kennedy promised further efforts to solve. They were (1) to enhance the welfare and well-being of the inhabitants of Okinawa and, for that purpose, to ask Congress to amend the Price Act to remove the present $6 million limit on assistance to Okinawa; (2) to enter into discussions with the Japanese government to work out the precise arrangements of a co-operative relationship between the United States and Japan in providing assistance to promote the welfare and economic development of the Okinawan people; (3) to make some modifications in the governmental structure and procedures of the administration of Okinawa which included (a) the appointment of a 'civilian' civil administrator (an office under the High Commissioner which had been previously occupied by military personnel), (b) restating the Executive Order to clarify the restricted purposes of the veto power of the High Commissioner, (c) provisions for nomination of the Chief Executive of the GRI by the legislature, (d) transfer, when possible, of certain governmental functions to the GRI, and so on.

Kennedy proposed these measures in order 'to discharge more effectively our [American] responsibilities towards the people of the Ryukyus, and to minimize the stresses that will accompany the anticipated eventual restoration of the Ryukyu Islands to Japanese administration'. This approach was new in its recognition that political and economic developments in Okinawa should be planned in step with those of Japan and should be carried out with the co-operation of the Japanese.

Kennedy's new Okinawa policy, however, met with considerable resistance from some parts of American political circles. This was most typically illustrated by Congress's hostile reaction to a bill to amend the Price Act to increase the maximum amount of annual grant to the High Commissioner of the Ryukyu Islands to $25 million. Although the bill was passed by the House of Representatives without modifications, the Senate Armed Services Committee showed great reluctance to its passage in its original form, insisting that the ceiling should be only $12 million. A final decision was taken along the line of the Senate Committee's recommendation.[35] The House of Representatives Appropriation Committee, which was not consulted on the amendment of the Price Act itself, took an unsympathetic attitude towards the Executive's request for a larger appropriation for Okinawa for the 1963 fiscal year. The strongest reason for their attitude to Kennedy's Okinawa policy was that it would be unwise to spend American money on the Ryukyus if they were to be returned sooner or later to Japan. From this viewpoint, they opposed any action that might weaken the American position on Okinawa. It seemed to them, therefore, that Dulles's reference to Japan's residual sovereignty over Okinawa was the cause of the whole trouble about Okinawa; they regarded as nonsense Kennedy's recognition of the fact that the Ryukyus were part of the Japanese homeland and also his allowing the people of Okinawa the right to hoist the Japanese flag.[36] The logical conclusion of this argument was that if the Executive were to ask Congress for a significant amount of money for Okinawa then it should take a firmer position on the American interests in Okinawa. Because the proposed increase of American assistance to Okinawa was to be the core of Kennedy's new Okinawa policy, the rejection of that proposal by Congress was a serious handicap.

Kennedy's promise for the political advancement of the Okinawan people was not fully carried out either. Although a civilian was appointed to the post of Civil Administrator and this was welcomed, his authority was so small that his appointment simply could not change the basic character of a military government in Okinawa. A much more important factor was the political approach of the High Commissioner himself, and in this regard the situation was not very hopeful.[37] It would not be very far from the truth to say that Caraway's policy was to resist as much as possible the tendency for Japan to have more say in Okinawan affairs. On one occasion he said unreservedly that the whole responsibility for the administration of Okinawa lay in the hands of the United States, the only possible alternative being to place the island under a trusteeship as specified in the Japanese Peace Treaty. Japan's residual sovereignty had, he added, nothing to do with the present question of administration of Okinawa, let alone its implication on the future disposition of the island. Although he did not deny either an eventual return of Okinawa to Japan or her offer of money to improve the present conditions of the Okinawan people, he stressed the necessity for disposing of such assistance from Japan in a way that would not 'interfere unacceptably with the orderly carrying out of the U.S. administrative responsibilities to the Free World'.[38]

This was a virtual denial of the idea (which was entertained by people like Ōta) of a gradual return of Okinawa to Japanese administration through increase of Japan's role in the U.S.-Japanese partnership over Okinawa. A high-ranking official of the Japanese government was annoyed with Caraway's rigid adherence to the principle of exclusive rights of the United States in Okinawa, and he regretted the High Commissioner's failure to comply with the Japanese proposal for a long-term programme of economic assistance to the Ryukyus. In this connection, the same official also criticized the half-heartedness of the American administration with regard to the Iriomote development programme—a programme which had been much publicized.[39]

Caraway also disappointed the Okinawan people's expectation of larger areas of autonomy for their own government. Rather the High Commissioner tightened and extended his 'direct rule' on virtually every aspect of the administration of Okinawa ostensibly because of the local leaders' 'inefficiency' and 'corruption'. That was indeed the main theme of another controversial speech of his in which he made a sharp comment on the Okinawan people's 'hue and cry after "autonomy" ': 'Autonomy at the present time is a myth; it does not exist. And it won't exist unless you Ryukyuans determine of your own free wills that you wish once again to become an independent nation-state.' The only possible alternative in the given circumstances, he contended, would be delegation of certain areas of governmental functions from a higher to a lower level of authorities, and this could take place only when the latter proved to be 'efficient' and 'responsible'.[40]

This speech caused a great commotion in Okinawa, partly because the High Commissioner spoke to members of the Golden Gate Club which was made up of graduates of American universities; its purpose was to encourage them to accept more leadership in Okinawan society. His speech was interpreted as an indication of his lack of confidence in the existing indigenous leaders. Caraway's argument (perhaps accidentally) did not touch the point that what people meant by 'autonomy' in Okinawa was a transitional state from complete American control to full Japanese sovereignty. His refusal of the Okinawan demands for 'autonomy' could be, therefore, another way of denying their hope of political reunion with the rest of the Japanese community. The High Commissioner's tough policy caused some friction in relations even with the moderates in Okinawa and Japan.[41]

The foregoing account should not, however, be taken to suggest that the President and the military differed seriously in their opinions of the fundamental purpose of American control of Okinawa. In the policy statement mentioned above, President Kennedy took cognizance of 'the importance the United States attaches to its military bases in the Ryukyu Islands', describing their importance in the following terms:

> The armed strength deployed at these bases is of the greatest importance in maintaining our [i.e. American] deterrent power in the face of threats to the peace in the Far East. Our bases in the Ryukyu Islands help us assure our allies in the great area from Japan through Southeast Asia not only of our willingness but also of our ability to come to their assistance in case of need.

In fact, the increased emphasis on the need for preparations for guerrilla warfare was one of the characteristics of the Kennedy administration's defence policy. In March 1961 President Kennedy said in his special message to Congress on the defence budget that the United States wanted to develop military resources 'in the form of strong, highly mobile forces trained in this type of warfare [i.e. guerrilla warfare], some of which must be deployed in forward areas, with a substantial airlift and sealift capacity and prestocked overseas bases'. In connection with this the United States had come to give more importance to Okinawa.[42]

The only difference, though not insignificant, was that the President saw the necessity of satisfying 'the desire of the Japanese people to maintain close contact with their countrymen in the Ryukyus' for the very purpose of securing the 'military imperative for continued United States administration' of the Ryukyu Islands. The military services responsible for the Okinawan administration

were more cautious; they did not want Japanese influence to grow
to an extent which might jeopardize the American military interests
there.

Under these circumstances U.S.-Japanese negotiations for creation of some kind of inter-governmental machinery through which
the two governments were to co-ordinate their aid programmes to
Okinawa made but little progress. It took nearly two years from
the time Kennedy announced that his government was prepared to
enter into discussion with the Japanese government for that purpose
to the final agreement which was reached between them in April
1964. It was decided by this agreement that a U.S.-Japan Consultative Committee and a U.S.-Japan-Ryukyuan Technical Committee
should be set up in Tokyo and at Naha respectively. The Consultative Committee was to consist (on the Japanese side) of the Foreign
Minister and the Director-General of the *Sōrifu* and (on the American side) of the U.S. Ambassador to Japan. The Technical Committee in Naha was composed of representatives of USCAR, the
Japanese government and GRI. The Consultative Committee first
met on 25 April 1964.[43]

In spite of these major obstacles to the implementation of Ken-

Table 2
BREAKDOWN OF JAPAN'S ECONOMIC ASSISTANCE TO OKINAWA
(in thousands of yen)

Fiscal year	Total*	Education†	Technical assistance	Industrial development	Social security
1952	2,160	2,160	—	—	—
1953	5,874	5,874	—	—	—
1954	7,722	7,722	—	—	—
1955	10,259	10,259	—	—	—
1956	1,145,788	14,418	—	—	—
1957	19,977	16,174	—	—	—
1958	33,576	18,326	—	—	—
1959	104,993	30,544	12,296	—	—
1960	81,095	39,320	21,880	—	—
1961	511,824	58,717	19,954	13,893	9,208
1962	1,012,831	77,882	29,285	526,117	78,097
1963	1,830,671	106,120	29,505	1,229,764	237,798
1964	1,864,358	183,478	32,329	1,123,253	371,265
1965	2,861,630	488,609	49,445	1,473,527	621,426
1966	5,800,971	2,870,035	69,730	1,275,884	1,078,216

SOURCE: Sōrifu, *Okinawa sankō shiryō* (mimeo, January 1966), pp. 456-7.
*The difference between the total and the sum of the figures in the other
columns in that year is the miscellaneous items which include expeditures
for *Nampō Dōhō Engokai*, solatium (from time to time) and others.
†Increase in the expenditures on education in later years is due to the
programme for the free distribution of textbooks for school children.

nedy's new Okinawa policy in every important aspect, there was a steady increase in Japan's economic assistance to Okinawa throughout the whole period of the Ikeda government. Its increase in the 1961 budget was especially significant because in this year two new items in Japan's economic assistance began. They were the promotion of industrial developments and the improvement of social security services in Okinawa. These two items account largely for the marked increase of Japanese assistance in the subsequent years (see Table 2).

Furthermore an important change in the nature of such financial assistance was taking place because these new items of assistance, unlike those in the previous stages, were to be transferred directly to the general account of the Government of the Ryukyu Islands. Although technically the Japanese government was not in a position to supervise the Okinawan government, as its contributions to GRI funds increased it began to have an important influence on Okinawan affairs. (For a comparison of Japanese and American contributions to GRI funds, see Table 3.)

Table 3

SHARE OF JAPANESE, U.S. AND RYUKYUAN FUNDS IN THE GENERAL
ACCOUNT OF THE GOVERNMENT OF THE RYUKYU ISLANDS

Fiscal year*	Japan $000	%	U.S. $000	%	GRI	%	Total
1958	—		817	3.3	23,778	96.7	24,595
1959	—		2,316	9.8	21,655	90.2	24,016
1960	—		2.456	9.6	22,996	90.4	25,452
1961	—		3,105	11.2	24,509	88.8	27,614
1962	55	0.2	4,821	13.6	30,434	86.2	35,310
1963	417	1.2	6,621	14.9	37,400	83.9	44,438
1964	2,664	5.2	5,220	10.1	43,585	84.7	51,469
1965	4,258	7.7	5,801	10.5	45,377	81.8	55,436
1966	5,890	8.9	7.091	10.7	53,424	80.4	66,405
1967	15,375	17.1	10,265	11.4	64,386	71.5	90,026
1968	23,715	19.8	16,668	13.9	79,369	66.3	119,752

SOURCE: Sōrifu, *Okinawa sankō shiryō* (mimeo, January 1966), pp. 426-7; Ryūkyū Seifu, *Okinawa yōran*, 1967, p. 147; *Okinawa Nenkan*, 1968, p. 598.
*The Ryukyuan fiscal year is the same as the American.

The amount and purposes of financial assistance from the Japanese government to the Ryukyus were to be determined annually through negotiations between the Japanese government and the American authorities in Okinawa. Since, however, the Americans were not ready to treat the Japanese as equal partners but instead regarded Japanese assistance as being merely supplementary to their own responsibilities in Okinawa, it was difficult for the Americans to accept the Japanese offer for a rapid increase in economic assistance to the Ryukyus. This was especially so when the American Executive's proposal for a larger appropriation for Okinawa met considerable resistance from Congress.[44]

Some of the difficulties arising from the problem of Japanese assistance to Okinawa were solved by the establishment of the Technical and Consultative Committees, but a difference of opinion still existed between the Japanese and the Americans regarding the means of economic aid. While the United States insisted on a package commitment of aid funds by the Japanese government, the latter wanted to know the uses to which the aid would be put. As one leading Japanese newspaper commented in an editorial, 'even though the administrative rights are in the hands of the United States, our [i.e. Japanese] aid to Okinawa is not aid to a foreign country but aid to a part of Japanese territory'.[45] In other words, Japanese assistance to Okinawa was, from the standpoint of Japan, something comparable to subsidies from the Treasury to a prefectural government, hence her demand for knowledge of the use of such funds. More important, the Japanese wished to enlarge the functions of the Consultative Committee so that it could handle political issues including the problem of the return of Okinawa. This attitude was unacceptable to the United States which insisted that subjects of discussion in the committee should be strictly limited to those related to economic assistance.[46]

The change of leaders in Tokyo and in Washington in 1963–4 did not add decisive new factors to the development of the U.S.-Japanese relations concerning Okinawa so far described. Both L. B. Johnson and Satō Eisaku, both of whom succeeded their respective predecessors unexpectedly, followed the established policies. The joint communiqué of Johnson and Satō which was issued after their conference in January 1965 was, as far as the Okinawa problem was concerned, little more than repetition and affirmation of what had been said in the Kennedy-Ikeda statement of June 1961 or the Kennedy statement of March 1962. The only noteworthy progress was that

> they agreed in principle to broaden the functions of the existing Japan-U.S. Consultative Committee so as to enable the committee to conduct consultations not only on economic assistance to the Ryukyu Islands but also on other matters on which the two countries can co-operate in continuing to promote the well-being of the inhabitants of the islands.[47]

It was generally understood that this agreement removed the outstanding difference between the two governments about the nature and functions of the Consultative Committee in favour of the Japanese opinion that not only economic but also 'political' matters, such as the extension of autonomy, the method of choosing the Chief Executive and the like, could be discussed by this committee.

The replacement of General Paul W. Caraway by General Albert Watson as the new High Commissioner for Okinawa in August 1964 was perhaps more important than the changes of top-level leaders. The relatively flexible approach of the new High Commissioner to various aspects of the Okinawa problem allowed a more co-operative frame of mind. Before proceeding to his new post, Watson visited Tokyo to exchange views on Okinawan affairs with Prime Minister Ikeda and other Japanese government leaders. This was welcomed by the Japanese press which contrasted the new High Commissioner's 'soft' lines with the high-handedness of his predecessor.[48]

The new High Commissioner also managed to avoid any action to worsen the political crisis of the last days of his predecessor over the leadership of the Conservative Party. Chief Executive Ōta had vetoed several important bills passed by the Legislature in which his own party held the majority. He had also withdrawn the income tax revision bill sponsored by the same Party. This invited hostile criticism not only from the Opposition parties but also from an important faction within the OLDP. They attributed Ōta's attitude to pressures from the High Commissioner and accused him of having yielded easily to such pressures. This led to the defection of the anti-Ōta faction from the OLDP and Ōta's resignation from the post of Chief Executive. The political confusion which followed finally ended when the two groups of Conservative politicians merged in December 1964 to form a Democratic Party with Matsuoka Seihō as its president.[49]

The basic trend of American policy to Okinawa which was established by Kennedy and followed by Johnson was to make concessions to desires of the Japanese and Okinawan people so long as such concessions would not jeopardize the United States' rights to use its military bases on the island. Two major areas in which such policy was pursued by the United States during the High Commissionership of General Watson were concerned with the question of 'self-rule' for the Okinawans and with that of co-ordination with the Japanese government.

As for the question of Okinawan 'autonomy', High Commissioner Watson seems to have paid heed to the criticisms levelled at his predecessor for his 'direct hands' in many areas of administration. Although he understandably refrained from making any open comment on his predecessor's methods, he emphasized that he would respect 'the will of the people'. While Caraway had bluntly declared that autonomy for Okinawa was a myth so long as the American rule continued, Watson took a pragmatic approach, pointing out that the question was not 'whether autonomy or not' but 'what percentage of autonomy'.[50] Thus he proceeded to carry out the programme announced in Kennedy's policy statement of March 1962 for the transfer to the Government of the Ryukyu Islands of such 'functions that need not be reserved to the United States as administering authority'. For instance, the High Commissioner rescinded the proclamation which required him to approve GRI department directors. The Chief Executive was thereby given a free hand to appoint executive officers of the GRI.[51] Also USCAR courts relinquished jurisdiction to GRI courts in certain areas. This policy, which the High Commissioner termed 'the step-by-step process of turning over functions to the GRI', continued to be pursued and, as a result, the number of outstanding items of USCAR legislation decreased from 145 on 1 August 1964 to 95 on 30 June 1966.[52]

It was difficult, however, for the United States to satisfy completely the desire of the Okinawa people for the expansion of autonomy, especially when the matter was concerned with the method of selection of the Chief Executive. This problem assumed a special importance because all major political parties in Okinawa pledged themselves at the 1965 legislative election to fight for the expansion of autonomy, especially the popular election of the Chief Executive. An *ad hoc* committee of five prominent Okinawan civic leaders, Yara Chōbyō among them, also campaigned actively for the popular election of the Chief Executive. The Opposition parties in Japan supported this, although the Liberal Democratic Party failed to take an unequivocal position of this particular issue.[53] Shortly before the date for the legislative election, the High Commissioner revealed at a press conference that the method of selecting the Chief Executive had for some time been under review in Washington; he added that a direct election by popular vote was not the only alternative to the existing method.[54]

The last point of High Commissioner Watson's remarks was interpreted by the local press as the American preference for an

4 Towards Partnership (1958–65)

indirect election, that is, the selection of the GRI Chief Executive by the Legislature which itself was an elective body. This conjecture proved to be true soon afterwards. On 21 December USCAR announced that President Johnson had amended the Executive Order so as to permit the Legislature to select the Chief Executive by a majority vote.[55]

This step failed, however, to mollify the Opposition parties which insisted that any method short of public election was unsatisfactory. They refused to participate in the first election of the Chief Executive under the new system on 16 March 1966; it was conducted only under the shelter of the police force which protected the Legislative Building from angry demonstrators. From the practical viewpoint, too, the new method did not provide a stable relationship between the two branches of the GRI, for the Legislature was not empowered to discharge the Chief Executive by a non-confidence vote, nor was the latter given the power to dissolve the legislature. Thus, despite the American efforts to satisfy the desire of the Okinawan people 'to have a greater voice in the management of their own affairs' (Kennedy statement), a satisfactory solution did not yet seem very near.

In the meantime there were some improvements in the relationship between the American authorities in Okinawa and the Japanese government. The High Commissioner, Watson, showed his respect for the Japanese feeling of national pride, while avoiding any action which might curtail the American interests. For example, when the 'flag incidents' occurred (American servicemen lowered and tore Japanese flags hoisted by the local population to welcome the arrival of torch-bearing runner of the Olympic flame; similar incidents occurred also in the New Year of 1965), the High Commissioner admonished the American soldiers not to damage Japanese flags, saying that an offender should be punished for 'an insult to the allied country of the United States'.[56]

As for Japanese assistance to Okinawa, the High Commissioner stated in his message to the Ryukyuan Legislature that the United States would accept the 'useful assistance' which the Japanese government was prepared to give and which could be usefully absorbed in the Ryukyus. With regard to the relative amounts of Japanese assistance and aid from the United States, he said he would not make it a matter of ratio.[57] Subsequently, the Japanese government increased its financial assistance to Okinawa at a remarkable rate; the United States government was hampered by the ungenerous Congress, and the rate of increase of its aid was not comparable (see Table 3).[58] In connection with this, the Japanese government progressively sought to have a say in the administration in Okinawa through the U.S.-Japan Consultative Committee.

A symbolic event of the American-Japanese relations regarding Okinawa in this period was the visit by Prime Minister Satō to Okinawa in August 1965. No official visit by a Japanese Prime Minister to the Ryukyu Islands had been made since the end of the war. (Ikeda had the idea of visiting Okinawa but he dismissed it because it was considered inappropriate in view of the relations between the United States and Japan at that time.) Although Satō's visit did not mean any immediate change in Japanese policy to Okinawa (and that is why he was confronted with the indignant demonstrators at Naha), it impressed upon public attention the importance the Satō government attached to the Okinawa problem.

While the United States showed its readiness to permit the Okinawan people to enjoy more autonomy and to respect the national feeling of Japanese,[59] it firmly refused to give in when it considered a vital national interest was at stake. A good example of this was provided by the American decision to use the Okinawan bases for B-52 bombers participating in the Vietnam war. Whether the American decision was intended to gauge Japanese reaction or was merely insensitive to local feeling, it gave a great shock to the Japanese government, for it was made shortly before the scheduled visit of the Prime Minister to Okinawa. Immediately it was notified by the U.S. government about the moving of the bombers to Okinawa, the Japanese government requested that the Okinawan base should not be used for bombing raids on Vietnam. When this request was made, however, the bombers had already started for Vietnam on a bombing mission.[60]

The episode of the B-52s showed again that the United States could and would use its military facilities in Okinawa regardless of Japanese opinion. American commitment to the Vietnam war had made the complete freedom of military base operations in Okinawa more valuable to their strategists than ever before. Such freedom in turn depended, the argument ran, upon the integrity of their administrative authority over Okinawa.

It was evident that, so long as the Americans continued to stand firm on this position, it would sooner or later come into conflict with the desire of the Okinawan people for autonomy which, to their mind, would not be completely fulfilled until administrative authority over the island was returned to Japan. Moderate elements in Japan and Okinawa—those who were not opposed to the American military presence in Okinawa but who were concerned for a lasting American-Japanese friendship—sought a solution which could satisfy at the same time the two different demands: Japan's demand for civil administration in Okinawa (which was identical, in the given situation, with Okinawa's demand for termination of alien, i.e. American, rule) and the American demand for maximum freedom in their use of the military base there.

Commenting on this so-called 'separation formula', the High Commissioner, General Watson, stated:

> There are considerable numbers of people in the Ryukyus and in Japan who advocate the slogan: 'Separate the administration of the island from the base' . . . I must say that I have never heard a plausible or convincing explanation of just how this could be accomplished without serious impairment of the ability of the United States to utilize Okinawa in pursuance of its treaty commitments . . . We need to be able to take without delay whatever action is ordered in pursuance of the treaty commitments of the United States, and *without consultation with a sovereign nation which might not be involved in the commitment or the necessary action.* Loss of administrative rights would reduce or destroy the freedom of our military forces to act, and would seriously impair the usability of Okinawa as a base in defense of the United States [my italics].[61]

Referring to the same question, he said on another occasion, 'If we can explain to the [Okinawan] people that they are contributing to the defense of freedom here in Free Asia, perhaps it will erase the emotional desire for reversion'.[62] This was, as far as the High Commissioner could see, the only solution. The problem was in convincing the Okinawan people, while Japan—the country which the Okinawan people regarded as 'theirs' and which the United States counted as an ally—was not wholly committed to the American concept of collective defence of Free Asia. The Okinawan debate in the subsequent years centred on this theme.

5

The '1970 Problem'

America's policy to Okinawa has always been one of buying time. It has never officially denied Japan's 'latent' sovereignty over Okinawa, but it has never said exactly when it will abandon its *de facto* sovereignty over the island in Japan's favour. Whenever necessity occurred, it made minor concessions (such as the return of Amami-Ōshima and, more recently, of Ogasawara to Japan) or simply repeated its pledge to respect Japan's special relations with Okinawa while striving to keep its own rights there practically intact. As one American professor put it, America's Okinawa policy has been one of indecision and inaction.[1] America's indecision is, however, not due to doubt about Okinawa's ultimate political status; any solution other than its return to Japan has never been seriously considered practical by American policy-makers. The problem is how long the United States can maintain the *status quo* before it has to hand the island back to Japan.

The official position of the United States on this point has changed little since Secretary of State Dulles declared in December 1953 that the United States would retain the Ryukyus 'so long as conditions of threat and tension exist in the Far East'. From the American viewpoint, such conditions have never ceased to exist; hence there has been no reason to change its policy toward Okinawa. For example, Thaddeus Holt, Deputy Undersecretary of the Army in charge of international affairs, reaffirmed this point when he stated in April 1967 before the Congress Armed Services Committee that 'the military importance of the Ryukyus and the continued tension in the Far East are the only reasons for our continuing the administration of the islands. Those reasons are compelling. They have been recognized [by the United States leaders] time and again'.[2]

To the Okinawans and Japanese, however, as time passed the *status quo* of Okinawa became more and more irritating; hence the increasing pressure for prompt or at least gradual return of the island to Japanese administration. President Kennedy and Prime Minister Ikeda endeavoured to work out a policy to conciliate these two different positions or rather postpone collision between them. Their policy of improving local conditions in Okinawa under U.S.-Japan partnership while leaving the basic problem of Okinawa's political status untouched was destined to become unsatisfactory as it fulfilled the promised 'improvements'. A time would come when the Okinawan people were no longer satisfied with the programme of economic and social welfare developments in the Ryukyus unless it was specifically and clearly geared to the ultimate goal—the return of the Islands to Japan. That is why the so-called *'ittaika'* (identification) programme worked out by the Japanese government was not very popular among the Okinawans.[3] The unstable, if not chaotic, political situation in Okinawa showed the Okinawan disappointment at American indecisiveness. Thus the United States was placed under increasing pressure to produce a more definite timetable for Okinawa's return to Japan.

Another factor which helped the Okinawa problem to assume special importance in Japanese politics, and consequently in U.S.-Japan relations, was the American commitment to the Vietnam war and the role played by Okinawa in it. Although the United States Forces in Okinawa had been a key factor in her counter-communist strategy in Asia ever since the Korean war, it was in the Vietnam war that the utility of the Okinawan bases was fully demonstrated in an actual war.

In February 1965 President Johnson decided to bomb military targets in North Vietnam. After this, the United States increased her military intervention in Vietnam by committing combat troops on a large scale. Shortly before the U.S. started bombing the North, General J. K. Waters, Commander-in-Chief, U.S. Army, Pacific, made a three-day inspection tour to Okinawa. About the same time Lt-General V. H. Krulak, Commander General, U.S. Fleet Marine Force, Pacific, also visited Okinawa for five days and then flew to Da Nang in South Vietnam.[4] In late January the *Morning Star,* an American-owned English-language newspaper in Okinawa, quoted Major-General William R. Collins of the Third Marine Division as having said that it was not beyond possibility that some elements of his division would be deployed to South Vietnam by the coming June.[5] Soon this turned out to be true. On 7 February when the American air raid on North Vietnam began, one battalion attached to the Third Marine Division and equipped with Hawk surface-to-air guided missiles was flown to Da Nang.[6] Other elements of the Third Marine Division were then moved to South Vietnam. Also sent to Vietnam was the whole of the 173rd Airborne Brigade of the U.S. Army which had been under training for counter-guerrilla operation since its formation in Okinawa in the fall of 1963.[7] These formerly Okinawan-based Marines (about 12,000 strong) and airborne troops (about 3,000 strong) constituted the core of the American combat forces in South Vietnam until more troops were sent from Hawaii and the American continent after mid-July 1965. Some of these reinforcements (e.g. the First Marine Division normally stationed at Camp Pendleton, California) were sent to Vietnam after a brief training period in Okinawa.

Okinawa also proved to be of great use as a fuelling station for Guam-based B-52 strategic bombers. This function was carried out by a squadron of KC-135 air-to-air tankers which had been transferred from Guam to Okinawa in January 1965. Occasionally, as mentioned in the previous chapter, B-52s themselves appeared at Kadena Air Base in Okinawa, ostensibly sheltering from typhoons. In August 1967 the United States began construction work to extend two 3,000-metre runways to 4,000 metres at Kadena Air Base. This was probably preparatory to stationing B-52s there permanently. On 5 February the following year about ten wings of B-52s arrived at Kadena and some more joined them later. In contrast to the previous occasions, no reason was given by the United States authorities for their arrival but the routine use of the Kadena Base by the American strategic bombers for air-raids in Vietnam has become common knowledge.[8]

Okinawa was useful to the American military efforts in Vietnam in many other ways. For instance the 2nd Logistical Command, with its headquarters in Okinawa, together with the 9th Command in Thailand (which had been stationed previously in Okinawa) and the 1st Command in Vietnam, were important in supplying the United States Forces in Vietnam. It is estimated that at Naha Military Port and White Beach, two major harbour facilities for the United States in Okinawa, some 310,000 tons of goods were loaded and unloaded during March 1967. This was an almost twofold increase over the average monthly figure in the previous year. This figure should be compared with an estimated monthly consumption of 400,000 tons of goods by the United States forces in Vietnam at that time.[9]

Also stationed at Okinawa were the 7th Psychological Operations Group, the 1st Special Forces Group and the U.S. Army Composite Service Group, all of which, it is believed, played their own parts in the Vietnam war.[10]

The usefulness of Okinawa in American military efforts in Vietnam was so great that General Albert Watson, the High Commissioner of the Ryukyu Islands and the Commanding General of the U.S. Army in the Ryukyus, stated in testimony to Congress that Okinawa's importance to the defence of the free world was demonstrated in the Vietnam war.[11] A similar view was also expressed by Admiral U.S. Grant Sharp, Commander-in-Chief, U.S. Forces, Pacific, when he told reporters that 'Okinawa is indispensable to our present posture in the Pacific' and that without the bases there the United States' war effort in Vietnam would have been infinitely more difficult and costly.[12]

The American involvement in the Vietnam war had a great impact on Okinawan life. Economically, the great increase in spending by the United States forces and its men caused a 'boom' in parts of the Okinawan economy. According to General F. T. Unger, who replaced General Watson as the High Commissioner for the Ryukyu Islands in November 1966, the Ryukyu's GNP grew at an average annual rate of 10 per cent between 1955 and 1965. It jumped to a record 13 per cent in real terms in the fiscal year 1965 and continued at that rate until 1968. 'This sudden upswing was,' the High Commissioner explained, 'due in great part to base construction expenditures necessitated by the Vietnam war'.[13]

On the other hand, however, the war had various undesirable effects. For instance, crimes committed against the Okinawan populace by American servicemen and civilian employees attached to the United States forces increased from 973 cases in 1964 to 1,003 in 1965 and to 1,407 in 1966 (total); from 265 in 1964 to 275 in 1965 and to 446 in 1966 (atrocious and violent crimes).[14] The considerable increase, especially in 'atrocious and violent' crimes, in recent years can be attributed to the state of mind of the American servicemen fighting in Vietnam.

Apart from such 'human' calamities, the Okinawan people suffered various forms of 'mechanical' disasters. To mention only a few: a trailer being carried by a Lockheed C-130 during its training flight was dropped to the ground and killed an Okinawan schoolgirl (11 June 1965); one man was killed when a KC-135 jet fuel tanker skidded at Kadena Air Base in an attempt to take off and crashed into his car on a nearby highway (19 May 1966); drinking water and crops were contaminated by the leakage of fuel oil from a pipeline in military use (4 January 1968); and a bomb-laden B-52, apparently on a mission to Vietnam, failed to take off and blew up at Kadena Air Base (19 November 1968). This latter incident was especially alarming. Fortunately, damage caused by the blast was not serious and there were few casualties. But the accident could have caused a holocaust if the plane had plunged into a densely populated area or, as was quite likely, it had flown for a few seconds longer and plunged into the nearby ordnance storage areas, where, it is believed, nuclear weapons are housed.[15]

That a crowded population lives close to or even amidst the huge and highly sophisticated American military base complex makes the Okinawan people very sensitive to the problem of their own physical security. A public opinion survey conducted by the *Ryūkyū Shimpōsha* in Okinawa in June 1967 revealed that 45.5 per cent of the respondents expressed strong anxiety for their safety because of the existence of the American military bases there; 30.0 per cent felt somehow insecure; 5.7 per cent did not feel insecure; 1.2 per cent felt their safety was secured by the American bases; 2.2 per cent gave other answers, and the remaining 15.4 per cent gave no opinion.[16]

The permanent stationing of B-52 bombers in Okinawa helped to intensify the inhabitants' sense of insecurity. Another *Ryūkyū Shimpōsha* survey conducted from late February to early March 1968 sought their feelings about it by asking the question: 'What do you think of the stationing of B-52s in Okinawa?' The question turned up the following answers: 'I feel insecure' (85.9 per cent); 'I do not mind' (3.5 per cent); 'I feel secure' (0.5 per cent); 'Don't know' and others (10.1 per cent).[17]

Also many Okinawans were not quite convinced that American involvement in the Vietnam war was justified. The *Ryūkyū Shimpōsha* survey of June 1967 showed that only 2.6 per cent of those who were interviewed thought the American intervention in the Vietnam war was justifiable compared to 44.5 per cent who did not think it was, while the remaining 52.9 per cent were either non-commital or ambiguous ('it cannot be helped': 7.5 per cent; impossible to answer in simple terms': 11.5 per cent; and 'Don't know': 33.9 per cent).[18]

Their sense of insecurity and anti-war feeling made them request, among other things, the prompt withdrawal of B-52s from Okinawa. In late 1968 the Ryukyuan Legislature, which included many pro-American Conservative members, unanimously protested against the use of Okinawa for B-52 missions and urged the United States to remove the bombers from the island immediately.[19] It also passed a resolution requesting the United States not to use Okinawan ports as a calling-station for its nuclear submarines.

On 23 December 1968 the Ryukyuan Legislature passed a resolution against nuclear submarines; this was preceded by public debate about possible radioactive contamination by U.S. nuclear submarines of Naha Military Port and its surrounding waters. A series of scientific analyses jointly conducted by the Government of the Ryukyu Islands and USCAR from June to November 1968 detected cobalt 60 and other radioactive materials from the mud and silt samples collected at Naha Military Port. The amounts were, it was explained, so small that they were harmless to the human body (the first test turned out 4-182 picocuries per kilogramme; the second 173-215; and the third 160-283). Japanese scientists claimed, however, that they had detected as much as 3,560-4,780 picocuries from some samples taken from the seabed in Naha Port. Although even that figure was meagre compared with 500,000 picocuries (the amount which was considered 'allowable' by the International Commission on Radiological Protection) the fact that such material was found on the seabed of Naha Military Port caused a great sensation among the Okinawan people. They counted 'nuclear contamination' among what they called 'public hazards stemming from U.S. military bases' *(kichi kōgai)*.[20]

These problems connected with the American military bases in Okinawa had their counterparts in Japan proper. The word *kōgai* (public nuisances) originally referred to various problems resulting from urbanization and industrialization such as traffic congestion, noise, air pollution, contamination of rivers and land by factory sewage, etc.; it came to be applied also to various problems related to the American military bases *(kichi)* or the U.S.-Japan Security Treaty *(ampojōyaku)* which allowed the United States to maintain such bases. Hence the new words *kichi kōgai* or *ampo kōgai*. In particular, the crash of a U.S. F-4C reconnaissance plane into a building of the Kyūshū University at Fukuoka (2 June 1968) and the discovery of an abnormal amount of radioactive material at Sasebo Naval Port which was said to be traceable only to U.S. nuclear submarines (6 May 1968) excited the sensitive Japanese public.[21] Thus there was mounting pressure on the government, both in Okinawa and Japan proper, to take necessary measures to protect citizens from 'public hazards' of this kind. The demand was especially great in Okinawa where, unlike Japan proper, the military facilities were extremely concentrated and almost inseparably interlocked with other fields of community life and where the national government was technically not in a position to speak for the affected public (see Table 4).[22]

In the meantime the United States authorities in Okinawa pursued the policy of mitigating Okinawan dissatisfaction, which culminated in the permission President Johnson at last gave the Okinawans to elect their own Chief Executive by popular vote.[23] The Okinawans responded to this American action by choosing as the Chief Executive the Opposition candidate, Yara Chōbyō, who

Table 4

COMPARISON OF THE LAND AREAS IN MILITARY USE BY THE UNITED STATES IN OKINAWA AND JAPAN PROPER
(in square kilometres)

	Total	*Military*	*Percentage*
Okinawa	2,196	210	9.56
Saitama	3,800	100	2.63
Kanagawa	2,375	27	1.12
Japan	369,661	360	0.09

advocated in his election campaigns 'immediate, unconditional and total reversion' of the Okinawan islands to Japan, although the conservative Okinawa Liberal Democratic Party retained its majority in the Legislative elections which were concurrently conducted. The Opposition candidate won also in the mayoral election for Naha, capital of Okinawa, which was held soon after the elections for the Chief Executive and the Legislature. A summary of these three election results was as follows:

Chief Executive:
　　　　Yara Chōbyō (Opposition) 　　　237,562
　　　　Nishime Junji (Conservative) 　　206,011
Mayor of Naha:
　　　　Taira Ryōshō (Opposition) 　　　　78,610
　　　　Furugen Sōtoku (Conservative) 　　38,722
Legislature:

	seats	*votes*
Opposition	14	51.88 per cent
Conservatives	18	48.12 per cent

Yara's victory was attributed by local political analysts to 'the impatience of many Okinawans with the twenty-three years of foreign rule' as well as to other factors including the candidate's 'impeccable personality' and career (a renowned former school-master, experienced education administrator, and ardent leader of the reversion movement) and the various public hazards connected with the U.S. bases outlined above. The Japanese government and its ruling Liberal Democratic Party were also considered responsible for the defeat of the Okinawan Conservatives because they were unable to clarify their position on the exact method and timetable for Okinawan reversion. On the eve of the election, LDP's Secre-tary-General Fukuda Takeo made a statement to the effect that, should Opposition candidates win the coming major elections, it would adversely affect the agreement to be reached between Japan and the United States on the timetable for the reversion of Okin-awa. This rather ill-considered statement had the wrong effect, since it offended the feeling of the Okinawan people who were inclined to place the reversion issue above party interests.[24]

It was against this background that the Okinawa problem came to the fore in connection with the so-called 1970 problem, namely the arguments calling for a general review of problems of Japan's national defence and especially the military arrangement with the United States if the U.S.-Japan Security Treaty was terminated in 1970.

The Treaty of Mutual Co-operation and Security between Japan and the United States of America which came into force on 23 June 1960 provided that 'after the Treaty had been in force for ten years, either Party may give notice to the other Party of its inten-tion to terminate one year after such notice has been given' (Article 10). This provision does not necessitate 'expiration' of the Treaty in June 1970. In other words, after the present Treaty 'expires', the Japanese (or the United States) government can adopt, theoretically, any of the following alternatives: (1) inform the other party of its intention to terminate the Treaty (abrogation); (2) conclude a new treaty which will replace the present one (revision); (3) extend the provisions of the present treaty for a certain specific period of time, say, for another ten years (renewal); or (4) not to do any-thing, in which case the Treaty will automatically remain in force in its present form until one party takes action (continuation).

Various arguments have been put forward in Japan for each of these alternatives but it looks as if the Satō government and the ruling Liberal Democratic Party intended to choose the last one.[25]

If that was the case, there would be no '1970 problem'. Nevertheless, what has happened in and outside Japan during the last decade seems to require a general review of Japan's foreign and defence policies. Externally, for instance, there is China's acquisition of nuclear weapons and probable development of their delivery system in the near future; the growing schism between China and the Soviet Union; the withdrawal of British power from Southeast Asia; and the recent trend towards decreasing commitment of the United States in Asia in military and economic terms: all these factors are producing expectations in some countries that Japan will take a larger role in the international scene.[26]

Some of the domestic conditions also seem to tend toward a more positive foreign policy. A remarkable economic success raised Japan's status in world economy to the third richest country in terms of gross national product. This economic success restored the confidence of the Japanese in their own power. Encouraged by this economic success, some political and industrial leaders began to challenge the fundamental principles which had governed post-war Japanese attitudes to national security. Thus the non-nuclear principle, the no-war clause of the Japanese Constitution and the *de facto,* if not *de jure,* prohibition of sending troops abroad under any circumstances were criticized by these people. They argued that recent international developments made these principles obsolete and insisted on the necessity of a new national 'consensus' about the country's defence policy. Although their bid for a new national consensus has not yet succeeded, their activities, together with the 'pluralization' of Japan's party politics and the growing divergence among the various mass organizations (especially the peace and the student movements), are undoubtedly contributing to the fluidity of Japan's political and ideological situation. Thus even if the government leaders decide on an automatic continuation of the Security Treaty, the '1970 problem' may well become a grave issue around which Japanese politics will be centred in the near future.[27]

What bearings then do the recent U.S.-Japan negotiations about Okinawa have on the 1970 problem? As mentioned in the previous chapter, some people in Japan and the United States advocated the so-called 'separation formula' to resolve the deadlock between the United States and Japan on Okinawa. This argument was, in essence, founded on the belief that the United States could and should return administrative rights over the Ryukyus to Japan, while retaining her military privileges there. They argued that if the United States was really ready to recognize Japan's sovereignty over Okinawa, it should be willing to retain its bases in Okinawa under an agreement with Japan. In a sense this was the contention underlying all the moderate arguments which had urged an early solution of the Okinawa problem ever since the San Francisco Peace Treaty. It was, however, not until fairly recently that such an argument began to have some practical influence on government leaders of both countries. Tokonami Tokuji, an active member of the Liberal Democratic Party Okinawa Committee and the Director-General of the Prime Minister's Office since November 1968, became renowned as an ardent advocate for the separation formula.[28] Under his influence, the LDP Okinawa Committee adopted an interim report (16 June 1966) which recommended a 'functional' return of administrative rights over Okinawa to Japan. It envisaged a gradual transfer of administrative functions in Okinawa from the United States authorities to the Japanese government, beginning with such fields as education, household registration and social welfare which were considered most remote from the military necessities.[29]

The idea of dividing military and civil functions between the United States and Japan in Okinawa was intended to be a substitute for a more simple version of the separation formula, that is, a 'geographical' separation of military and non-military areas—an idea which was totally unrealistic in a place like Okinawa with such a high degree of military concentration. But this new concept of functional division rested on an eventual restoration to Japan of full sovereignty over Okinawa, and a crucial question had to be answered before the United States could take it seriously: what sort of military privileges could the United States expect in a Japanese-controlled Okinawa? Conditions were not yet ripe for U.S.-Japanese negotiations for the return of Okinawa to Japan via functional division: this was shown by the failure of a proposal by Mori Kiyoshi, the then Director-General of the Prime Minister's Office, for the transfer of authority for education to Japan.[30]

As the outcome of the Mori proposal showed, the real problem was the great gap between the United States and Japan regarding the free use of Okinawan bases by the United States. In Japan proper where the United States was allowed to use military facilities under the terms of the U.S.-Japan Security Treaty, there were certain 'restrictions' upon the military freedom of the United States. They were exemplified by the so-called 'prior consultation' pledge. In the joint communiqué of Prime Minister Kishi and President Eisenhower on the conclusion of the new Security Treaty of 1960,

71

the President had said 'the United States government has no intention of acting in a manner contrary to the wishes of the Japanese government with respect to the matters involving prior consultation under the treaty'. According to the Japanese-American agreement, three things were subject to prior consultation: major changes in the deployment into Japan of U.S. Forces, major changes in their equipment, and the use of Japanese bases by U.S. combat troops for the purpose of conducting military operations outside Japan.

In connection with this, the Japanese public also tended to interpret rigidly the term 'the Far East' in the Security Treaty (Article 4 provided that the United States was granted the use by its land, air and naval forces of facilities and areas in Japan 'for the purpose of contributing to the security of Japan and the maintenance of international peace and security in the Far East'). Since the conclusion of the Treaty, the Japanese government was never completely free from the public's critical scrutiny of the *modus operandi* of that Treaty, especially the provisions for prior consultation and the Far East. These provisions were, to the Japanese mind, too loose to restrain the United States effectively, and Japanese sensitivity to involvement in foreign wars and especially to nuclear arms was obviously felt by the United States to be too restricting.[31]

If the United States were to be subject to similar restrictions in Okinawa when it was returned to Japanese administration, the United States would have to make a sacrifice too great to be tolerable. This had been the major stumbling block in past attempts to solve the Okinawa problem. Why then did the United States begin to show its readiness to talk about a return of administrative rights over Okinawa, if not those over the military bases?[32]

This is still a matter of conjecture. The United States leaders probably saw a danger, from the recent developments in Okinawa, that the rising dissatisfaction of the Okinawan people might jeopardize the smooth operation of the military bases unless a timely solution was made. It may well be also that the American decision to 'de-escalate' the Vietnam war had some effects on her Okinawa policy. Perhaps most important were the Japanese government's efforts to close the gap between the United States and Japan on collective security.

The arguments in Japan on Okinawa took a dramatic turn in early 1967. While campaigning for the general elections to the House of Representatives, Prime Minister Satō told the newspapermen that he would consider it more desirable to solve the Okinawa problem by the return of what he termed 'comprehensive admin- istrative rights' rather than of certain specified administrative func- tions (e.g. education).[33] Satō's statement was interpreted by observers as an open disavowal of his former Director-General's modest plan of recovering Japanese authority over education in Okinawa first. It was welcomed by some who regarded it as an indication of the government's intention to take more positive steps towards solving the problem. If so, what made Satō come to this ambitious plan?

Various statements made by Japanese government officials in the following months showed that Satō's statement was not a mere slip of the tongue. Most revealing and most controversial were a series of statements made by a top-level *Gaimushō* official, Shimoda Takezō. As the Permanent Undersecretary for Foreign Affairs (al- though he was quoted at that time only as a high-ranking official of the *Gaimushō*), Shimoda expressed the view, at a press con- ference on 1 February 1967, that for an early return of the administrative rights over Okinawa to Japan, the contracting parties to the San Francisco Peace Treaty had to be sure that it would not endanger 'the maintenance of international peace and security in the Far East'. Elaborating his view, Shimoda stated that it would be difficult for the United States to fulfil its treaty commitments to its Pacific allies if the public was as hostile to its military activities in a Japanese-controlled Okinawa as it had been to those on the Japanese mainland. From this point of view, he counselled the Japanese people to abandon their narrow-mindedness about the freedom of military action of the United States in Okinawa.

Shimoda, who was soon afterwards appointed to the post of Ambassador to Washington, iterated a similar view on various occasions. On one of those occasions, he even went on to say that the United States should be allowed to store nuclear weapons in Okinawa (if not in Japan proper) if it made that a condition for its return. Ambassador Shimoda also told the American audience quite outspokenly about the support of 'a majority of Japanese people' for the American military actions in Vietnam.[34]

These statements by Undersecretary (and later Ambassador) Shimoda were unusually outspoken and polemical for a diplomat (not a politician). Naturally, they aroused much criticism in Japan and Okinawa. The government leaders made gestures to disasso- ciate their views from Shimoda's, but it seems possible that his statements reflected the official views of the Japanese government in essence, if not in details: Shimoda was never recalled from his post nor punished in any other way for his provocative statements.

The attitude the Satō government took towards the United States over the various problems of the Security Treaty (e.g. its consent to the visits of U.S. nuclear submarines and the nuclear-powered aircraft-carrier, *Enterprise*, to Japanese ports) also seems to support the view that it was the Satō government's policy to co-operate closely, when the circumstances permitted, with the United States government in the latter's efforts to maintain 'international peace and security in the Far East'.

It is questionable whether such a policy on the part of the Japanese government was a result of any suggestions made by the United States leaders. Also one may ask whether an early solution of the Okinawa problem was the most important objective of that policy. It is certain, however, that the Satō government tried to 'educate' the public about the necessity of defending their own country if they wanted to see an early return of Okinawa to Japanese administration.

The government campaign for a national consensus about the place of Okinawa in the future defence of Japan has not yet attained much success. Most of the people in Japan proper and Okinawa are certainly in favour of the earliest possible return of Okinawa.[35] When it comes, however, to the problem of the types of bases which the United States should be allowed to maintain in a Japanese-controlled Okinawa, opinions are divided. The results of an *Okinawa Taimusu* opinion survey (August 1968) may be taken as a convenient guide to the Okinawan feeling on this question. They are compared with the results of the previous survey carried out jointly by *Asahi Shimbun* and *Okinawa Taimusu* in September 1967.[36]

1. Are you in favour of the return to Japan of administrative rights over Okinawa, with the U.S. given free use of military bases in Okinawa—including possession of nuclear weapons?

	per cent	
	1968	*1967*
Yes	15	9
No	60	63
Unavoidable	9	4
Don't know	14	} 24
No answer	2	

2. Do you agree with another opinion which supports an early reversion in exchange for the free use of military bases—without nuclear weapons?

	per cent	
Yes	41	32
No	30	31
Unavoidable	13	9
Don't know	14 }	28
No answer	2 }	

3. Do you support the proposal for an early reversion through a formula by which the U.S. bases are scaled down to the same status as in Japan, with the government restrictions put on them?

	per cent	
Yes	68	57
No	14	13
Don't know	16 }	30
No answer	2 }	

4. Another opinion is that a reversion with even some military installation intact is meaningless for the Okinawans. Do you agree?

	per cent	
Yes	39	40
No	34	25
Don't know	23 }	35
No answer	4 }	

5. Under which of the following do you want the Japanese government to negotiate with the United States for the reversion of Okinawa?

	per cent	
Free use of bases with nuclear arms	0	2
Free use of bases without nuclear arms	5	9
Restricted use of bases as in Japan	47	32
Removal of bases	28	26
Don't know	17 }	31*
No answer	3 }	

*Including those who gave other answers.

A majority of the people wanted to see the U.S. bases in Okinawa 'downgraded' to the same status as in Japan. In particular, many of them were strongly opposed to the return of Okinawa with U.S. nuclear weapons intact.

Negotiations on Okinawa were started by Foreign Minister Aichi's visit to Washington in June 1969 and ended in the Nixon-Sato conference in November of the same year. They had, from the Japanese point of view, three objectives: to obtain an American promise to return Okinawa to Japan by a specified date in the near future; to place Okinawa, on its return to Japan, under the same conditions as the rest of Japan with regard to the U.S.-Japan Security Treaty; and, more specifically, to make it clear that no nuclear weapons were to be stored on Okinawa after its return to Japan.

The joint communiqué issued after the meeting of President Nixon and Prime Minister Sato in Washington on 22 November 1969 satisfied, prima facie, all of these Japanese desires. It stated that the two leaders 'agreed to expedite the consultations with a view to accomplishing the reversion [of Okinawa] during 1972'.[37] It also recorded their agreement 'that, upon return of the administrative rights, the Treaty of Mutual Co-operation and Security and its related arrangements would apply to Okinawa without modification thereof'. As for the sensitive problem of nuclear weapons, the joint communiqué stated:

> The Prime Minister described in detail the particular sentiment of the Japanese people against nuclear weapons and the policy of the Japanese government reflecting such sentiment. The President expressed his deep understanding and assured the Prime Minister that, without prejudice to the position of the United States Government with respect to the prior consultation system under the Treaty of Mutual Co-operation and Security, the reversion of Okinawa would be carried out in a manner consistent with the policy of the Japanese Government as described by the Prime Minister.

Despite Sato's claim that his purposes were completely satisfied, it would be premature to conclude that the communiqué has dispelled all doubts about the Okinawa problem. One of the important assumptions underlying the agreement is that the war in Vietnam would be concluded before the return of Okinawa to

Japan. What if this presumption was not fulfilled? According to the
joint communiqué, the leaders of the two governments

> agreed that, should peace in Vietnam not have been realized by
> the time reversion of Okinawa is scheduled to take place, the two
> governments would fully consult with each other in the light of
> the situation at that time so that reversion would be accomplished
> without affecting the United States efforts to assure the South
> Vietnamese people the opportunity to determine their own
> political future without outside interference.

The United States may still retain her rights to use Okinawa as a
base from which B-52s, for example, can launch an attack on
Vietnam. If this happens to be the case, it would mean a major
modification of the terms of the Security Treaty as far as Okinawa
is concerned.

The communiqué is evasive about the future deployment of
nuclear weapons on Okinawa. As the recent announcement of
removal of the Mace-B missiles from Okinawa by the United
States government indicates, the nuclear weapons at present stocked
there would be removed by the time of reversion. But the wording
of the communiqué makes it possible for the United States, after
consultation with the Japanese government under the Security
Treaty, to arm Okinawa with nuclear weapons.

This brings us to the problem of the 'prior consultation system'.
As before mentioned, the fact that this system was taken to be
tantamount to Japan's veto had hindered the United States from
giving up Okinawa in favour of Japanese sovereignty. In the Diet
debate preceding the Okinawa negotiations, the Japanese government leaders made great efforts to disavow this interpretation, saying that the Japanese government should be governed only by the
consideration of 'national interests' in deciding 'yes' or 'no' to an
American move. It was hinted that the Japanese government might
allow, for example, United States combat troops to use Japanese
bases to conduct military operations outside Japan, if the Japanese
government considered such an action essential for Japan's own
security. The same would apply to major changes in the deployment in Japan of American forces and major changes in their equipment, including nuclear weapons.

With these facts as background it is very significant that the
Prime Minister affirmed, in his joint communiqué with President
Nixon, 'the recognition of his government that the security of Japan

could not be adequately maintained without international peace and security in the Far East and, therefore, the security of countries in the Far East was a matter of serious concern for Japan'. The Japanese government's official recognition that Japan's security was identical with that of the 'Far East' was a revolutionary departure from its past policy. The Nixon-Satō communiqué specifically mentioned the Korean peninsula and the Taiwan areas as those areas whose peace and security Japan would regard as a matter of her own concern. This means that Japan now openly committed herself to maintaining the *status quo* in these areas.

In conclusion, the keynote of the Okinawa agreement at the Nixon-Satō conference was that Japan adopted a new and broader outlook on problems of international peace and security in the Far East in exchange for the American promise to return the administrative rights over Okinawa to Japan. In this way it has brought about a significant change in the *modus operandi* if not the letter of the U.S.-Japan Security Treaty.

If the Okinawa settlement means, as Prime Minister Satō stated, the end of Japan's post-war era, does it also indicate a turning point in her foreign policy from an economic to a political and military one? Japan's pledge to support the United States' efforts to maintain the *status quo* in the Korean peninsula and the Taiwan area has already invited an accusation by Peking and Pyongyang of the 'revival of Japanese militarism and of the old dream of a Greater East Asia Co-Prosperity Sphere'.[38] Although the recent emphasis in Japanese opinion on 'a greater responsibility to protect its own country' is primarily aimed at moral effects, it is quite likely that such an argument will influence Japan's future defence policy. The next five-year plan of national defence (1972–6) is now under consideration. It is reported to envisage the gradual undertaking of local defence of Okinawa by Japan's Self-Defence Forces after 1972. But it also provides for a substantial improvement of Self-Defence Forces so that they can meet a 'direct and indirect threat on a local scale' alone, while relying as before on the United States' nuclear deterrent for Japan's defence in a total war.[39] The question is how Japan's new commitment to the defence of South Korea and Taiwan affects her concept of national defence *vis-à-vis* local threat.

Another problem of military significance is the continued existence of the American bases on Okinawa after its return to Japan. This was made clear in the joint communiqué of President Nixon and Prime Minister Satō who agreed that 'the United States would retain under the terms of the Treaty of Mutual Co-operation and

Security such military facilities and areas in Okinawa as are required in the mutual security of both countries'. There is a strong American feeling, reflected in Congress, against relinquishing American military privileges in Okinawa and there is also still a strong suspicion in Japan about the American alliance in the military field. Because of this, it would be difficult for the two governments to arrange the operation of Okinawan bases in a way that would not offend domestic opinion in either country. Okinawa might in this way continue to be a controversial issue in American-Japanese relations.

Finally, the people in Okinawa are the ones most directly affected by return of the island to Japan. It seems inevitable that changes in the status of U.S. forces in Okinawa would require a substantial readjustment and perhaps cause confusion in local economy which has been so heavily dependent on the American military bases. Such a problem has already manifested itself in the form of strikes of Okinawan military workers who are demanding retraction of a wholesale dismissal plan.[40] The removal of customs and other economic barriers between the Japanese mainland and Okinawa might also, unless carefully regulated, help to make Okinawan society a prey to metropolitan economic magnates. Again it is a question of how long the Japanese government will keep up its interest in the welfare of the Okinawan people once the Okinawa problem is 'settled'. After all, the reversion movement was, from the Okinawan viewpoint, their quest for civil liberties and social and economic welfare under the Japanese Constitution. Not the American but the Japanese government's efforts to protect their rights as Japanese citizens will be subject now to critical scrutiny by the local population. Whether a new era in Okinawan history will be a happy one for the Okinawan people will depend on their own persistent efforts to uphold their rights as well as on the sincerity and farsightedness of the Japanese government in assisting such Okinawan efforts. In this sense, the Okinawa problem still remains unsettled.

PART TWO

6

Government Departments
and the Making of Policy

In this chapter we shall discuss what attitudes different branches of the Japanese government took towards Okinawa. What is the machinery for the formulation and conduct of Japan's Okinawa policy? A superficial answer would be the entire Cabinet. In the Cabinet, the Minister of Foreign Affairs might be expected to be the one most concerned. The Okinawa problem is not, however, a purely foreign policy matter for the Japanese government, but rather a quasi-internal matter. This is because relations between Japan and Okinawa are, in Japanese eyes, the relations between national and local authorities in a single political community.[1] Hence virtually all agencies of the Japanese government are involved in the formulation and conduct of Okinawa policy.

It appears that at Cabinet level there is a difference in attitude between the Ministry of Foreign Affairs on the one hand and more 'domestic-oriented' ministries on the other. The establishment of agencies within the Prime Minister's Office (Sōrifu)[2] to attend specifically to matters related to Okinawa has made this more discernible. Generally speaking, the Prime Minister's Office takes a tougher line than the Ministry of Foreign Affairs. Government policy vacillates between these two poles reflecting the dual character of the Okinawa problem itself, namely its half-foreign and half-domestic nature.

Before we proceed to case studies let us first outline the growth of the governmental institutions concerned with Okinawa policy.

Until the end of World War II Okinawa, like the other forty-six prefectures comprising metropolitan Japan, was administered by a Prefectural Governor (chiji) appointed by and accountable to the

Home Ministry *(Naimushō)*. With the invasion of the American forces, however, Japanese administration over Okinawa came to an abrupt end and the island was placed under the control of the American military government. After the Japanese surrender Okinawa continued to be administered *directly* by the American military, whereas on the Japanese mainland the Occupation authorities governed *indirectly* through the Japanese government.

Initially repatriation and other miscellaneous business concerning Okinawa was handled by an agency created for that purpose within the Ministry of Foreign Affairs *(Gaimushō)* in co-operation with the remnants of the Tokyo Office of the Okinawa Prefecture. In September 1948, however, when the immediate business was settled, these institutions were abolished.[3]

In the meantime officials from the *Gaimushō* preparing for the eventual negotiation of a peace treaty drew up a very detailed case for the return of Okinawa (and Chishima) to Japanese sovereignty.[4]

In August 1952 after the Peace Treaty (which continued U.S. administration of Okinawa) had come into effect, the Japanese government, in response to a suggestion by SCAP, set up a liaison office in Naha, the *Naha Nihon Seifu Nampō Renraku Jimusho* (popularly abbreviated to '*Nanren*'), to deal with trade and travel between Okinawa and the Japanese mainland and other quasi-consular business. It was made clear on the one hand that it should exercise no political or administrative jurisdiction over the inhabitants but on the other hand that its personnel should not possess diplomatic or consular titles of immunities.[5] Simultaneously there was established in the Prime Minister's Office a liaison bureau, *Nampō Renraku Jimukyoku*, to direct its activities. In 1958 this office developed into the *Tokubetsu Chiiki Renraku Jimukyoku* ('*Tokuren*' for short) with enlarged functions covering not only Okinawa and Ogasawara but also Chishima and the islands north of Japan occupied by the Soviet Union. There have been no substantial changes in the status and functions of *Nanren*, although in 1962 the Japanese government decided to appoint a diplomat rated as 'Minister' to that post. More recently, it was decided in accordance with the agreement reached between President Johnson and Prime Minister Satō in November 1967 that the function of the Japanese Government Liaison Office be expanded to permit consultations with the High Commissioner and the United States Civil Administration of the Ryukyu Islands on matters of mutual interest.[6]

Another important development was the creation in September

1957 of a semi-governmental body, the Association for Relief of
our Compatriots in the Southern Areas, *Nampō Dōhō Engokai*.[7]
Largely subsidized by the Treasury and staffed by government-
appointed officials, this association has been engaged in a wide
range of activities including educating the public about the problems
of Okinawa and Ogasawara[8] and providing various kinds of
assistance to students, war-bereaved families, retarded children and
physically handicapped people in Okinawa. It operates under the
supervision of the *Sōrifu*.[9]

Until 1957 the Prime Minister had been assisted by his Chief
Cabinet Secretary, *Kambōchōkan* (a member of the Cabinet), in
superintending the *Sōrifu*. In August 1957, however, the office of
Director-General *(Sōmuchōkan)* was created to assist the Prime
Minister in his function as Chief of the *Sōrifu*. Originally the status
of *Sōmuchōkan* was similar to that of Permanent Undersecretary
(Jimu jikan) in ordinary ministries (although he was entitled to
attend Cabinet meetings). His status, however, has been recently
enhanced to that of a Cabinet Minister.[10] The raising of his status
had nothing to do with the Okinawa problem, but it was to have
considerable effect on the making of Cabinet policy for Okinawa.
In view of the fact that Okinawa is one of the more important
'political' matters assigned to him, he can be regarded in fact as a
Minister for Okinawa Affairs.[11]

Some other ministries maintain specific sections or working
groups to deal with administrative business related to Okinawa.
Even the ministries that do not maintain such specific agencies are
often involved in Okinawan affairs. There was no inter-departmental body to formulate policy on Okinawa until 1965 when the
Satō government decided to create the Committee of Ministers concerned with Okinawa Problems, *Okinawa Mondai Kakuryō Kyōgikai*.[12]

Government policy towards Okinawa is formulated among these
bodies; diplomatic negotiations with the United States are conducted through the *Gaimushō*. A most important diplomatic channel is meetings between officials of the *Gaimushō* and those of the
American Embassy in Tokyo. Even at this point, however, officials
from the *Sōrifu* and *Nampō Dōhō Engokai* sometimes play a substantial role, because *Gaimushō* officials rely upon them for technical details. An institutional expression of this is the establishment
of the U.S.-Japan Consultative Committee Concerning Economic
Assistance to the Ryukyu Islands, consisting (on the Japanese side)
of the Foreign Minister and the Director-General of the *Sōrifu* and

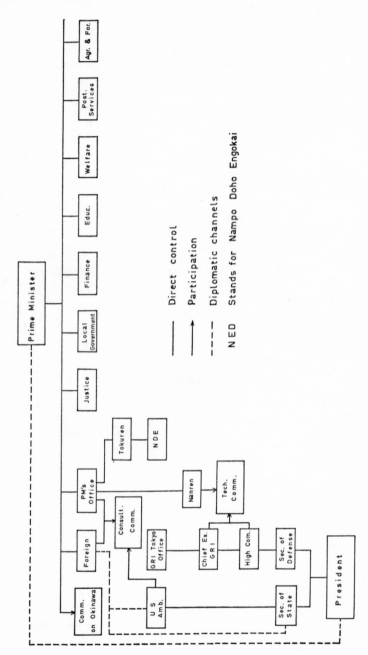

Fig. 1 Government institutions involved in Okinawa policy

(on the American side) of the American Ambassador. An official designated by the Director-General of the *Sōrifu* also represents the Japanese government in a U.S.-Japan-Ryukyu Technical Committee set up for the same purpose in Naha with a representative of the High Commissioner as Chairman and the Chief Executive of the GRI or his representative being its other member.[13]

Besides the normal diplomatic channels between the two countries, *ad hoc* conferences of leaders of the two governments, especially those between the Japanese Prime Minister and the American President, are quite important. This is so partly because there are so many government institutions concerned with formulating and conducting Okinawa policy both in Japan (see Fig. 1)[14] and in the United States where the Departments of State and Defense are involved.

Let us now look at some case studies in the making of policy on Okinawa. Two principal cases are typical: the controversy in 1956 between the *Gaimushō* and the *Hōmushō* (Ministry of Justice) over the legal grounds for protection of the inhabitants of Okinawa by the Japanese government, and the differences of opinion between the *Gaimushō* and the *Sōrifu* over the establishment of U.S.-Japanese Committees for Okinawa in 1962–4. A few other cases will be briefly discussed to support the general argument.

Gaimushō v. Hōmushō

In mid-1956 the Japanese press, social groups and political parties exercised strong pressure on the Japanese government. They wanted it to make the United States rescind its policy of paying lump sums as compensation for Okinawan land needed for military purposes. The Hatoyama government disagreed as to whether the Japanese government was in a position to raise this issue in diplomatic negotiations with the United States. At a Cabinet meeting on 19 June 1956, the Foreign Minister, Shigemitsu Mamoru, expressed the view that the land problem in Okinawa was an internal affair of the United States and that therefore the Japanese government could not raise this matter diplomatically. All it could do, he added, was to use its good offices to convey to the United States the Okinawans' desire for reconsideration of the land policy. The Cabinet approved Shigemitsu's view.[15] In line with this decision, Shigemitsu on 21 June discussed the matter with the American Ambassador, J. M. Allison. The latter issued an official statement in which he reaffirmed Japan's residual sovereignty over the Ryukyu Islands and strongly denied any American intention to acquire permanent possession of the islands.[16]

These diplomatic exchanges failed, however, to satisfy some Cabinet members. The Minister for Justice, Makino Ryōzō, had expressed his dissatisfaction with the view put forward by the Foreign Minister at the Cabinet meeting on 19 June.[17]

The difference of opinion between them developed into an open controversy when the *Hōmushō* made public its own viewpoint in a statement issued on 21 June. The *Hōmushō* maintained that the land problem was important to all the inhabitants of Okinawa and that it was the concern of the Japanese government. Its argument consisted of three points: there was no doubt about the Japanese nationality of the inhabitants of Okinawa; their legal status under American control was not different from that of Japanese citizens abroad; the Japanese government had as much right of protection over the inhabitants of Okinawa as it had over Japanese residing, for example, in the United States. The statement concluded that the Japanese government should exercise the right of protection over the Okinawans in connection with the land problem and strongly demand that the United States government rescind the policy of payment in lump sums.[18]

The *Gaimushō* and the Cabinet's legal advisers (the *Naikaku Hōseikyoku*) were against the *Hōmushō's* view.[19] A Cabinet meeting on 29 June failed to reach an agreement on this point. Further efforts to resolve inter-departmental differences were unsuccessful.[20] In the end a Cabinet meeting on 3 July reaffirmed the Foreign Minister's view that the legal question raised by the *Hōmushō* was an unimportant factor in the problem.[21]

In the course of debate in the Diet, however, it became apparent that this Cabinet decision had not settled the difference of opinion between the two departments. Before the House of Representatives Standing Committee for Foreign Affairs, Murakami Chōichi, head of the Civil Affairs Bureau of the *Hōmushō*, said that the Japanese government had sound legal grounds for conducting diplomatic negotiations with the United States over the land problem in Okinawa and that such action would not infringe the rights of the United States. Shimoda Takezō, head of the Treaty Bureau of the *Gaimushō,* admitted Murakami's conclusion, although unlike Murakami he did not deduce it from the right of protection over citizens abroad.[22] Instead he based it on the argument that Japan, as a sovereign state, had the right to defend the interests of its own people by diplomatic measures.[23] This shows that Shimoda agreed with Murakami on the most crucial point, namely, that the inhabitants of Okinawa were Japanese nationals whose fate was the concern of the Japanese government.[24]

This debate is significant because it showed that, even in the executive branch of the Japanese government, there was strong criticism of the weak diplomacy of the *Gaimushō* in connection with the Okinawa problem. Although the opinion of the *Hōmushō* officials was not adopted by the Cabinet as its official view, it had considerable impact on the attitude of the *Gaimushō*. (*Hōmushō* officials' opinions on Okinawan affairs carried considerable weight because they were familiar with legal aspects of the Okinawa problem through their handling of family registrations.)[25]

The importance of the expert opinion of *Hōmushō* officials was again demonstrated in 1959 by the new penal code for Okinawa, although this time the *Hōmushō* favoured American policy. On 13 May General Booth, the High Commissioner, promulgated Ordinance no. 23, a new Code of Penal Law and Procedure for the Ryukyu Islands, to be effective from 5 June. This was to replace the old penal code set forth in Civil Administration Ordinance no. 144 of 16 March 1955. The official explanation for this revision was improvement: rules of evidence were modified so that they would be more favourable to accused persons and licensing requirements for publication were removed, as were restrictions on access to the Naha port area.[26]

The proposal was at first received with indifference by the Okinawan community. It caused, however, serious anxiety on the Japanese mainland and subsequently also in Okinawa. Faced with this situation, the High Commissioner was cautious. On 4 June 1959 he deferred the date on which the Ordinance was to come into effect from 5 June to 15 August. In the meantime, he solicited the views of the *Hōmushō* on the matter. The *Hōmushō* replied that various provisions of the new code were neither unreasonable nor unduly harsh considering the nature and purpose of the law; they suggested some improvements, such as removal of the restrictions on the display of the Japanese flag for public purposes, would be desirable.[27] Their view was endorsed by the Kishi Cabinet at its meeting on 17 July.[28]

Informal exchanges of opinion on the matter took place between the *Gaimushō* and the American Embassy in Tokyo, but the matter did not become a diplomatic issue between the two countries.[29] The Japanese government's attitude was favourable, but the Ryukyuan Legislature officially requested ample time to study and evaluate the provisions of the code. In response, the High Commissioner postponed implementation indefinitely.[30]

In this case there was no disagreement between the *Gaimushō* and the *Hōmushō*. The reason for the latter's favourable attitude is not known. It is significant, however, that the Americans regarded the opinion of the *Hōmushō* as important. Its conciliatory attitude together with the flexible policy of the High Commissioner was responsible for the successful handling of the penal code issue.

Gaimushō v. Sōrifu

Sōrifu did not play a significant role in either of these cases. With the advent of the Ikeda Cabinet, which adopted a policy of financial aid for Okinawa, the *Sōrifu* acquired a greater significance as a government agency dealing with Okinawan affairs.

Symbolic of this was the visit of Fujieda Sensuke, Director-General of the *Sōrifu*, to Okinawa in late 1960. This was the first visit to Okinawa by a Japanese minister since the end of the war. Since then each of Fujieda's successors has followed his precedent. The *Sōrifu* had become a key factor in the making of Japan's Okinawa policy; this was clearly illustrated by its role in deciding to establish U.S.-Japan Committees for Okinawa following President Kennedy's announcement of policy on 19 March 1962.

There was an important difference of opinion between the United States and Japan over the scope the committees should have. Generally speaking, the Japanese wished to include political problems such as an extension of political freedoms in Okinawa and removal of restrictions on travellers to and from Okinawa, while the Americans tried to limit the discussions to problems of economic aid. This is not to say, however, that the Japanese government was determined and consistent in its policy. On the contrary, there was considerable vacillation in its diplomatic position. This may be attributed to differences of opinion between the *Gaimushō* and the *Sōrifu*.

The Japanese government established an inter-departmental committee to formulate proposals to be put forward to the United States. This committee consisted of officials of the rank of Chief-of-bureau from relevant ministries and the Board of Audit, and was chaired by Tokuyasu Jitsuzō, the Director-General of the *Sōrifu*.[31] Its report was submitted to the Prime Minister on 8 September 1962 and approved by the Cabinet on 13 September.[32]

It was in his discussion with the American Ambassador (E. O. Reischauer) which followed later on the same day that the Foreign

Minister (Ohira Masayoshi) formally proposed establishing inter-governmental organs for Okinawa.[33] In reply Reischauer on 2 November put forward a proposal which included the following points: a consultative committee composed of the Japanese Foreign Minister and the American Ambassador should be set up in Tokyo; a technical committee should be set up in Okinawa with the High Commissioner as chairman and attended by representatives of the governments of the Ryukyu Islands and Japan; these committees should deal only with problems of economic aid to Okinawa and should not handle any political questions.[34]

It took nearly five months for the Japanese government to produce a counter-proposal. One of the reasons for this delay was apparently differences of opinion between the *Sōrifu* and the *Gaimushō*. The former maintained that as its Director-General was actually in charge of Okinawan affairs, he, as well as the Foreign Minister, should be on the consultative committee. The *Gaimushō* opposed this on the ground that it would be improper for anyone but the Foreign Minister to represent the government diplomatically. Finally, however, the *Sōrifu's* view was adopted by the Cabinet and incorporated into the proposal presented to the United States delegate on 2 April 1963.[35]

The American reply reached the Japanese government on 22 July. The Americans agreed on the inclusion of the *Sōrifu's* Director-General on two conditions: the committee in Tokyo should consist officially of the Japanese Foreign Minister and the American Ambassador, with the Director-General and the Minister at the U.S. Embassy as observers; the functions of the two committees should be limited to problems of economic assistance to Okinawa, and matters concerning the political status of Okinawa should not be put on the agenda.[36]

The Japanese government was again divided over this American proposal. The *Gaimushō* wanted to agree to the American offer. The *Sōrifu* argued that it would be unrealistic to separate the problem of economic aid from other political questions, and that a committee in which the Director-General did not have full membership would achieve little more than the ordinary diplomatic channels.[37]

It is not known how these differences were settled within the Japanese government. Nor do we know the contents of the resultant proposal that the Japanese government handed to the United States on 27 September 1963. After another six months the two countries finally reached an agreement by exchanging official notes on

25 April 1964.[38] The Americans conceded to the Japanese plan on the status of the Director-General, while the Japanese gave in on the scope of the committees' work.

A similar difference between the *Gaimushō* and the *Sōrifu* developed over the *Sōrifu's* plan for the Prime Minister to visit Okinawa in mid-1963. This plan originated from Tokuyasu, the Director-General, who proposed that the Prime Minister should attend the anniversary of the end of the fighting in Okinawa (22 June). Some *Gaimushō* officials were afraid of adding another obstacle to the negotiation for establishing the Okinawa committees; they opposed this proposal on the ground that such a visit might stimulate the movement to have the island returned to Japan. Because Ikeda, the Prime Minister, did not show much interest in this plan it proved abortive.[39]

Although the *Sōrifu* had thus emerged as a key factor in the Japanese government's apparatus for making decisions on Okinawa, it did not exclude other ministries from initiating policy from time to time. An example of this was the role of the *Jichishō* (Ministry of Local Government) in a proposal to provide seats in the Japanese Diet for representatives from Okinawa.

In October 1963 the Election System Inquiry Commission *(Senkyo Seido Shingikai)* recommended amendments to the electoral law. One was that four Lower House seats should be created for the old prefecture of Okinawa, the elections to be held when administrative power over Okinawa was returned to Japan.[40] The *Jichishō* seemed sympathetic to this plan at first. The Cabinet's legal advisers said there were no legal objections to it. However, *Gaimushō* officials resisted it because they had been unofficially informed that the United States would dislike the plan. Leaders of the Government Party accepted the *Gaimushō's* view.[41] As a result the *Jichishō*, with the approval of the Prime Minister, dropped this proposal.[42]

We have examined several cases which illustrate the way in which Japan's Okinawa policy was decided. A summary of information relating to these is given in Table 5. What are the characteristics of this decision-making process?

One common factor is the conciliatory policy of the *Gaimushō*. Some other government agencies resisted it (or rather, courses of action which they initiated were hindered by the *Gaimushō*). Although different agencies played this role from time to time, the *Sōrifu* emerged as the principal one. Presumably the main reason for this is the increased scope and importance of the *Sōrifu's*

administrative functions in supplying financial and technical aid to
Okinawa. The upgrading of its chief also contributed, although it
was not originally connected with the Okinawa question.

The difference of attitude between the *Gaimushō* and the *Sōrifu*
is not fundamental. There is neither ideological disparity nor
difference of opinion about the legal status of Okinawa (compare
the controversy between the *Gaimushō* and the *Hōmushō* in 1956
which was fundamental). The difference of opinion between them is

Table 5
PATTERN OF DECISION-MAKING ON OKINAWA POLICY

Issue	Intensity of difference	Parties to dispute	Prime Minister	Cabinet decision	Name of PM
1 Diplomatic protection	4	G v. H	pro G	pro G	Hatoyama
2 Penal code	0	G v. H	—	—	Kishi
3 U.S.-Japan committees	3	G v. S	?	pro S	Ikeda
4 PM's visit to Okinawa	1	G v. S	pro G	—	Ikeda
5 Representation in the Diet	2	G v. J	?	pro G	Ikeda

G, H, S and J stand respectively for *Gaimushō, Hōmushō, Sōrifu* and
Jichishō. The degree of intensity ranged from 0 (non-existent) to 5 (tension
strong enough to produce the dismissal of Ministers concerned or the
resignation of an entire Cabinet).

a result of their different functions. For the same reason, however,
the difference is inherent and permanent. In other words, it is little
affected by changes in Cabinet leaders.

However, the opinion of civil servants, especially officials of the
rank of Chief-of-bureau, carries considerable weight. They are
often influential even in political decisions as distinct from administration; Ministers are often spokesmen for their officials rather
than members of the supreme decision-making organ. A Cabinet
decision sometimes does not resolve inter-departmental disagreement. Such was the case with the dispute between the *Gaimushō*
and the *Hōmushō* over initiating diplomatic discussions with the
United States on its land policy in Okinawa.

What is the relative importance of various agencies in deciding
Japan's Okinawa policy? Judging from the above, it seems at first
that the *Gaimushō* carried a greater weight than others: the final
decisions were generally in favour of the *Gaimushō*. Viewed from
another angle, however, this is a reflection of Japan's relatively weak

diplomatic position *vis-à-vis* the United States. For this reason the *Gaimushō* is often criticized severely for its 'weak-kneed' diplomacy. Frustrated desires look for compensation in the more positive attitudes of some other agencies; the Okinawans' high expectations of the *Sōrifu* or its Director-General are an instance.[43] In some circumstances conciliation is intended to facilitate more important negotiations.

The foregoing analysis may suggest poor leadership by the Prime Minister in formulating Japan's Okinawan policy. It is certainly difficult to discern decisive action by a Prime Minister to settle inter-departmental conflict. His role is, however, important in two ways. In the first place, summit conferences between the United States and Japan have provided opportunities for reviewing the problem of Okinawa in the light of developments in international and U.S.-Japanese relations. In fact, every Prime Minister since the Peace Treaty (with the sole exception of Hatoyama) visited Washington at least once during his tenure to discuss a wide range of problems outstanding between the two countries. The Okinawa problem has always been included in such conferences, although the importance attached to it has varied from time to time. Sometimes the conference did not produce any concrete result, but sometimes the results were significant. For example, the Ikeda-Kennedy talks in mid-1961 gave a fresh start to the policy of providing economic assistance to Okinawa through a co-operative relationship between the two countries. Because of the plurality of the policy-making machinery for Okinawa both in the United States and in Japan, it is quite likely that an important decision, if made at all, will be made at summit level.

A Prime Minister can lay down a broad line for foreign policy in general and for Okinawa policy in particular. Such was the case, at least, with the Kishi and Ikeda Cabinets. It may be said that they represented two types of conservative diplomacy in contemporary Japan. While Kishi tried to solve the Okinawa problem by modifying security arrangements with the United States, Ikeda's aid to Okinawa policy accorded with his general method of 'economic diplomacy', i.e. a diplomacy based on economic strength.

The development of Okinawa policy under the Satō administration confirms our conclusions about the pattern of Japan's policy-making on Okinawa. Satō, the brother of Kishi and close friend of Ikeda, showed great interest in the Okinawa problem from the beginning of his administration. In his talks with President Johnson in January 1965, not long after the formation of his Cabinet, great importance was attached to it. Another indication of his special concern was his visit to Okinawa, which was the first by a Japanese Prime Minister since Okinawa was placed under American control. The marked increase of the amount of Japanese aid to Okinawa in the fiscal year 1965 and after, and the establishment of the Committee of Ministers Concerned with the Okinawa Problems in September 1965 were among the concrete achievements of his administration in its early years. These steps on the whole accorded with the policy of his immediate predecessor.

From about the end of 1966, however, it became obvious that Satō was inclined to link the Okinawa problem with national security. The Prime Minister's disavowal of the Mori plan (see chapter 5) in January 1967 was the first clear sign of this change.

The Mori plan was a logical conclusion of Ikeda's policy of increasing Japan's involvement in Okinawan administration without questioning the military bases. Its disavowal by Satō meant a departure from the method established by Ikeda. It also meant that the *Gaimushō*'s view had triumphed over the *Sōrifu*'s, since Satō was most probably influenced by the *Gaimushō* experts in adopting the new policy (see chapter 5). Since then a group of *Gaimushō* officials, nicknamed the 'Security Treaty team' or 'Shimoda group',[44] have continued to advocate that administrative rights over the Ryukyu Islands should be returned to Japan in exchange for the promise to the United States of a more flexible interpretation of the terms of the Security Treaty.

The recent 'high posture' of the *Gaimushō* may appear to deviate from its traditional role of restraining the various domestic pressures for the return of Okinawa. But it is because of diplomatic considerations that the *Gaimushō* officials have been actively engaged in the Okinawan negotiations of recent years. They believed that an early solution of the Okinawa problem would not only help to remove a thorny issue in U.S.-Japanese relations, but would also bring the two countries closer if, as they hope, their negotiations for it resulted in a better understanding between them about the problems of collective security in the Far East. Whatever its motivations may be, the *Gaimushō*'s 'high posture' with regard to Okinawa is unlikely to be seriously opposed by any other Departments of the government. It is the task of the Prime Minister and other political leaders to weigh diplomatic considerations against domestic ones.[45] It still remains to be seen to what extent the Satō government will succeed in balancing them.

7

The Diet

Most of the observers of contemporary Japanese politics will agree in thinking that the share of the Diet—the Japanese parliament—in making government policies, especially in the field of foreign relations, is very small. The predominance of the executive over the legislature is common in the contemporary world. This tendency is, however, amplified in contemporary Japan under political conditions peculiar to the country. Although the new Constitution of 1946 makes the Diet 'the highest organ of the state power', the theory of parliamentary supremacy has not taken deep root in Japanese soil. What is more, under the so-called one-and-a-half-party system which is characterized by the semi-permanent predominance of a particular party, the government is apt to be identified with the party in power. Sharp and wide disparity between the government and the Opposition prevents the latter from contributing significantly through parliamentary debate to many fields of government. Really important decisions are made through direct channels between the government and the Party, such as Cabinet-Party Liaison Meetings and constant contact between the government departments and various organs of the Party, well before the matter comes to the Diet.[1] This situation may be described as a party government rather than a parliamentary government.

This pessimistic view of the work of the Diet applies generally also to its function in Okinawan affairs. But the Diet has been influential in shaping public opinion, if not very effective in forming government policy. We shall therefore examine in this chapter the methods available to the Diet for that purpose.

Debate on the Peace Treaty

The most important method of parliamentary control over the administration of foreign relations is the approval for the conclusion of treaties. What attitude did the Diet take to the Japanese Peace Treaty, Article 3 of which provided for the political separation of Okinawa from Japan?

The Japanese Peace Treaty, together with the U.S.-Japan Security Treaty, was passed by the House of Representatives on 26 October 1951, and by the House of Councillors on 18 November. The voting in the House of Representatives is given in Table 6. The vote was divided strictly along party lines, with only a little cross-voting among one section of the Conservatives, the Democrats.[2] The pros and cons of the treaties were largely determined by Members' opinions about the problem of Japan's position in world politics, namely her political and military alignment with the United States. Because of this, some concrete problems involved in the Peace Treaty, such as reparations and the territorial settlement, were relegated to second place and had little bearing on the final votes for ratification of that Treaty. As a result, it is very difficult to discern in their votes Members' opinions about these problems. It must be pointed out, however, that there were quite a few abstentions among the Conservative Members. Although not all of these abstentions were evidence of dissatisfaction with the treaties, the abstention rate was extraordinarily high among Members from Kagoshima Prefecture (which has geographically and politically close ties with Okinawa and especially with Amami-Ōshima).[3]

The feeling in the Diet on the territorial clauses in the Peace Treaty was more clearly expressed during the debate especially in the Special Committee on the Peace and Security Treaties in each House. Twelve out of fifty members of the Committee of the Lower House and eleven out of thirty-five members of that of the Upper House questioned the government on Article 3 of the Peace Treaty.[4]

These questions can be classified into two broad categories. The first concerned the relationship between Article 3 of the Japanese Peace Treaty and principles governing the territorial settlement. The government took the position that Japan was bound to accept any decision made by the Allied Powers because of the Potsdam Declaration. This provided that Japan's sovereignty should be limited to the four main islands of Honshū, Hokkaidō, Kyūshū and Shikoku and to 'such minor islands as we [the Allied Powers] determine'. Although nobody dared to challenge this view squarely, some Members maintained that, in spite of the Potsdam Declaration, the Allied Powers had to observe the Atlantic Charter and other wartime international documents. These laid down the principle of non-aggrandizement, and that territorial changes must accord with

Table 6

ANALYSIS OF VOTES ON THE JAPANESE PEACE TREATY AND THE U.S.-JAPAN SECURITY TREATY
(HOUSE OF REPRESENTATIVES, 26 OCTOBER 1951)

Peace Security	1 pro pro	2 pro abst.	3 pro con	4 abst. pro	5 abst. abst.	6 abst. con	7 con pro	8 con abst.	9 con con	Total
Liberals	224	—	—	12	51	—	—	—	—	287
Democrats	46	3	1	—	14	—	—	—	3	67
Right-wing Socialists	—	1	23	—	3	—	—	—	1	28
Left-wing Socialists	—	—	—	—	2	—	—	—	15	17
Rōnōtō	—	—	—	—	—	—	—	—	4	4
Communists	—	—	—	—	1	—	—	—	21	22
Minor groups*	7	2	—	—	3	—	—	—	3	15
Total	277	6	24	12	74	—	—	—	47	440

Peace Treaty
Approval (1-2-3) 307
Disapproval (7-8-9) 47
Abstention (4-5-6) 86
440

Security Treaty
Approval (1-4-7) 289
Disapproval (3-6-9) 71
Abstention (2-5-8) 80
440

*Minor groups include *Kyōdōtō, Daisan Kurabu, Nōmintō,* and Independent.

the freely expressed wishes of the people involved.[5] Some Members questioned the compatibility of Article 3 of the Peace Treaty with Articles 76 and 77 of the United Nations Charter; they implied that a trusteeship for Okinawa, an integral part of Japan, would be incompatible with the 'spirit' of the provisions of the Charter.[6] These discussions showed that many people were not convinced of the justice of the peace conference's decision on Okinawa.

The second group of questions focused on the problem of residual sovereignty. When he expounded Article 3 of the Peace Treaty before the Diet, the Prime Minister, Yoshida, assured the Diet that sovereignty over Okinawa and Ogasawara would remain with Japan. He cited Dulles's statement at the San Francisco Conference that the Treaty would 'permit Japan to retain residual sovereignty' over these islands. Yoshida also said that, while Article 2 provided specifically for the detachment of the islands of Chishima and Karafuto from Japan, there was no such provision in Article 3, which referred to Okinawa and Ogasawara.[7]

Most questioners demanded that the government explain the effects of this provision on Japan's relations with Okinawa. What would 'residual sovereignty' actually mean for Japan? The government gave two answers, which were not incompatible but were slightly different in emphasis. One was that the United States would, under this provision, eventually return the islands to Japan, although she would exercise administrative power over them as long as she liked. Japan's sovereignty over the islands would be, so to speak, frozen until that time.[8] Another interpretation of residual sovereignty was that, even before such complete return of the islands took place, Japan might have some share in certain fields of administration in Okinawa.[9] The government tried to impress on the Diet that no final decision had yet been reached as to how the Americans would exercise the rights given them by Article 3 and that, therefore, much depended on a future arrangement in which Japan's interest would be taken into account.[10]

There were a few Members who disagreed with the government's optimistic expectation of a friendly attitude on the part of the United States towards Japan's special interests in Okinawa. They asked why it was necessary to the security of the United States and Japan for the Americans to control the islands on such terms while the United States was given the rights of free use of military facilities on the Japanese mainland under the Security Treaty.[11] People like Ashida Hitoshi, a former Prime Minister, went on to say that the control of Okinawa by the Americans could be explained only by America's suspicion of Japan. It would, Ashida argued, be extremely difficult for anybody to persuade the Japanese people that the American forces' continued occupation of the island was imperative for the security of the West.[12]

Throughout the Treaty debate in the Diet there was no sharp division of opinion about the Okinawa problem between the conservatives and the radicals. Members from virtually all political parties took part in the debate on the subject.[13] Neither in the intensity nor in the content of their arguments was there any substantial difference between the left and the right. They were almost all alike in expressing regret over the territorial arrangement. As one Member of the House of Representatives put it, the 'extremely harsh' territorial provisions of the Peace Treaty were incompatible with what Dulles called 'the peace of trust, the peace of reconciliation'.[14] This feeling was expressed also in the resolution carried by the Diet on the implementation of the Peace Treaty which called for a 'just settlement' of the territorial question.

Resolutions

Perhaps the most positive means by which the Diet can influence foreign relations is the resolution, through which it expresses its opinion on an important matter. Such resolutions are not binding on the executive branch; they are usually submitted to the Cabinet merely as a suggestion. But they can warn or encourage the negotiators on either side.

The Japanese Diet, since its establishment under the new Constitution in 1947, has passed many resolutions on the Okinawa problem. The Diet's resolutions on the territorial questions are outnumbered only by those for promoting repatriation of the Japanese nationals abroad in the early post-war period (particularly those who were believed to be detained in the Soviet Union); the

Table 7

DIET RESOLUTIONS ON FOUR MAJOR ISSUES, 1947–60

Subject	Lower House		Upper House		Total	
	moved	passed	moved	passed	moved	passed
Repatriation	17	12	10	9	27	21
Territorial questions	22	11	4	2	26	13
Nuclear bombs	5	3	5	4	10	7
Japan-China trade	6	4	3	2	9	6

next-largest groups are those protesting against the production and testing of nuclear bombs and those for promoting Japan-China trade (see Table 7).[15]

In the earlier resolutions (to 1953) on territorial problems, apart from those sponsored by local interests, the problem of the southern islands (Okinawa, Ogasawara and Amami-Ōshima) was not distinguished from that of the northern territories (Chishima, Habomai, Shikotan, and including sometimes the southern half of Karafuto); later these two territorial problems came to be treated separately but concurrently in a pair of resolutions. This method was adopted for the first time in 1953. These resolutions became a product of political manœuvring between the left and the right in Japanese politics.

The process by which the resolutions were carried in 1962 provides an illustration. The Socialists took the initiative in moving a resolution about the Okinawa problem and suggested that the Conservatives join with them. The latter proposed including the northern territories. The Socialists did not agree. Meanwhile the Democratic Socialists were prepared to move a resolution on the Okinawa problem on their own initiative, opposed to both the Socialist and the Conservative plan. Finally these three parties compromised and the Diet passed two resolutions, one on the Okinawa problem and the other on the northern territories.[16]

The resolutions on the Okinawa problem were always passed by a unanimous vote, whereas the resolutions on the northern territories were not unanimous. This is because the leftist groups oppose the Conservatives on the territorial issue *vis-à-vis* the Soviet Union while there is unanimity on the Okinawa problem.

There is a close relationship between some of the Diet resolutions and those of the Okinawan Legislature. For example, the Diet resolution on 7 November 1953 was passed in response to the appeal made by the Okinawan Legislature on 30 September of that year. Similarly, the March 1962 resolutions were carried in response to the famous 1 February resolution of the Okinawan Legislature, which cited the December 1960 Declaration of the United Nations on the right of independence to all dependent peoples. Again the Socialist and Democratic Socialist proposals in 1958 and 1964, although unsuccessful, were presumably moved under the stimulus of the appeals of the Okinawan Legislature of 11 April 1958 and 27 April 1964.

All this suggests a pattern of political manœuvring in the making of the Diet resolutions on the Okinawa problem in recent years.

The Opposition, particularly the Socialists, are so receptive to public pressure, especially appeals from the Okinawan Legislature, that they initiate proposals that the Diet express its desire for the earliest possible return of Okinawa to Japan. The Conservatives are embarrassed and try to reject the Socialist proposals. When they are unable to resist the public pressure behind the Socialists, they try to offset the effect of such resolutions by combining the problem of the northern territories with that of Okinawa. The Opposition has to succumb to this tactic because they are not strong enough to have their own wish carried.[17] The only exception to this rule is the resolution of 2 June 1956 which was carried without being coupled with a resolution on the territorial issue *vis-à-vis* the Soviet Union. This was made possible by the existence of bi-partisan concern about the military land problem of Okinawa.

There is an obvious difference between the Conservatives and the Socialists in their attitude toward the Diet resolutions on the Okinawa problem. But the two parties agree on one thing, and this is embodied in the resolutions. The wording 'return of administrative power' is suggestive; it has two connotations. In the first place it is used to mean the fact (or the belief) that the problem of sovereignty or territorial rights in Okinawa and Ogasawara has already been settled and that the question pending between Japan and the United States is merely when and how the latter should return the actual power over the islands. The constant use of the words 'return of the territories and territorial rights' with reference to the 'northern islands' should be remembered in this connection. To pro-American elements this sounds good because they can maintain that the Americans are generous enough to recognize Japan's sovereignty over Okinawa, while the Russians, in contrast, have deprived Japan of the sovereign right to the northern islands. On the other hand those who are critical of the American position on Okinawa think that Japan has a sound reason to demand that the United States return the power to Japan. For this reason both sides are happy about this terminology.

The other connotation of this wording is related to the argument that the use of military installations in Okinawa by the United States would not require that America exercise administrative power over civil affairs in the island. Those who interpret thus, argue that the Japanese are prepared to concede the American military interests in Okinawa if the Americans are ready to return the 'administrative power' of the island to Japan. Some sections of the Conservatives advocate this argument; the Socialists can also use it to attack the government for failing, in the face of the firm American objection on military grounds, to demand that the United States return administrative power.

Although a Diet resolution does not bind the government, it can be used as a test of the government's diplomacy over Okinawa, especially when public opinion reinforces it. At least the government is often asked in the Diet whether it has informed the United States government of these resolutions and how they have been used in the conduct of its diplomacy.

Committees

Another important area of the Diet's functions lies in what is called the legislative investigation into the activities of the executive. This function is performed mainly through committees.[18] The government's Okinawa policy has been investigated by various committees of the Diet.

For obvious reasons the Committee on Foreign Affairs of each House shows the greatest concern about this subject. This is so in spite of the fact that the investigation of the *Sōrifu* (Prime Minister's Office), including Okinawan affairs, is in principle a matter for the Committee on the Cabinet. Customarily, however, matters related to Okinawa are discussed more frequently in the Committee on Foreign Affairs.[19] The Okinawa problem also comes before other committees, particularly the Budget Committee.

To give some idea about the Diet's activities in this respect, we shall compare the work of the 24th session (December 1955 to June 1956) and the 40th session (December 1961 to May 1962).[20] During the former session the nation became concerned about the Okinawa problem because of the Okinawan people's determined objections to the American policy of land acquisition; the latter session saw the launching of the 'Kennedy new policy' on Okinawa. Thus in these two sessions more Members spoke about, and more hours were spent on, the Okinawa problem than in any others: sixty-nine Members and 1,463 minutes in the former and sixty-six Members and 1,434 minutes in the latter.

Analysis of these figures shows that there are some differences between the activities of the two sessions. In the first place, the importance of the Budget Committees increased in the intervening years. In the 24th session the Foreign Affairs Committee of the Lower House (44 speakers, 815 minutes) played a prominent role in the discussion about the Okinawa problem.[21] In the 40th session, while the Foreign Affairs Committees of both Houses continued to be important (10 speakers and 349 minutes in the Lower House; 7 speakers and 187 minutes in the Upper), the Budget Committees had assumed equal importance (7 speakers and 112 minutes in the Lower; 20 speakers and 213 minutes in the Upper).

There are two factors which account for the increased importance of the Budget Committees in this field. One is that the Budget Committee is generally regarded as the most important of all committees in either House. It is numerically the largest: fifty in the Lower and forty-five in the Upper House. All matters of broad policy as well as the technical problems of the budget come before it. With the decline of Plenary Meetings, the Budget Committee has now become the place for high policy debates, particularly on 'general questions' which follow the submission of a budget to the Committee. Thus the Budget Committee's great concern with the Okinawa problem indicates that it has become a matter of high policy.

Another reason for the Budget Committee's concern with Okinawan affairs is the fact that financial aid to Okinawa in recent Japanese budgets has been substantial.

In terms of the party affiliation of those who spoke on the Okinawan problems there was also a considerable change from the 24th

Table 8

PARTICIPANTS IN THE OKINAWA DEBATE BY PARTY AFFILIATION
(JAPANESE DIET, 24th AND 40th SESSIONS)

Party Affiliation	Lower House Speeches	Lower House Speakers	Upper House Speeches	Upper House Speakers	Total Speeches	Total Speakers
		24th Session				
Liberals	—	—	1	1	1	1
Democrats	20	10	—	—	20	10
R. Socialists	16	7	1	1	17	8
L. Socialists	25	12	—	—	25	12
Rōnōtō	3	1	—	—	3	1
Communists	1	1	—	—	1	1
Ryokufūkai and Independent	—	—	2	2	2	2
Total	65	31	4	4	69	35
		40th Session				
Liberal-Democrats	3	2	1	1	4	3
Democratic Socialists	5	3	4	3	9	6
Socialists	22	18	20	11	42	29
Communists	1	1	3	1	4	2
Independent	—	—	7	3	7	3
Total	31	24	35	19	66	43

to the 40th session (see Table 8). In the former session, participants in the discussion came from both the Conservatives and the Socialists, although nineteen out of the twenty Conservatives who took part in the discussion were former Democrats. The situation was very different in the 40th session where Conservatives had only an insignificant share in the debate. This trend shows that the Diet's role in formulating policy, particularly policy on Okinawa, was changing. In 1956 the government leaders had only loose control over their own party because it had only recently been unified and was now seriously divided about the policy of its new leader, Hatoyama Ichirō, towards the Soviet Union. In addition, the government leaders were not prepared to take any effective measures on Okinawa. Under these circumstances the Diet acted on a bi-partisan basis in advocating a positive policy towards Okinawa. That was the case when the Diet strongly criticized the Hatoyama Cabinet's weak diplomacy in the political crisis caused by the American land policy in Okinawa in 1956.

In 1962, on the other hand, the government leaders enjoyed a fairly firm command of their party. Regarding Okinawa, the Ikeda Cabinet was well equipped with a new policy of 'partnership' between Japan and the United States. In this situation members of the Government Party had little say in forming policy through debate in the Diet. An illustration may be seen in the compilation of the budget: the opinions of the members of the Government Party were considered in the earlier stages so that the debate in the Diet had little significance for them.[22] The role of the Diet is to criticize rather than to control the policy and actions of the government, and only the Opposition Members are interested in this task. The same applies to the debate on Okinawa in recent sessions of the Diet.

In recent years some efforts were made to improve the functions of the Diet with regard to Okinawan affairs. For example an *ad hoc* Committee on Okinawan Problems was set up in each House of the Diet in February 1967. This step was taken after the Opposition parties had advocated it for many years.[23] The Okinawan Legislature had also petitioned for such a committee in the Diet.[24] The ruling Liberal Democratic Party was, however, afraid that the Committee would become the theatre of leftist propaganda. In order to alleviate this fear, the Committee adopted a round-table method. The Socialists also seem to have been cautious of bringing the Committee to a standstill by excessive arguing. As a result the Committee proved to be quieter than expected.[25]

Another proposal which has been long advocated but so far without success is that for the direct representation of the Okinawan people in the Diet. Before the war the Okinawa Prefecture used to send its own representatives to the Imperial Diet (two members from 1912 to 1920; five thereafter). When the election law for the House of Representatives was substantially amended shortly after the surrender, it was provided that two Members could be elected although actual elections for them should be suspended for the time being. In other words Okinawa remained, at least on paper, a constituency in the Japanese parliamentary system. In 1947, however, when a second amendment was made to that law, Okinawa was completely deleted from it.[26] There was no change in this when Japan regained her independence in 1952.

Although there have subsequently been some isolated efforts to restore Okinawa to its original status in the Japanese Diet, it is only recently that vigorous efforts for that purpose have been resumed. A resolution passed by the Okinawan Legislature in April 1961 was evidence of this. Resolutions to the same effect have been carried by the Okinawan Legislature six times, including this one.[27] Despite the difference between the moderates, who might be satisfied with sending observers to the Diet, and those who insisted on having representatives with full membership, there is developing among the Okinawans a strong desire to have a voice in the Japanese government.[28]

The appeals of the Okinawan people have met with a sympathetic response among some quarters of Japanese society. For example, the Election System Inquiry Commission, an advisory body for the Japanese government, recommended in its report of October 1963 that four Lower House seats be created for Okinawa provided that elections were held on the return of the island to Japanese administration.[29] As mentioned in the previous chapter, this recommendation was turned down by the government for diplomatic reasons.

The issue was revived in 1967 when the three Opposition parties (the Socialists, the Democratic Socialists and the *Kōmeitō*) jointly proposed to give the Okinawans the 'latent' rights to elect five representatives for the Lower House and two members for the Upper House. Some members of the LDP, especially its Okinawa Committee, reportedly favoured the proposal. The objection came from the senior members of the Party including the Secretary-General, Fukuda Takeo, who thought it unwise to irritate the Americans with the Prime Minister's visit to Washington near at hand.[30] As a result the matter again came to nothing.

The Okinawan hope came near fulfilment in October 1968 when

the Americans consented to the Japanese government's proposal that Okinawan observers (without voting rights) be permitted to attend the Diet. It was widely believed that the Japanese government and the United States agreed on this hoping that it would help the Conservative candidate in the forthcoming election of the Chief Executive in Okinawa.[31] Whether this was true or not, the election result was disappointing to the Liberal Democrats. Thereafter they seem to have lost interest in the implementation of the agreed policy. The bill for that purpose was shelved in the 1968–9 session of the Diet and the Okinawan hope was again frustrated.[32]

The work of the Diet depends, to a great extent, upon the nature of the political parties. The conclusion of the Japanese Peace Treaty and the land controversy in Okinawa in 1955–6 excited considerable attention in the Diet. Its debates in these periods were comparatively non-partisan. This was partly because participation in the discussion in the Diet was the most effective, or rather the best conceivable, means available to those back-benchers who wanted to influence the government's policy. The existence of non-ministerial Conservative Members (i.e. the Democrats) was, in particular, responsible for this.

As regimentation of political parties along the ideological line proceeded, however, the Diet's activities came to be greatly affected by this development of party government. Conservative back-benchers were uninterested in discussions in the Diet because various party machines, such as the LDP's Committee on Okinawa Problems, provided them with a more direct and more effective means of influencing the government. This is clearly shown in the work of the parliamentary committees in recent years; their debates on the Okinawan affairs are almost completely dominated by the Opposition. Another explanation for this phenomenon is that the return of Okinawa, which was merely a matter of national aspiration in the earlier days, has become part of a broader and more controversial problem, namely that of Japan's security and the American alliance.

Although the Diet has been not as effective in forming government policy towards Okinawa as it has been in other policy matters, it has helped to awaken public attention. Quite frequently the Diet's debate on Okinawa is fully reported in the press. The government is constantly subject to critical scrutiny by the Opposition Members of the Diet. Moreover, the Diet, whose most articulate expression is made in resolutions, sometimes succeeds in expressing a 'common concern' with the Okinawa problem. Whatever the process up to the passing of the resolutions, once carried they are to be regarded as the will of the Japanese nation, and as such affect the government's course of action. Since the main reason for the negative government policy on Okinawa is presumably the existence of factors outside its control (i.e. the unwillingness of the United States to make concessions), the government may well approve when the Diet expresses a more forceful policy than the government itself is able to implement. By this means the government might hope to bring indirect pressure to bear on the United States.

8

Political Parties (1945–55)

The role of political parties in formulating policy since the war can be divided into four periods.[1] The first was the period from 1945 to 1950, which includes most of the Occupation; the political parties took virtually no part in government policies, particularly in its foreign policies. This was followed by a brief but important period (1950–2) during which there were vigorous debates on the Peace and Security Treaties. It was in this period that Japanese political parties established their fundamental orientation. In the few years (1952–5) which followed the nation's independence, Japanese politicians devoted themselves almost entirely to political reorganization which produced the 'two-party system' in 1955. Throughout these first three periods Japan's diplomacy was largely formulated and conducted by a single person, Yoshida.[2] The advent of the Hatoyama Cabinet and the subsequent merger of the conservative parties opened a new era in the pattern of foreign policy formulation in post-war Japan. A feature of this period (after 1955) is the growing participation of the Government Party (or its various factions) in the making of foreign policy. This was first and most dramatically illustrated by the Hatoyama-Kōno diplomacy in the normalization of relations with the Soviet Union. 'Amateur diplomacy' is perhaps one of the characteristics of the new era.[3]

As discussed in the previous chapter, the decline of the Diet as a policy-making organ was largely a result of the growth of political parties. It was only after the war that political parties gained such an important place in Japanese politics. Before the war they never controlled the bureaucrats who ruled the country in the name of the Emperor. In this sense the advent of a party state in post-war Japan was a corollary of the parliamentary supremacy established by the new Constitution.

Against this general picture of Japan's post-war foreign policy formulation, we shall discuss in the present chapter the development of each political party's attitude to the territorial questions and especially to the Okinawa problem during the first three periods. The few years around the conclusion of the Japanese Peace Treaty (i.e. the second period, 1950–2) are particularly important in discussing this question. Problems in the fourth period will be treated in the next chapter.

In the early post-war period, it was generally difficult for any political party to pay due attention to the current and future status of Okinawa. There is no evidence to show that any of the parties, except the Japanese Communist Party, were concerned with Okinawa.

This lack of concern is understandable: people in all walks of life were preoccupied with their own economic rehabilitation. Moreover the Allied solidarity, which people believed still existed, seemed to leave little room for diplomatic manœuvring by a defeated nation.

As the Cold War developed, however, various political elements had more to say about international affairs in general and the territorial problems in particular. Allied negotiations for a Japanese peace treaty provided the Japanese political parties with an opportunity to discuss these questions.

The Liberals

The Liberal Party (*Jiyūtō*),[4] the party which was in office when the Peace Treaty was conducted, did not fail to take advantage of this opportunity. It made an open attack on the Yalta Agreement. In late 1949 a Liberal Member of the House of Representatives advanced the theory that, according to international law, the Japanese government was not bound by the Yalta Agreement because it was not informed about it when signing the surrender terms.[5] *Gaimushō* officials agreed with him and the U.S. State Department responded sympathetically.[6]

Shortly after this event, a senior member of the Party, Hoshijima Nirō, with the acquiescence of the government, violently attacked the Yalta Agreement, insisting that the Potsdam Declaration should be the sole guide in settling the Japanese territorial problems in peace negotiations.[7] This was the first time that the Japanese government denounced by name a particular member of the Allied Powers. The main objective of this speech was to refute the argument for an 'over-all peace' sponsored by, among others, the Communists. The Yalta Agreement and the Chishima problem were used to channel the popular feeling against the Soviet Union. But it was a double-edged instrument: it raised also the question of Okinawa and Ogasawara.

Like the other parties, the Liberal Party began to formulate its policy towards a peace treaty in June 1950 immediately after Dulles's first visit to Japan. For this purpose a Committee (*Kokusai Mondai Chōsakai*) was set up within the Party with Uehara Etsujirō as chairman.[8]

The policy it worked out, endorsed at the Executive Council (30 January 1951), was a request to Dulles to modify on some points, including the territorial arrangements, the policy announced by the United States.[9] With this decision as a basis, the Party's delegation, which met Dulles on 2 February, claimed Japan's territorial rights to Ogasawara, Okinawa and Chishima.[10] It is likely, however, as a newspaper commented, that the Liberals did not push the matter and remained satisfied with conveying to Dulles the Japanese people's feelings on Okinawa.[11] There is no evidence to show that the Liberals put pressure on the government. It seems that Yoshida enjoyed almost complete freedom of action so far as his own Party was concerned.

A problem which is of interest here is the attitude of Hatoyama Ichirō, Yoshida's successor, towards a Japanese peace treaty. Although as a result of a purge he was technically prohibited from engaging in politics, Hatoyama was given an opportunity to meet and discuss the peace treaty with Dulles when he visited Tokyo. He showed no particular concern with the territorial problems except to favour a deferment of the final settlement on former Japanese territories (he mentioned Taiwan, Chishima and the southern half of Karafuto).[12]

The Democrats

It was the Democratic Party[13] that expressed the most articulate opinion on territorial questions at that time.

It is not easy to determine the nature of this Party. Some people regard it as a party of the 'progressive conservatives', others label it as the most reactionary section of Japanese society.[14] As far as international policy is concerned, however, it appears fair to say that leading members of this Party represented the most 'nationalistic' elements in post-war Japan. Their nationalism assumed a classic form: they regarded the maintenance of an independent defence force as an essential prerequisite to the nation's political independence. From that point of view, they advocated 'strengthening the independent capacity for self-defence', in opposition to the government's policy of military reliance on the United States.[15]

The Party's position on the Okinawa problem (and the territorial questions in general) was quite in line with this trend of thought. An *ad hoc* Committee on Foreign Policy set up in the Party met thirteen times between June and October 1950 to determine the Party's position on the Japanese Peace Treaty.[16] Its report, which was endorsed at the January 1951 Party Convention, said the following in reference to the territorial problems:

> In the light of the spirit of the Atlantic Charter, Japan should be allowed to retain those areas which are recognized as her territories upon the principle of nationality and from the historical point of view, such as Chishima, Ryūkyū, Amami-Ōshima, Iwō-Jima, etc.[17]

The Committee's resolution of 26 January 1951 elaborated on the Party's position towards the problem of Okinawa and Ogasawara by saying, 'In case of a UN trusteeship being proposed for Okinawa and Ogasawara, Japan should concur in that proposal *subject to* the eventual return of these islands to Japan after a certain period of time' (my italics).[18] A few days after, representatives of the Party presented to Dulles their views on the Treaty including this point during an interview which lasted an hour and a half.[19]

Since information is not available about the discussion within the Party on the territorial questions, it is hard to decide what elements espoused this attitude. However, in view of the strong influence of Ashida Hitoshi upon the Party's foreign policy at that time, it would not be unreasonable to attribute it largely to Ashida and a militant group centred around Kitamura Tokutarō.[20]

The Party did not give its unqualified approval to the ratification of the Treaty because it was dissatisfied with the territorial clauses. After frequent meetings at various levels in October 1951, the Party finally decided to approve both the Japanese Peace Treaty and the U.S.-Japan Security Treaty but it recorded its belief that Chishima should eventually be returned to Japan, and that sovereignty over Okinawa, Amami-Ōshima and Ogasawara rests with Japan even though these islands were placed under a trusteeship system.[21]

Although the Party officially approved the two Treaties, some of its members did not agree with its decision; this resulted in a split vote by the Democrats on the ratification of the Treaties in the Diet.[22]

Also the Democrats, together with the Socialists, sponsored a resolution in the Diet which expressed its desire for a 'just settlement' of the territorial questions.

The desire for a revision of both the Peace Treaty and the Security Treaty was inherited by its successor, the *Kaishintō*. The outline of policy adopted at the inaugural convention of that Party (8 February 1952) stated that the Party would demand an early return of Karafuto, Chishima, Okinawa, Amami-Ōshima and Ogasawara and that it would promote the revision of the Peace and the Security Treaties.[23] The December 1952 convention of the Party passed a resolution expressing its desire for the return of these territories.[24] The convention of January 1954 again urged a prompt return to Japan of Chishima, Habomai, Shikotan and the southern half of Karafuto, as well as a recovery of Japan's full sovereignty in Okinawa and Ogasawara.[25] On this occasion the term 'unequal treaties' was used of the Peace Treaty, the U.S.-Japan Security Treaty and the U.S.-Japan Commercial and Navigation Treaty. The convention advocated revision of these 'unequal treaties' and the replacement of the existing 'unilateral' agreements by new treaties on a 'bilateral' basis. In view of the historical associations of the movement for revision of the unequal treaties in the Meiji era (*jōyaku kaisei undō*), the slogan 'revise the unequal treaties' had highly nationalistic overtones.

To sum up, the Democrats' position on the territorial problems expressed their nationalistic orientation which sought to put Japan on an equal footing with other foreign countries, including the United States. The national aspiration of the time found candid expression, as far as the territorial questions were concerned, in the Democratic Party; it was not bound, like the ruling Liberal Party, to defer diplomatically to the United States or, like the left-wing Opposition, by ideological considerations in relation to the Soviet Union.[26]

The Socialists

The Japanese Socialist Party (JSP) was seriously divided between the left-wing and right-wing groups over the ratification of the Peace and the Security Treaties; the effects of this split the Party in 1951. Evidence shows, however, that the territorial question was unimportant in this dispute. Nevertheless one can see a difference in the two sides' approach to the territorial problems.

In late 1949 when the JSP formulated its general attitude concerning the Peace Treaty issues, the Party said nothing about the territorial questions.[27] It was not until September 1950 that the Socialists took up a position on that question. The Party policy was decided by its Central Executive Committee on 18 September 1950; its statements on the territorial problem were: (1) in accordance with the Cairo Proclamation, the independence of Korea, the return of Manchuria, Formosa and the Pescadores to China and the relinquishing of the former Japanese Mandate in the Pacific must be considered as unavoidable; (2) sovereignty over Okinawa, Ogasawara, Chishima, Habomai, Shikotan and the southern half of Karafuto should rest with Japan because it was one of the fundamental conditions for the maintenance of a peaceful existence by the Japanese people;[28] these areas should remain Japanese because of their historical affiliation and close economic relations with the Japanese mainland.[29]

The January 1951 convention of the Party endorsed this policy which, together with other documents, was submitted by the Party delegates to Dulles on 1 February of that year, during his second visit to Japan.[30]

Up to that time there was no internal conflict in the Party over the Peace Treaty issue. As the time of ratification of the Treaty approached, however, the right-wing group challenged the Party's official line. This finally split the JSP: the right-wing Socialist Party favoured the Peace Treaty but opposed the U.S.-Japan Security Treaty; the left-wing Socialist Party opposed both.

A subcommittee of the Party's Foreign Policy Committee had been set up specifically to conciliate different views on the Treaties. At one stage of the debate within the Party which produced the final split, five proposals were put to this subcommittee, all agreeing that Japan was not bound by the Yalta Agreement (of which Japan had not been informed at the time of her surrender) and that Japan's claim to Okinawa, Ogasawara, Chishima and the southern half of Karafuto should be admitted.[31]

Despite the fundamental agreement on the territorial issues between the right-wing and the left-wing Socialists, the former were more persistent and consistent than the latter. For example, some right-wingers criticized the Party's official memorandum to Dulles and urged the Party to take a more 'positive and resolute' stand on the territorial questions.[32]

After the split, developments in the policies of these two groups of Socialists showed their different approaches to the territorial problems. The right-wing Socialists' position was close to that of the Democrats; the position of the left-wing Socialists remained ambiguous.

The right-wing Socialists advocated, like the Democrats, the 'revision of unequal treaties'. The term 'unequal treaties' had various connotations. In the beginning, it referred mainly to the one-sidedness of the U.S.-Japan Security Treaty (especially the problem of jurisdiction over U.S. Forces in Japan); it gradually extended to include all the treaties governing U.S.-Japanese relations. The territorial problems were the target for the Party's propaganda for the revision of the treaties.[33]

The right-wing Socialists showed their enthusiasm also by setting up a Special Committee for the Territorial Problems (later the Special Committee for the National Movement for the Revision of the Unequal Treaties) with Asanuma Inajirō as chairman; it included all members of the Party in both Houses of the Diet. They intended to appeal to the national aspiration of the people and by so doing to strengthen the Party which was inferior to the left-wing Socialists.[34]

In the meantime, the left-wing Socialists remained silent on the territorial questions despite a great deal of debate on the Security Treaty issue. It is interesting to see that the Party officials had difficulty in justifying their argument against the Peace Treaty.[35] They hardly referred to the territorial clauses in their Treaty debate. It was only in 1954 that the Party took up 'the return of territorial sovereignty over Okinawa to Japan' in its Action Policy.[36]

The difference between the left-wing and the right-wing Socialists on the territorial questions was expressed in their discussions for the reunification of the Party. The former insisted on the revision of the Japanese Peace Treaty on its *military* clauses (i.e. articles 5 and 6 relevant to the Security Treaty), while the latter wanted to see the Treaty revised on its *territorial* and *reparation* provisions.[37] It is hard, however, to find any positive reason against the reversion of Okinawa among the left-wing Socialists. It was not Okinawa but Chishima and Karafuto that caused the divergence between the two groups of Socialists at that time.[38] In spite of this difference they agreed to reunite the Party in late 1955. In the general election immediately before, the two groups had campaigned under the same slogans, one of which read, 'A complete return of Ogasawara and Okinawa to Japan. A reinstatement of Habomai, Shikotan,

Chishima and the southern half of Karafuto'.[39] Judging from its wording, the right-wing groups were primarily responsible for this attitude.

The Communists

While the other parties tended towards a gradual increase in concern about Okinawa during the first decade of the post-war period (apart from the difference in the intensity of their concern), the Communist attitude towards Okinawa during the same period changed drastically. At first they inclined to political separation of Okinawa from Japan; later they vigorously supported its return to Japan. The Communists were unique also in that they expressed their opinion on Okinawan affairs in the early days of the post-war period.

Although the Japan Communist Party (JCP) did not formulate or proclaim any official policy on Okinawa in this period, substantial evidence points to strong support within the Party for Okinawa's separation from Japan. The February 1946 National Convention of the JCP congratulated the *Okinawajin Remmei*, an association of Okinawan residents in Japan, on making their way towards independence and freedom.[40] In July 1947 when Ashida Hitoshi, the Foreign Minister, told a press conference that it was the aspiration of the Japanese people that Okinawa and Chishima be returned to Japan, the Communists, as well as some Socialists, strongly criticized him.[41]

While the Communists' reaction to Ashida's claim to Japan's sovereignty over Chishima is not very surprising,[42] their attitude towards Okinawa in the early post-war period merits some explanation. In the first place, one must remember the climate of opinion against every Japanese establishment of pre-war origin, whether it was associated, as in Marxist thinking, with the bourgeoisie or, as in some others' view, with Japanese militarists. In this situation the Communists preferred to place Okinawa under the control of international 'democratic forces' rather than call for its return to Japanese administration. Whether consciously or not, they were also influenced by Nosaka's theory of 'peaceful revolution', i.e. the theory that Japan could achieve a revolution by peaceful means with the sympathetic support of international democratic forces, including the United States. The overthrow of the old establishment was given priority over other considerations.[43]

To this general outlook of the Japanese Communists in the early post-war period were added some other factors such as the belief that the Okinawan people were a different stock from the Japanese mainlanders (*naichijin*) and were suppressed and exploited by the latter in pre-war Japan.[44] The personal background of Tokuda Kyūichi, the Secretary-General of the JCP, an Okinawa-born Japanese, apparently contributed to this line of thinking.[45] Under these circumstances, a small group of people who were devoting themselves to the cause of the return of Okinawa to Japan were regarded by the Communists, and by the *Okinawajin Remmei* under their influence, as 'reactionary and treacherous'.

The Cominform's criticism of Nosaka's theory of 'peaceful revolution' urged the Party to depart radically from its previous strategy.[46] This affected the Party's position on the territorial question *vis-à-vis* the Soviet Union and, more inconspicuously, on its Okinawa policy as well. In the debate over the Yalta Agreement opened up by the ruling Liberal Party, the Communists firmly defended the Soviet Union, condemning the government's attitude as 'fascist-like irredentism'.[47] This was the first time that the Japanese Communists firmly committed themselves to support the Yalta Agreement.

It took a few years, however, for the JCP to formulate a new Okinawa policy in line with the Cominform's criticism. The slowness of this change can be explained by the aftermath of the theory of national minority applied to Okinawa's relations with Japan. For example, Okinawan affairs together with Korean and Chinese (Taiwan) problems were dealt with, even in this period, by the Party's Division of Minority Affairs, *minzoku taisakubu*.[48]

A feature of the Party's Okinawa policy of this period was the growing emphasis on the need to fight against the United States' military use of Okinawa, while avoiding a definite commitment on the problem of Okinawa's political status. 'We demand', a document of the Party said in March 1951, 'withdrawal of all military forces from Okinawa. It should be for the Okinawan people freely to decide their political status'.[49]

The earliest sign, as far as can be ascertained, of a change in the Party's Okinawa policy is found in the Action Programme in October 1953. This recognized 'the liberation of the Okinawan people as an inseparable and highly important part of the liberation of the Japanese people from American imperialism'.[50] This policy was finally endorsed at the central level of the Party in April 1954 and again in January 1955.[51]

In conclusion a few points deserve mention. In the first place Japanese politicians were conspicuously slow to form opinions on the Allied decisions about Japanese territory. Passivity and apparent indifference prevailed and lasted for half a decade among them. It was not until 1950–1 when Dulles sought the ideas of Japanese leaders that the Japanese political parties began to consider the matter seriously. A superficial explanation of this slow response is that they were preoccupied with the immediate tasks of the economic and social rehabilitation of Japan. This does not explain, however, why the Japanese were so much slower than the Germans and the Italians.[52] Two factors, one psychological and the other economic, contributed to the Japanese attitude. Japan had suffered a national defeat for the first time in her history. This unprecedented experience was such a great shock to the Japanese people that they temporarily lost their sense of direction. They were not accustomed to taking a subordinate position and asserting their rights under the most unfavourable circumstances. In addition to this psychological consideration, the territorial problems were not regarded as vitally relevant to the economic recovery of the nation which was the matter of utmost concern at the time.

Another characteristic of the Japanese attitude towards the territorial problems was the initial indifference among the left-wing elements. This was quite different from the situation in post-war Germany where the Social Democrats took the initiative in advocating the return of the Saar. In connection with this, attention should be directed to the fact that the JCP's position on the territorial problem *vis-à-vis* the Soviet Union presented an interesting contrast to that of the Italian Communists who openly defended the Italian character of Trieste against the Yugoslav claim. In Japan it was the right-wing Conservatives who opened up the debate on the territorial problems by attacking the Yalta Agreement. If this tactic was useful to attack the Soviet Union and the Japanese Communists, it also endangered the political and moral concepts upon which the war-time international agreements concerning Japan were based. The American position on Okinawa seemed to the Japanese just as shaky as the Soviet claim to Chishima. While the ruling Liberal Party was not in a position to push the Okinawa problem too far, the Democrats and the right-wing Socialists loudly championed the return of both Chishima and Okinawa. It was only when the problem of American bases in Okinawa loomed large that the left-wing began to be seriously concerned with the matter. Thus Japanese attention to the territorial problems moved politically from right to left and geographically from north to south.

It is also important that the Japanese government was free from pressure from the ultra-rightists (cf. irredentist sentiment advanced by neo-Fascists who were dissatisfied with the Italian Peace Settlement after World War II). The lack of strong opposition from the right as well as from the left moderated the tone of Japanese arguments on territorial problems.

9

Political Parties (after 1955)

When considering the involvement of Japanese political parties in the Okinawa problem, the years 1955–6 form a watershed which distinguish the following period in many ways from the preceding one.

In the first place, the party in office has come to be important in formulating foreign policy in general and Okinawa policy in particular. Secondly, events in Okinawa have brought the political parties in Japan into direct contact with those in Okinawa. Thirdly, the Okinawa problem has become a matter of public concern; political parties, whether in office or not, can no longer afford to ignore public opinion.

As the last of these three aspects will be analysed in the next two chapters, here we shall be concerned largely with the first two.

This period witnessed three major events with regard to Okinawa: the political crisis which developed in Okinawa over the American land acquisition policy (1956–8); the revision of the U.S.-Japan Security Treaty (1958–60); and the development of 'Kennedy's new Okinawa policy' (1961–4). Let us first examine the ways in which political parties were involved in these developments. This will be followed by a brief review of the parties' positions in the debate about Okinawa and the implications for Japan's future defence policy.

As we have seen in the previous chapter, the Democrats had been loudly advocating revision of the San Francisco Treaties, including the security and territorial arrangements therein. It was when they took office that the military land issue in Okinawa began to assume its most serious aspect. The Okinawa problem became the test of the Democrats' diplomacy *vis-à-vis* the United States.

The Japan Democratic Party was established with Hatoyama

Ichirō as its head in November 1954 and took office the following month. It was composed of three groups whose merger is best explained in terms of a power struggle against Yoshida Shigeru rather than any agreement on policy matters.[1] They were, however, in accord in criticizing Yoshida's diplomacy and advocating an 'independent' foreign policy. The literature of the new Party was full of such colourful expressions as 'an assertive and independent diplomacy backed by public opinion', 'consummation of national independence' and so on.[2]

What was the attitude of the Democrats towards the territorial problems and, more specifically, towards Okinawa? The new Party did not commit itself to a definite position on these problems except to say vaguely that it would endeavour to regain the territories which used to be an integral part of Japan.[3] Since the Party leaders had advocated an 'independent' foreign policy, it appears strange that they should have failed to take an assertive stand on these questions. This may be explained to a large extent as deliberate caution because they foresaw difficulties arising in the coming territorial negotiations with the Soviet Union. In the election campaign followed by the formation of the Hatoyama government, the Liberals (now in Opposition), gave prominence to 'recovery of territories' as the substance of their slogan 'consummation of national independence', while the Democrats remained silent on the subject.[4] In short, the Liberals turned the tables on the Democrats by adopting the latters' argument regarding the territorial problems. This divergence in views was carried into the unified Conservative Party (the Liberal Democratic Party) where it was expressed as factional differences on, among other things, the restoration of diplomatic relations with the Soviet Union.[5]

It was apparent that the territorial problem was mainly that of the northern territories and that Okinawa was not expected by the Party leaders to become an urgent policy matter in the near future.

In mid-1956 when the Price Report produced public discontent over the U.S. military land acquisition in Okinawa, the government leaders showed little interest. They were unprepared for the Okinawa problem, and preoccupied with the restoration of diplomatic relations with the Soviet Union; their freedom of action was further restricted by dissentients within the Party who were critical of the Hatoyama-Shigemitsu diplomacy. This indecisiveness on the part of the Hatoyama government was sharply criticized by the Opposition, the press and the public.

The Democrats were very vulnerable to criticism because, after all, they themselves had accused the Yoshida government of 'weak-kneed' diplomacy towards the United States. For example, Shige-mitsu, Foreign Minister in the Hatoyama government, had belittled the Yoshida government's success in securing restoration of the Amami-Ōshima group; the fact that the Americans had returned only Amami-Ōshima, he claimed, showed their lack of confidence in Yoshida. The solution of the problem, he added, had been delayed by Japan's failure to build up a self-defence force of significant size.[6]

Under these circumstances some of the Party officials supported the Okinawan landowners. In June 1956 the Executive Board (*sōmukai*) of the Liberal Democratic Party (LDP) resolved that the Japanese government should ask the United States government to reconsider its land acquisition policy.[7] Kishi Nobusuke, Secretary-General of the LDP, together with Nomura Kichisaburō, Chairman of the newly established Okinawa Committee of the LDP, visited the Commander-in-Chief of the U.S. Far Eastern Forces on several occasions to discuss the Okinawa problem. The Liberal Democratic Party also participated in the mass rally which took place on the Socialists' initiative in early July 1956 which called for a prompt and satisfactory solution of the land problem.[8]

Although the positive attitude of the Party officials and some Party members produced little immediate effect upon the diplomatic posture of the Hatoyama government on the Okinawa problem, it had a long-term effect on government policy in the following two ways.

First, Kishi was sympathetic to the Okinawan landowners. His positive attitude was in marked contrast to the indifference of Hatoyama and some members of his Cabinet and the Party. Kishi complained of U.S. Okinawa policy to the Commander-in-Chief, Far East Forces, to the U.S. Ambassador and to the press.[9] He was also among the proposers of a Diet resolution (2 June 1956) requesting the return to Japan of administrative power over Okinawa and Ogasawara. Neither Kishi's social background nor his career as a civil servant explains his stand. Nor does he appear to have been influenced by any specific groups either within or outside the Party. His attitude, however, is not inconsistent with his liking for an 'independent' foreign policy. He—like other leaders of the Hatoyama government—was not politically committed to the San Francisco Peace Treaty (Okinawa was one of its consequences), because at the time the Treaty was concluded he was purged from public life under the Occupation policy. Unlike the government leaders he was not preoccupied with the restoration of diplomatic relations with the Soviet Union and other impending policy matters. Lastly, as Secretary-General of the LDP, he was obliged to defend the Party against the accusation of indifference to the fate of compatriots in Okinawa. Kishi's concern with the Okinawa problem seems to have been formed at this time. He showed a positive attitude towards the Okinawa problem as Foreign Minister and Prime Minister shortly afterwards.

The second factor which was to have a long-term effect on the government's Okinawa policy was the establishment of a special committee of the LDP on the Okinawa problem (hereafter referred to as the LDP Okinawa Committee). It was set up in late June 1956 with Nomura Kichisaburō as chairman.[10] On 26 July 1956 it resolved that effective measures should be taken to protect the livelihood of the Okinawans because it would take time to settle the land problem satisfactorily. It proposed the following steps: (1) setting up of an association, partly subsidized by the government, to promote a national movement for the solution of the Okinawa problem, improving domestic and international public opinion, urging the government to find a solution to the problem, and rendering various kinds of assistance to the inhabitants of Okinawa; (2) the extension of the military pensions system to Okinawa; (3) the appointment of a minister in charge of Okinawa and Ogasawara affairs.[11]

These proposals were modified by the LDP's Executive Board as follows (they were particularly worried lest the 'national movement' be channelled into anti-American activities): (1) the Party should encourage the government to achieve the return of the administrative power over Okinawa to Japan and a solution of the land acquisition problem. It should promote an *effective and constructive movement* and endeavour to arouse domestic and international public opinion (emphasis added); (2) a non-governmental association, the *Nampō Dōhō Engokai* (Association for Relief of our Compatriots in the Southern Areas), should be established to promote a solution to the Okinawa problem and to engage in relief activities; (3) the government should enlarge its office, the *Nampō Renraku Jimukyoku* (Liaison Bureau for the Southern Areas); (4) a delegation from the Diet should be sent to Okinawa to investigate the local situation; (5) to facilitate diplomatic negotiations with the United States on the Okinawa problem, a delegation from the Diet should, if necessary, be sent to the United States.[12]

This decision was important in the sense that the Liberal Democrats rejected 'bi-partisanship' (the movement for the return of Okinawa had thus far been under the leadership of the Socialists) and recognized the necessity for taking the initiative from the Socialists. It foreshadowed the future development of the LDP's Okinawa policy, namely, financial aid by the Japanese government for the welfare of the inhabitants of Okinawa. The *Nampō Dōhō Engokai* was in fact established in November 1956 in accordance with this policy and began to function as an important instrument in the government's aid to Okinawa.

However, it was some years before the policy of financial aid to Okinawa was really launched. The immediate task with which the LDP Okinawa Committee was confronted was to work for a compromise on the land issue.

The LDP Okinawa Committee which heard petitions from the Okinawan landowners warmly supported the Four Principles (see p. 37. The Committee recommended that the Japanese government concentrate its diplomatic efforts on persuading the United States to review the payment of land rentals.[13] The Party's position on this matter remained unchanged until the United States finally gave way and acceded to the desires of the Okinawa landowners in mid-1958. It is not easy to evaluate exactly the extent to which the Party's position caused the final modification of American policy, but it is at least possible to say that it was a contributing influence.

With the ending of the political crisis over the land issue in mid-1958, the Okinawa problem entered a new phase. There were at that moment two possible courses along which Japan's Okinawa policy could develop. First, the opinion was growing among the Liberal Democrats that the Japanese government should actively participate in the administration of Okinawa, especially in the field of social and economic welfare. There was an important obstacle to this: under the Japanese Peace Treaty all power over Okinawa was vested in the United States; from a strictly legal standpoint, Japan's participation in the civil administration of Okinawa might be regarded as interference in the internal affairs of the United States. To remove this obstacle, it was felt that the Japanese government should reach an understanding with the United States.[14]

Another step to be taken was to negotiate with the United States for the conclusion of a new joint defence treaty whereby the United States would be granted the right to use military facilities in Okinawa and Ogasawara, while the administrative power over civil affairs in these islands would be transferred to Japan.[15]

A meeting between Foreign Minister Fujiyama and Secretary of State Dulles in September 1958—shortly after the settlement of the land problem in Okinawa—was significant, because they agreed that their governments would open negotiations through diplomatic channels on these two questions. Of these two lines of negotiations which began almost simultaneously, the Treaty negotiations attracted much attention at the time.

In revising the Security Treaty, the negotiators could either conclude a new treaty of a 'joint defence' type, or make a partial amendment to the existing treaty to give Japan more say. Kishi, the Prime Minister, was believed to favour the first, while the Foreign Minister, Fujiyama, preferred the second.[16]

After the first meeting of the *Gaimushō* officials and the American Embassy in Tokyo about revising the Security Treaty, the Japanese government was considering various proposals. The *Asahi Shimbun* revealed that one of them was a joint treaty under which Japan would render the United States military help (short of sending troops overseas) in exchange for an explicit commitment by the United States to defend Japan.[17] This would mean that Japan was committed to defend Okinawa and Ogasawara. To this the Socialists objected strongly. There was an existing alliance between the United States and Taiwan, South Korea and the Philippines (the American forces in Okinawa were the linchpin of the system) which might constitute a *de facto* NEATO (North-East Asia Treaty Organization). This, together with the proposed treaty, could involve Japan in Far Eastern or Southeast Asian international conflicts.[18] Kishi, the Prime Minister, replied that, by extending her self-defence rights to Okinawa, Japan could increase her actual power over Okinawa and accordingly 'depress' the United States administrative power. The Japanese press divided on this point, but some of the leading newspapers like the *Asahi Shimbun* bitterly accused the Kishi government of playing a dangerous game. A similar criticism came also from a group within the Party led by Miki Takeo and Matsumura Kenzō.[19]

In the face of these objections the Kishi government began to shift its position from the first to the second alternative, namely from the 'Kishi plan' to the 'Fujiyama plan'. A meeting between the Prime Minister and the Foreign Minister of 3 December 1958 produced a compromise: Japan would offer the United States 'joint defence' against armed attacks on the United States Forces stationed in Japan proper instead of undertaking the defence of Okinawa and Ogasawara, the areas outside Japanese jurisdiction.[20]

This change of policy was warmly welcomed by the press as well as by the Miki-Matsumura group. The group led by Kōno Ichirō, chairman of the Executive Board of the LDP, was henceforth the most determined opponent of Fujiyama's diplomacy.[21] There were various reasons for their opposition to the Treaty negotiations conducted by Fujiyama, one of them being the decision to exclude Okinawa and Ogasawara from the new Treaty. Their argument was that, whereas it was difficult to include these islands in the defence area at the present time, it should nevertheless be made clear in a written agreement with the United States that these islands would automatically come under the Treaty area on their return to Japan. By so doing, they argued, the Japanese government would be able to defend itself against the reproach that it had forsaken its compatriots in Okinawa.[22] Although the basic policy of the Japanese government to the Treaty revisions remained unchanged, the forcefulness of these arguments was partly responsible for its expressions of concern for the defence of Okinawa and Ogasawara in a minute attached to the revised Security Treaty with the United States.[23]

In the meantime, there had been an inconspicuous but important development in another aspect of Okinawa policy—the aid programme for its inhabitants. As mentioned above, the agreement in September 1958 between Fujiyama and Dulles opened the way for the participation of the Japanese government in the welfare policy in Okinawa. As a result, the Japanese government appropriated some 10,000,000 yen for economic and technical assistance to the Government of the Ryukyu Islands (GRI) in the 1959 budget. When Ikeda took over the government from Kishi in 1960, he directed its main efforts in Okinawa policy to the enlargement of financial aid.

The LDP Okinawa Committee was chiefly instrumental in obtaining a greater budget allocation to Okinawa. In this process it effectively bridged Tokyo and Naha and thus compensated for the poor communication at the governmental level.[24]

Through its activities in the past the LDP Okinawa Committee has produced some politicians especially interested in Okinawa. There are not many of them, and they do not constitute a solid group which could be called an Okinawa lobby. Nevertheless they significantly influence the formulation of the LDP Okinawa policy. They have been recruited from four different groups: (1) the Members of the House of Representatives from the constituencies of Kagoshima Prefecture (which historically and geographically has close ties with Okinawa); (2) those with some political or administrative experience in Okinawa before the war (e.g. former Prefectural Governors of Okinawa); (3) post-war civil servants whose work has been concerned with Okinawa (e.g. Director-Generals of the Prime Minister's Office); (4) those who, while not belonging to any of the above categories, are interested in Okinawa for ideological reasons (including nationalism).

Because an exhaustive list of the Committee members since its establishment is not available, it is impossible to show a classification of its members by categories. It is possible, however, to describe one or two persons typical of each group: the first is represented by Tokonami Tokuji (M.H.R. from Kagoshima) who has served as chairman or vice-chairman of the Committee and has been one of the most active members of it. Recently he was appointed Director-General of the Prime Minister's Office. Itō Ryūji, Representative from Amami-Ōshima, was also an important member of the Committee until his death in March 1968. The second is represented by Fuchigami Fusatarō (former Prefectural Governor of Okinawa), one of the leading figures of the Committee in its earlier days. He is still an influential person as a director of the *Nampō Dōhō Engokai*. There are very few in this group. Kosaka Zentarō (former Foreign Minister and chairman of the LDP Okinawa Committee in 1963–4), Usui Sōichi (former Director-General of the Prime Minister's Office and chairman of the Committee in 1964–5 and again since 1968) and Yasui Ken (former Director-General of the Prime Minister's Office and chairman of the Committee in 1967–8) are examples of the third group. Representative of the fourth is Takaoka Daisuke, another leading figure of the Committee in its earlier days. He is also a director of the *Nampō Dōhō Engokai*.

Turning to the attitudes of the Socialists towards Okinawa, one finds the leadership of the Party policy towards Okinawa has gradually shifted from the right-wing to the left-wing elements within the united Socialist Party. The turning point roughly coincided with the settlement of the Okinawa land problem in mid-1958 and the introduction of a new issue—revision of the Security Treaty —in the latter half of that year. In the course of debate on revision of the Treaty, the predominance of the leftist over the rightist leadership became obvious. Towards the end of the debate, differences again split the Socialists into two separate parties. The pattern was very similar to that of the ratification of the San Francisco Treaties in 1951.

As we have seen in the previous chapter, the right-wing Socialists emphasized territorial problems (including Okinawa and Ogasa-wara) more than the left-wing did. This tendency continued in the approach of the united Socialist Party to the Okinawa problem in its earliest stages. Possibly the best illustration of this is the Party's response to the political crisis in Okinawa over the land issue.

The basic policy of the Japan Socialist Party (JSP) to the land problem was decided at a meeting of Party leaders in early July 1956. It consisted of two parts: a maximum and a minimum policy. The former included the withdrawal of American forces from Okinawa; the latter included the settlement of the land issue based upon the Four Principles advocated by the Okinawan landowners, and the return of administrative power over Okinawa to Japan.[25] It is significant that the return of administrative power was treated separately from the withdrawal of the military forces. The minimum policy was in fact adopted in order to facilitate agreement with the Liberal Democrats on this matter.[26]

To implement this policy, the JSP established a special Com-mittee on the Okinawa Problem (hereafter referred to as the JSP Okinawa Committee) with Asanuma Inajirō as chairman. In this Committee the right wing was better represented than the left. Throughout the first three years of its existence, the Committee was chaired by right-wing Socialists.[27] The connection between the JSP and the Okinawa Socialist Masses Party (which is closer to the right-wing than to the Socialists) shows the rightist orientation of the JSP Okinawa policy at this stage. In April 1958 the JSP Okinawa Committee warmly welcomed the announcement by the United States High Commissioner of the Ryukyu Islands, General Moore, that the United States would cancel its lump-sum payment policy.[28]

From about that time leftist opinion became more and more articulate in the JSP Okinawa policy. 'Stagnation' of the movement for the return of Okinawa was frequently mentioned and attributed to the rightist leadership of the movement. Criticisms were levelled at the 'inadequate' management of the *Okinawa-Ren,* the Party's front organization (see chapter 10).[29] Political and military aspects of the Okinawa problem were increasingly stressed at the expense of its humanist-nationalist aspects.[30] These tendencies resulted in a reorganization of the *Okinawa-Ren* in early 1959 on the basis of the exclusive leadership of the JSP, with specific emphasis being placed on the abolition of nuclear bases in Okinawa.[31] The establishment of the Okinawa Socialist Party by dissentients from the Okinawa Socialist Masses Party in early 1959 was also in line with this tendency. It was not surprising, therefore, that the September 1959 national convention of the JSP declared that the Party would tackle the Okinawa problem as part of its struggle against the Security Treaty. Further, the JSP opposed the Kishi proposal to include Okinawa in the defence area of the new Security Treaty.

Unlike the Liberal Democratic Party who were divided on the subject of Okinawa's status in the security arrangement, the Socialists remained outwardly united on the matter. But once they split into two separate Parties in 1959–60 each one developed its own Okinawa policy in line with its general attitudes towards the American alliance. The Japan Socialist Party (i.e. the left and larger segment of the Socialists) came to insist more explicitly that a final solution to the Okinawa problem (as well as to the Chishima problem) would be possible only if Japan withdrew from the American alliance.[32] The Democratic Socialists (the right and smaller segment) maintained that the problem of administrative power should be solved separately from the problem of the military bases. The Democratic Socialists favoured the government policy of increasing Japan's contribution to Okinawan welfare, expecting that it would facilitate the return of administrative power. The JSP were rather sceptical of the effect this would have on the solution of the fundamental problem of Okinawa.[33]

The left-wing Socialists were facing keen competition from the Communists in propaganda activities calling for the return of Okinawa to Japan. By about 1959 the Communists had overcome their initial setback *vis-à-vis* the Socialists in this field.[34] In the evolution of the Communist policy on Okinawa in this period, two points should be noted. First, the Communists seem to have been more vigorous and, perhaps, more successful than the Socialists in amalgamating two different policy conceptions: pacifism in terms of anti-military or anti-nuclear policy and nationalism in terms of anti-colonialism. Secondly, possibly as a result of the recent pluralization of the international Communist movement,[35] the Japan Communist Party came to speak more openly of Japan's legitimate claim to Chishima. They insisted that neutralization of Japan (her withdrawal from the American alliance) would create a new situation in which the Soviet Union and Japan could make a fresh approach to a solution of that problem.[36] Although this factor has no direct bearing on the Communist attitude towards Okinawa, it may well have made them less reserved in their policy towards the territorial problems in general.

Increasing interaction between the political parties in Japan and those in Okinawa was characteristic of this period.

In October 1959 the Okinawan Conservative politicians, who had been divided into three groups, merged into a united Conservative Party under the name Okinawa Liberal Democratic Party (OLDP).[37] It is not known to what extent the Liberal Democratic Party in Japan intervened in this merger. More importantly, it was the outcome of struggles among local politicians for the office of Chief Executive. In 1959 with a plurality in the Legislature the OLDP succeeded in gaining that office for one of the three candidates whom it recommended to the High Commissioner.

Led by the newly appointed Chief Executive, Ōta Seisaku, who also assumed the chairmanship of the OLDP, the Party cultivated close relations with the Conservative leaders in Japan. Ōta officially visited Tokyo in July-August 1960; he took this opportunity not only to ask the government leaders for increased financial aid to the GRI but also to ask leaders in political and business circles to give moral and financial support to the OLDP in the elections for the Legislature in November 1960.[38] In response to Ōta's request, the Liberal Democratic Party and business circles supported the OLDP in various ways.[39] Similar collaboration between the LDP and the OLDP occurred in the Okinawan elections in 1962.[40] In the course of these activities, the OLDP came to be regarded as a *de facto* prefectural chapter of the LDP.[41]

The relationship was, however, unstable. The split of the OLDP in 1964 exposed some of the inherent weaknesses in their relations. The LDP leaders offered to use their influence to rejoin the two segments of the Conservatives in Okinawa, but they did not succeed. Instead, the crisis was saved by the direct intervention of the U.S. High Commissioner. These events challenged the relationship between the local and the metropolitan leaders of the Conservative Party. There were three factors involved.

First, the High Commissioner displayed his objection to, or at least his disapproval of, direct intervention by the Japanese leaders in the 'internal' affairs of Okinawan political parties.[42]

Secondly, the personalities of the leaders were important. Ōta Seisaku (who had served as an official under the Japanese government before the war and had little support among the local politicians) was inclined, understandably, to look to the metropolitan authorities for assistance and leadership.[43] Matsuoka Seihō, who succeeded Ōta as leader of the Okinawan Conservatives, made a contrast with his predecessor in many ways. A graduate from an

American university, and a man who had built his career almost exclusively in Okinawa, Matsuoka had always been influential in politics in post-war Okinawa. If Ōta was an 'imported' bureaucratic politician, Matsuoka was an 'indigenous' party politician. Although, with the change of leader in Okinawa, the relationship between the Conservatives in Naha and those in Tokyo did not suffer serious deterioration, their relationship was not quite harmonious.

Thirdly, there was a subtle but unmistakable difference between the attitudes—or at least the emphasis—of Conservative leaders in Okinawa and those in Japan. Local leaders were more militant and impatient than the metropolitan leaders about the political status of Okinawa. For example, the Okinawan Legislature, in which the Liberal Democrats held a comfortable majority, carried a unanimous resolution (1 February 1962); it accused the United States of practising colonial rule in defiance of the December 1960 declaration of the U.N. General Assembly which had called for a prompt eradication of all forms of colonialism.[44] While the Chief Executive Ōta as well as the Japanese government expressed their disapproval of the resolution, the OLDP leaders endorsed it.[45] The revolt of anti-Ōta elements within the OLDP split the Party and caused Ōta to resign. This expressed the Okinawan dissatisfaction with the 'weak-kneed' diplomacy of the Japanese government.[46]

Despite these factors which hindered close affiliation between the Okinawan Conservative Party and the LDP, there was a tendency to more intimate association between them. This was because the stability of Okinawan politics depended to a large extent on Japan's contribution to the economic and administrative assistance to Okinawa. The dependence of the Okinawan Conservative Party (which regained its old name, Liberal Democrats, in December 1967) on the metropolitan leaders was demonstrated by the latter's vigorous assistance with the 1968 elections in Okinawa.

The relationship between the Opposition parties in Okinawa and those in Japan is more complicated. The Okinawa Socialist Masses Party (OSMP), the Okinawa Socialist Party (OSP) and the Okinawa People's Party (OPP) resemble in their ideological positions the Democratic Socialist Party (DSP), the Japan Socialist Party (JSP) and the Japan Communist Party (JCP) respectively. But, with the exception of the JSP-OSP combination, there are no clear relations between each pair in organization and in action.

In 1957 the Japan Socialist Party came into contact with the Okinawa Socialist Masses Party.[47] In early 1958 a conflict developed within the OSMP over the Naha mayoral election.

Kaneshi Saichi, the successful candidate, left the Party to form a separate group called the Okinawa Socialist Party, and the JSP supported Kaneshi.[48] Kaneshi himself left the OSP a little afterwards, but the JSP continued to assist the OSP candidates for legislative elections after 1960. The OSP were soon designated the Okinawa prefectural chapter of the JSP, with the right to send representatives to national conventions of the JSP.[49] It is significant that this process coincided with the leftwards tendency of the leaders of the JSP Okinawa policy.

In the meantime, the Democratic Socialists who formed a separate party in 1960 did not establish close contacts with the OSMP. One reason for this is the reluctance of the OSMP to enter direct association with any particular political party in Japan.[50]

There is no doubt that friendly relations existed between the Okinawa People's Party and the Japan Communist Party. This is not to say, however, that the OPP is a local organization of the JCP.[51] The OPP leaders believe their Party exists in order to obtain the return of Okinawa to Japan. They envisage a time when their Party will be dissolved once this supreme objective is fulfilled. For this reason they distinguish their Party from the Japan Communist Party which aims to seize political power in Japan.[52]

The *Kōmeitō,* political organization of an emerging Buddhist group (*Sōka Gakkai*), as yet has no seats in the Legislature, but it made an impressive advancement in the Naha city assembly (four out of thirty seats in the July 1965 elections and five seats in the July 1969 elections).[53] As in Japan proper, it may well become an important factor in Okinawan politics in the near future.

To sum up, the growth of political parties in post-war Okinawa has been determined more by the social and political factors peculiar to Okinawa than by Japanese influences. This is true although rapidly increasing interaction between Okinawa and Japan in recent years (especially since 1960) has had a considerable impact on the behaviour of Okinawan political parties. In this sense the political parties in Okinawa are now in a transition period.[54]

The return of Okinawa to Japan is a concern common to all political parties in Japan and in Okinawa. Differences among them lie in the manner in which they relate this particular objective to a broader policy of maintaining Japan's national security.

Generally speaking, the political parties in Okinawa give priority to the return of Okinawa to Japan as soon as possible, and differences among them are frequently submerged for the common cause. On the other hand, differences among the Japanese political parties in their views about the American connection and Japan's role in it are so deep that they are not ready to act in concert for the return of Okinawa. It is a great paradox that a political issue for which national consensus is easily attained—the return of Okinawa to Japan—is intrinsically entangled with another over which the nation's opinion is sharply divided—the wisdom of the American alliance.

This latter point was clearly demonstrated by the different positions which Japanese political parties took in the debate over the status of American military bases in a Japanese-controlled Okinawa. The ruling Liberal Democratic Party failed to decide its official position on this subject except to say vaguely that it would examine carefully the trend of public opinion before the final decision was taken.[55] The LDP's indecision seemed, however, due more to division within the Party itself than to any other factors. For example, people like Kaya Okinori, a close friend of the ex-Prime Minister Kishi Nobusuke and leader of the 'hawks', stressed the importance of Okinawan bases in the security arrangements against Communist China, arguing that the free use of these bases, including nuclear arms, by the United States was indispensable.[56] If this is representative of right-wing views within the LDP, those of the Party's left wing were expressed by Nakasone Yasuhiro who insisted on the return of Okinawa by 1970 with the American bases there being scaled down to the same standard as those in Japan proper.[57] The difference of opinion on this point was believed to be one of the factors involved in the Party's presidential election of November 1968. It was fought between the incumbent Prime Minister Satō Eisaku, who was cautious about making his standpoint clear, and his former Foreign Minister Miki Takeo, who appeared to be taking a view close to that of the Nakasone group.[58]

With the U.S.-Japanese top-level discussion on Okinawa just ahead, the LDP set up the Okinawa Affairs Council whose function was to co-ordinate the various views within the Party on the future status of American bases in Okinawa and their implications for the U.S.-Japan Security Treaty. The Council was chaired by the Party's vice-president Kawashima Shōjirō. It included among its members Funada Naka, chairman of the LDP Council on National Security and advocate of a positive defence policy. On the other hand there were people like Miki Takeo and Nakasone Yasuhiro.[59]

The Socialists and Communists both advocated twin slogans: 'the abrogation of the U.S.-Japan Security Treaty' and 'the immediate, unconditional and complete return of Okinawa'.[60] The Democratic Socialists and the *Kōmeitō* took middle-of-the-road positions; both favoured the return of Okinawa by 1970 with substantially reduced and non-nuclear bases subject to Japanese government restrictions as bases are in Japan proper.[61]

10

Individuals and Groups

We shall be concerned here with the activities of non-governmental associations and individuals in Japan who try to influence government in order to further the return of Okinawa to Japan. Who are they? What are their methods? How have their activities affected the course of events?

Public involvement in the political process regarding the Okinawa problem can be divided roughly into two periods: the first decade (1945–55) in which organized activities were barely apparent and only a few isolated individual activities were discernible; and the period since 1955 in which various group activities have emerged. The description of the earlier period in this chapter centres on an individual, Nakayoshi Yoshimitsu; that of the later period is centred on a complex of group activities. One could regard the whole Okinawan community as an 'interest group' for the present purpose, but we shall not, because it is too various to be treated as one unit. Instead, attention will be paid, wherever necessary, to the interaction of group activities on the Japanese mainland and those in Okinawa.

It is natural to assume that the Okinawans resident on the Japanese mainland form a basic stratum of the Japanese public's interest in Okinawa, although they should be regarded as a 'latent' rather than a 'manifest' interest group. It is hard to ascertain the size and distribution of this population. It was estimated on the eve of the 'repatriation' of the Okinawans to their home islands (i.e. August 1946) that there were some 150,000 Okinawans resident in Japan.[1] Soon after the Japanese surrender, the Patriotic Okinawan Society (*Hōkoku Okinawa Kyōkai*), a war-time organization, became the Okinawan Association (*Okinawa Kyōkai*), with Baron Ie Chōsuke, former Member of the House of Peers, as president. Those who disliked the 'reactionary' colouring of the Okinawan Association formed another group called Okinawan Federation (*Okinawajin Remmei*) with Iha Fuyū, celebrated Okinawan historian, as its president. The main function of these associations was to assist in the rehabilitation and repatriation of Okinawans.[2] The repatriation of the Okinawans commenced on 15 August 1946, exactly one year after the surrender. According to one source, 140,000 registered as wanting to return to Okinawa and 121,000 of these were actually repatriated by the end of that year.[3] It can be seen that only a relatively small number decided to remain on the mainland.

During the repatriation there was no definite plan for the future status of Okinawa. But on 29 January 1946 the Occupation authorities issued a directive which separated the administration of the Ryukyu Islands and some other outlying areas from Japan. Not very much is known about the reaction of the Okinawans to this step. An articulate section among them, especially those who became the leaders of the *Okinawajin Remmei,* were inclined to favour the governmental separation of Okinawa from Japan. It seems safe to say that there was no strong opinion among them against the political separation, whether temporary or not, of Okinawa from Japan.

The first voice calling for the return of Okinawa to Japan came from an entirely different quarter—from Nakayoshi Yoshimitsu.[4] He survived the war as the mayor of the capital, Shuri, which had been one of the fiercest battlefields in the Okinawan campaign. As early as 4 August 1945 he petitioned the U.S. military government in Okinawa asking that Okinawa should be allowed to remain part of Japan in the future peace settlement. Nakayoshi said that the Okinawa Advisory Council, whose advice was sought by the American authorities, reported that his view did not represent majority opinion.[5] He was told by the Americans, however, that his petition had been forwarded to Washington. On the suggestion of an American officer that he should appeal to GHQ, he left Okinawa for Tokyo in July 1946.

In Tokyo, he told a public gathering held at the Kyōbashi Public Hall about the political and economic conditions obtaining in Okinawa. This was the first time since the end of the war that the Japanese public, including the Okinawan residents in Japan, had had a first-hand report on Okinawa.

Nakayoshi also met two *Gaimushō* officials, Tsuruoka Senjin and his superior officer, Hagiwara Tōru (head of the Treaty Bureau), who told him they intended to ask the Allied Powers to consider Japan's desire for the retention of her territories including Okinawa. Encouraged by their suggestions he gathered men of the same mind and formed an organization later known as the Association for the Realization of the Return of the Okinawa Islands to Japan (*Okinawashotō Nihon Fukki Kiseikai,* or *Kiseikai* for short). Most of its members were moderates.[6]

From that time to the conclusion of the Japanese Peace Treaty, Nakayoshi made unswerving efforts to place his view before the relevant American and Japanese authorities. In autumn 1946 he submitted to GHQ and the government petitions signed by members of *Kiseikai* and other prominent persons from Okinawa such as Irei Hajime, former Member of the House of Representatives (1928–45), and Ōhama Nobumoto, then a professor at the Waseda University and later its president.

The *Kiseikai* also tried to make the Japanese Diet adopt a resolution calling for the return of Okinawa to Japanese control; but this attempt was vain. Officials of the Diet, when approached by Nakayoshi and his friends, informed them that the Diet had been told by GHQ not to touch matters embarrassing to the United States such as the Okinawa problem.[7] On 23 June 1947 (i.e. the day of the inauguration of the first session of the Japanese Diet under the new Constitution) a most celebrated Member of the House of Representatives, Ozaki Yukio, had proposed that the coming peace settlement for Japan should not be on the basis of victor and vanquished but should be based on 'rational principles as befitted the present stage of human civilization'. In particular the principle of self-determination was to have priority over the national interests of the victors in former Japanese territories (Taiwan, Okinawa, Korea and Manchuria were specifically mentioned here).[8]

It is quite unlikely that Nakayoshi's petition would have been treated more favourably by the leaders of the Diet than Ozaki's proposal was. We must remember that the latter followed a statement by the Foreign Minister Ashida (6 June 1947) which had revealed Japan's position on various issues, including territorial problems, relating to a peace settlement for Japan and which caused considerable and generally unfavourable repercussions in various quarters.

As these events showed, Nakayoshi's movement for the return of Okinawa to Japan encountered various difficulties in this period. Besides the indifference of politicians, there was the wide difference of opinion among the Okinawan residents in Tokyo. They were divided into three groups, namely: (1) proponents of independence for Okinawa, (2) those who wanted a United States trusteeship for Okinawa and (3) those who wanted to retain traditional bonds between Japan and Okinawa.[9] Among them the first group was the most vigorous and articulate. The *Okinawajin Remmei* and its youth group, the *Okinawa Seinen Remmei,* provided them with organizations for these purposes. These bodies were apparently influenced by leftist elements, especially the Communists. Nakayoshi's movement was harshly condemned by this group as 'militaristic and ultra-nationalistic'.[10] Nakayoshi was hampered also by the almost complete lack of any kind of communication between the Japanese mainland and Okinawa.

By 1950–1 when the time was approaching for a Japanese peace settlement, the domestic and the international situation had changed considerably in favour of Nakayoshi's movement. In January 1950 the Secretary of State, Acheson, made public the American intention of proposing trusteeship for Okinawa. On this information Nakayoshi visited Okazaki Katsuo, former Permanent Under-secretary of the *Gaimushō* and the then chairman of the House of Representatives Foreign Affairs Committee, and asked his advice. Okazaki encouraged Nakayoshi to persist in his activities and added that the Secretary of State's pronouncement was not the final decision of the United States. Okazaki also drew Nakayoshi's attention to the remark of the GHQ officials that, apart from the opinion of the Okinawan residents in Japan, they had so far not heard expressions of opinion by the inhabitants in Okinawa. On the advice of Okazaki, the *Kiseikai* decided to petition the Secretary of State asking him to reconsider the matter, and also to urge their friends in Okinawa to enter the movement.[11]

These activities of Nakayoshi were at least in part responsible for the beginning of the movement in Okinawa. The election of Taira Tatsuo, a friend of Nakayoshi, as the Governor of Okinawa *Guntō* in September 1950 and the formation of the Okinawa Socialist Masses Party (OSMP) by his supporters provided a landmark in the development of the movement. On this group's initiative the Association for the Promotion of the Return of Okinawa to Japan, sister organization of Nakayoshi's *Kiseikai,* was formed in Okinawa in May 1951.

The Okinawans resident in the Japanese mainland also began to unite against the American proposals of trusteeship for Okinawa. They held a mass rally in Osaka in May 1951 which was the first meeting of this kind. The *Okinawajin Remmei* which was reorganized under the leadership of Kamiyama Masayoshi, a friend of Nakayoshi, petitioned President Truman.[12] Nakayoshi himself lodged petitions with the member countries of the Far Eastern Commission and the countries participating in the San Francisco Peace Conference asking for the complete removal of the Okinawa trusteeship clause from the Treaty.[13]

These activities began to influence Japanese politicians. When Dulles visited Tokyo in January-February of 1951 to discuss the problem of the Peace Treaty with Japanese leaders, he heard an almost unanimous expression of opinion from the Japanese government as well as from representatives of various quarters of Japanese society irrespective of party affiliation, calling for the return of Japanese sovereignty over some pre-war Japanese territories, including Okinawa.

One of the characteristics of the movement for the return of Okinawa in this period was that it was limited to a relatively small number of people directly concerned with their own lot. Its method was also limited, with a few exceptions, to personal contact with *Gaimushō* officials and a few interested Members of the Diet. In other words, they had so far not succeeded in gaining the interest of the general public or the press. The group pressing for the return of Okinawa at this stage was also behind other groups which enlisted relatively active sympathies of Members of the Diet representing regional interests (e.g. Amami-Ōshima) or which prefectural organizations could sponsor (e.g. Habomai and Shikotan).[14] For example, the Diet passed three relevant resolutions (one concerning Amami-Ōshima, one Habomai, and one the territorial problems in general) during the months before the conclusion of the Peace Treaty. The Okinawan groups endeavoured to make the Diet pass a resolution requesting the reversion of Okinawa but without success.[15]

The movement in Okinawa was also hindered by internal weaknesses (e.g. the defection of one sector of the Socialist Masses Party from the movement) and by the hardening of the American attitude towards it. This state of affairs lasted for a few years.

As serious friction developed between the local population and the American authorities over the military land issue, the Okinawa problem rapidly began to attract public attention. The process of public involvement can be divided into three stages. The first stage saw the participation of some professional associations not primarily interested in the Okinawa problem but concerned with universal objectives such as liberty, justice and equality. In March 1954 the

Japan Civil Liberties Union (*Nihon Jiyū Jinken Kyōkai*)[16] received a letter from Roger N. Baldwin, president of the American Civil Liberties Union (ACLU) and chairman of the International League for the Rights of Man (a non-governmental organization with consultative status with the United Nations).[17] He pointed out that, according to a recent newspaper report, there was growing popular discontent in Okinawa over the attempt of the United States authorities to expropriate land for military purposes at a unilaterally determined, cheap price. He asked the JCLU for further information.[18] At this request the JCLU after ten months' study produced a report on the human rights problems in Okinawa. The report was sent to the ACLU in New York, while in Japan it received great publicity through the *Asahi Shimbun*.[19]

It should be noted here that the report approached the problem as one of vindication of human rights: how were civil liberties to be defended in relation to security considerations? The writers of the report stressed that no *political* problems should be involved. They meant by this that the intervention of the Japanese government was neither practical nor desirable. Instead they intended to appeal to an attentive public in the United States and, if necessary, in the United Nations, to move the United States government towards a solution of the problem. This implied that, legally, administrative problems in Okinawa were U.S. problems.[20] In this sense their presentation of the matter was of universal rather than of nationalist orientation.

There was, however, another way in which the problem was aired. The JCLU brought the matter before the Asian Lawyers' Conference which met in Calcutta in late January 1955.[21] The Asian Countries' Conference in New Delhi in April 1955 also heard a report from a Japanese delegate, Kamiyama Masayoshi (Chairman of the *Okinawa Sokoku Fukki Sokushin Kyōgikai*), on human rights in Okinawa.[22] This was part of the effort to rouse Asian attention. In this section of world opinion the Okinawa problem was seen as part of the task of eliminating colonialism. Baldwin showed that he disliked this approach when he warned the JCLU against entering into collaboration with the International Democratic Lawyers' Association on the ground that the latter was communist oriented. Possibly this caused the failure of the attempt to dispatch an investigation group to Okinawa by an international committee set up by the Asian Lawyers' Conference.[23]

The situation changed rapidly and entered a new phase characterized by nationalist orientation. When the issue was raised as a

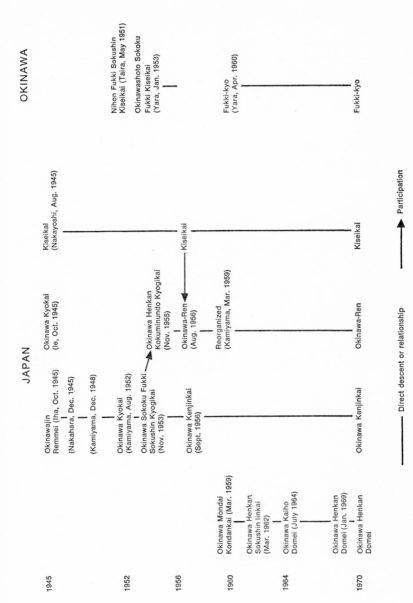

Fig. 2   Lineages of major pressure groups concerned with Okinawa

141

national one, various powerful organizations supported the movement calling for solution of the Okinawa problem.

The release of the Price Report in June 1956 provided the immediate reason for the movement. By then three groups directly concerned with the Okinawa problem had come into action: Nakayoshi's *Kiseikai*, the recently organized Council for the Promotion of the Solution of the Land Problem in Okinawa (*Okinawa Tochimondai Kaiketsu Sokushin Kyōgikai*) with Ie Chōsuke as its chairman and the Council for the National Movement for the Return of Okinawa (*Okinawa Henkan Kokuminundō Kyōgikai*). The last of these three groups was itself a federation composed of five organizations in support of the movement of Kamiyama's Council for the Promotion of the Return of Okinawa to the Fatherland.[24]

On 26 June the three groups had a joint meeting; they decided to hold a mass rally and called for the participation of various groups in it. An executive office was set up for this purpose, comprising representatives from, besides the above three groups, the Liberal Democratic Party, the Japan Socialist Party, the General Council of Japanese Labour Unions (*Shōhyō*), two student organizations (the *Zengakuren* and the *Shigakuren*), the Japan Council of Youth Organizations (*Nisseikyō*) and the All Japan Buddhists' Association. The Liberal Democrats agreed to participate in the rally on three conditions: the Communists should not take part in the rally, red flags should not be used, and the problem of the United States military bases should not be involved.[25] The Communists were persuaded by the Socialists to accept these terms.[26] Thus the mass rally took place successfully. One of the most striking characteristics of the movement in this period was that the Japanese government was now urged to intervene vigorously in the solution of the Okinawa problem. In other words, those frustrated in their activities now began to appeal not to the United States but to the Japanese government for action.

The 'national front' for the Okinawa problem had only a short life. Despite the Conservatives' efforts to prevent it, the issue of American military bases came to be involved, and sharp cleavages developed among the participants. Groups now formed on a party, rather than on a national, basis. The third stage of the development was characterized by the efforts of the ruling Liberal Democratic Party to 'governmentalize' the group interests on the one hand and the 'monopolization' of the movement by the Opposition on the other.

The cleavage began after the mass rally over a question of

organization. The executive officer of the organizing committee for
the rally proposed to make the existing *ad hoc* committee into a
standing organization for furthering the movement. Representatives
from the LDP were lukewarm towards this proposal. They were
apparently afraid that the organization would be dominated by the
radicals. After repeated meetings the Socialists persuaded the LDP
to remain in the newly organized Liaison Conference for the
National Movement for the Solution of the Okinawa Problem
(*Okinawa Mondai Kaiketsu Kokuminundō Renraku Kaigi* or *Okinawa-Ren* for short).[27] At the same time, however, the LDP decided
to set up a separate association to further 'an effective and constructive' movement for the return of Okinawa to Japanese administration and for a solution of the land problem. This decision
resulted in the formation of the *Nampō Dōhō Engokai* in November
1956.

As mentioned before, the bi-partisanship of the movement for
the solution of the Okinawa problem in July 1956 was realized at
the expense of the Communists' participation in it. The Communists
were also omitted from the *Okinawa-Ren*. Although they did not
manage to participate formally in the organization, their influence
on the movement gradually grew: Nosaka Sanzō, leader of the
JCP, was asked to speak at a mass rally held by the *Okinawa-Ren*
in February 1957. On this occasion the LDP did not take part in
the gathering. At last in April 1957 the LDP formally withdrew
from membership of the *Okinawa-Ren* on the grounds that the
radicals had brought the question of the American military bases
into the movement.[28]

In the meantime the *Okinawa-Ren* was inactive because of wide
differences of opinion among its members. For example, it failed
to decide 'common attitudes' towards the Senaga affair and the
Naha mayoral election in 1957–8.[29] This situation lasted until
March 1959 when the *Okinawa-Ren* was reorganized under the
exclusive leadership of the Socialists.[30] By that time the Communists had changed their tactics: rather than co-operate with the
Socialists within the *Okinawa-Ren* they created in mid-1959 a rival
organization, the Discussion Group on the Okinawa Problem (*Okin-
awa Mondai Kondankai*). It developed into the Committee for
Promoting the Return of Okinawa (*Okinawa Henkan Sokushin
Iinkai*) in 1962, which was in turn merged into the League for the
Liberation of Okinawa (*Okinawa Kaihō Dōmei*) in July 1964 and
again into the League for the Return of Okinawa and Ogasawara
(*Okinawa Ogasawara Henkan Dōmei*).[31] This consummated the

pluralization of group interests in Okinawa in accordance with party affiliation.[32]

What bearing does this strong party affiliation have on the activities of the groups we have studied? It is noticeable that the Conservatives succeeded in institutionalizing interest representation by establishing the *Nampō Dōhō Engokai* which collaborates closely with governmental departments. It works especially with the *Sōrifu*, which is concerned with Okinawan matters, such as the budget allocation for the Okinawan people. The LDP Okinawa Committee provides a necessary link between them. Here interest representation has become part of administrative routine rather than pressure outside the government. Although the *Engokai* is not primarily concerned with promoting the return of Okinawa to Japan, an important aspect of its functions is to improve the social and economic welfare of the Okinawan people. It can be better described as a 'protective' rather than a 'promotional' group.

The groups affiliated with the Opposition are not satisfied with, nor do they influence, the government's policy. Instead they concentrate on creating a climate of opinion, domestic and international, in favour of their final goal, namely the return of Okinawa to Japan. Their activities are directed to the whole public rather than to the government. In other words they are typically 'promotional' groups.[33]

Their tactics aimed at arousing or keeping alive public attention in Japan over Okinawa range from mass rallies and processions, to collecting signatures. One of the notable characteristics of their activities in recent years has been the choice of a particular date, 28 April, for the events. It was on this day in 1960 that the Council for the Return of Okinawa Prefecture to the Fatherland (*Okinawa-Ken Sokoku Fukki Kyōgikai*, or *Fukkikyō* for short) was founded in Naha with the participation of seventeen organizations.[34] Since then the *Fukkikyō* has held mass meetings each year on this day. On the Japanese mainland also various events have been held mostly on this day. The meaning of this is obvious: this was the day when the Japanese Peace Treaty came into effect in 1952, by which the separation of Okinawa from Japan was established. Thus it is often termed by them 'Humiliation Day' in an attempt to remind the Japanese people and the government of what they regard as the Japanese government's betrayal of Okinawa to the United States.[35]

The second point to be noted concerns the rivalry, covert and overt, between the Socialists and the Communists in leading the campaigns. The general trend seems to be a gradual increase of Communist, at the expense of Socialist, influence over the movement, particularly since about 1959. In 1964 the rivalry between them reached such a point that the Organizing Committee for the National Movement Demanding the Return of Okinawa (*Okinawa Henkan Yōkyū Kokuminundō Jikkō Iinkai*) split and two meetings were held in latitude 27° N. in Okinawan waters: one on 28 April by the Socialists and the other on 15 August by the Communists.[36] This resembles a split which occurred in the anti-nuclear movement in Japan about this time. The division in the case of the Okinawa problem is not, however, over policy (as is the case of the anti-nuclear movement) but largely over tactics and degree of enthusiasm. This is best illustrated by their different attitudes towards the wisdom of organizing processions. Generally speaking, the Socialists and the *Okinawa-Ren* have been reluctant to take part in processions initiated by Communist-oriented groups.

The fragmentation of the movement in Japan complicates its relationship with the movement in Okinawa. In Okinawa as in Japan proper, the united front of 1955–7 against the American land policy did not revive in 1960 when the *Fukkikyō* was formed without the LDP's participation. Within the Opposition camp, however, a relatively united front has been maintained, embodied in the formation of the *Fukkikyō*. One of the recent tendencies is a growing interaction between the movement in Okinawa and that in Japan proper, as instanced by the demonstrations at sea at 27° N. near Okinawa (which is the 'invisible boundary' between Japan and Okinawa) held jointly by the *Fukkikyō* and friendly associations in Japan each year on 28 April. Sometimes difficulties are caused by diversity in Japan and unity in Okinawa. For example, in 1964 the difference between the *Okinawa-Ren* and the Communist-affiliated groups (see above) was carried into the local movement so that the Okinawa People's Party and its affiliated groups refused to take part in the 28 April demonstration held by the *Fukkikyō* and the *Okinawa-Ren* and decided to participate in another meeting held on 15 August (the anniversary of Japan's surrender) by the pro-Communist groups. So far a split has been prevented, but the inherent difference within the movement sometimes makes the operation of joint enterprises very difficult.[37]

The promotional groups try to arouse public attention not only in Japan and Okinawa, but also throughout the world. As previously stated, some attempts were made as early as 1955 to present their case to various pan-Asian conferences. Since then the Organization for Afro-Asian People's Solidarity has been giving continuous attention to the Okinawa problem. For example the first conference on Afro-Asian People's Solidarity (Cairo, December 1957) adopted a resolution on Okinawa at the motion of a Japanese delegate who submitted a lengthy report on that subject.[38] Its third conference held in February 1963 (at Moshi, Tanganyika) decided to make 28 April Okinawa Day and appealed to its affiliated organizations throughout the world to campaign for the liberation of Okinawa each year on that day.[39] It is apparent that these activities are aimed at influencing world opinion, particularly in the United Nations, so that measures may be taken by the United Nations for the return of Okinawa to Japan. The United Nations' declaration on the granting of independence to colonial countries on 14 December 1960 provided them with a good weapon. As mentioned before, the Okinawan Legislature based its resolution demanding Okinawa's return to Japan (1 February 1962) upon this declaration of the United Nations. Nakayoshi's *Kiseikai* also repeatedly petitioned

Table 9

NUMBER OF ARTICLES ON OKINAWA APPEARING IN FOUR REPRESENTATIVE JAPANESE OPINION JOURNALS, 1950–65

Year	Kaizō*	Bungei Shunjū	Chūō Kōron	Sekai
1950	1	—	1	—
1951	1	—	—	—
1952	1	1	—	1
1953	2	2	—	—
1954		—	—	1
1955		—	1	—
1956		1	—	6(0)
1957		1	—	9(0)
1958		—	3	9(1)
1959		1	2	9(1)
1960		—	—	5(0)
1961		—	—	1(3)
1962		—	—	5(3)
1963		—	—	5(3)
1964		—	1	3(3)
1965		—	1	2(3)
Total	5	6	9	56(17)†

*The *Kaizō* was discontinued in 1954.
†Figures in brackets show the number of articles which appeared in *Nihon no Ushio,* a column in the *Sekai* (created in 1956) where anonymous columnists' comments on selected important current topics on Japanese affairs appear (usually four topics a month).

the United Nations for the same purpose. It is likely, however, that these voices will only embarrass the Japanese government, because it regards their opinions as illegitimate and also because other Afro-Asian governments which know the Japanese government's position will not take measures which would upset it.[40]

Finally some Japanese journals offer a very important field of activity for those who are interested in the Okinawa problem. Table 9 shows the appearance of articles on this subject in four representative monthly journals during the period from 1950 to 1965. Except for the initial six years, when the *Kaizō* showed a considerable concern over the subject, the *Sekai* has always been the principal forum on this topic.

Forty people contributed fifty-eight articles on this subject to the *Sekai* during this period (see Table 10). The most outstanding among them was Senaga Kamejirō, leader of the Okinawa People's

Table 10

ANALYSIS OF CONTRIBUTORS TO THE *SEKAI* ON THE OKINAWA PROBLEM, 1950–65

Categories	Number of writers	Number of articles
Okinawans:	17	25
OPP	2	14
*Minren**	2	2
OSMP	2	2
OLDP	1	1
OSP	1	0†
Organization leaders	3	0†
University teachers	1	1
Journalists	1	1
Writers	1	1
Critics	1	2
Others	2	1†
Japanese:	23	33
JCLU lawyers	3	5
Other lawyers	4	6
Journalists	4	6
Photographers	4	5
Critics	3	5
Writers	2	2
Others	3	4
Total	40	58

*For a description of the *Minren*, see chapter 11.
†Joint authors and discussion participants are counted for each person; the items which they contributed are counted elsewhere.

147

Party and the central figure of the Senaga affair, whose articles appeared fourteen times in this journal, particularly between 1958 and 1960. Seventeen people from Okinawa, including Senaga, contributed twenty-five items, about 43 per cent of the total. Among the Japanese contributors lawyers held first place, followed by journalists, critics, photographers and writers. It is noteworthy that lawyers who belong to the Japan Civil Liberties Union have also made a significant contribution in this field.[41]

What are the characteristics of the movement for the return of Okinawa to Japan as a political movement?

As regards its historical origins the movement sprang from discontent over the state of affairs imposed upon the Okinawan people by the Peace Treaty with Japan. It became nation-wide only in 1955–6 with the land issue as the turning point. In the first decade following the end of World War II there had been hardly more than activities by individuals. The lack of collective action in that period is partly explained by people's preoccupation with more immediate issues but more importantly by the current mental climate ('immobilization of nationalism': Professor Maruyama)[42] in which the movement's objective was apt to be labelled illegitimate. In such circumstances it found advocates only among those men with a strong sense of tradition to whom a separation of Okinawa from Japan seemed a violent and intolerable break in the nation's history. It is significant that the Okinawa problem came to the fore for the first time during Hatoyama's premiership when nationalist sentiment emerged as a reaction to Yoshida's regime which was too closely identified with the Occupation. The movement against the American land policy in Okinawa provided one of the earliest examples of the 'national movement' in post-war Japan.

One of the most interesting characteristics of the groups concerned with Okinawa is their dual nature. As sectional (or protective) groups they are primarily concerned with the presentation of local interests of Okinawa. They have little chance to wield significant influence in Japanese politics because they are numerically very small. The Okinawa problem is not a vote-raising issue.[43] They do, however, successfully present their case to the public as a matter of national concern so that people feel it involves not only the lot of the Okinawans but also a national cause well worthy of their support. In this respect their movements become promotional and propaganda bodies. It is because of this that Okinawa presents a dynamic issue in Japanese politics.

The movements of the latter kind are characterized by their

increasingly pro-Opposition orientations and decreasing contact with the government and the Government Party. When they restrict themselves to *ad hoc* objectives they maintain contact with the Conservative government, but when they advocate fundamental changes in Okinawa's status this becomes impossible. This is because a fundamental change involves ideological and highly political issues which naturally attract the interest of the Opposition parties. This tendency is strengthened by the political situation characterized as a 'one-and-a-half party' system (i.e. a virtually permanent monopoly of power by one party), because, in such circumstances, a 'permanent Opposition' which has little hope of governing is likely to make wild promises to outbid the government.

The movements are characterized not only by being pro-Opposition but also by the division and competition within the Opposition camp. This is in a sense a difficulty inherent in any promotional groups which compete for the same members as political parties do. The cause of the movements (i.e. the return of Okinawa to Japan) itself is not a controversial one, but people cannot easily agree on means to achieve that end. This can be seen in promotional movements in contemporary Japan. 'National movements', as they are commonly called,[44] are composed of various combinations of existing large national organizations such as the *Sōhyō* (labour), *Zengakuren* (students), *Nisseikyō* (youth) and *Chifuren* (women) which are brought together for various purposes at different times. As the issue varies, the name of the organization and the mode of combination vary too, but the entity remains more or less the same. This type of federation is used as a substitute for subordinate organizations of political parties which lack wide grassroots membership. This leads to a furious competition for the hegemony of the movement among the political parties which sponsor it and at worst results in a split of the organization. The movement for Okinawa seems to be no exception to this usual course.

11

The Press

When discussing the development of Japanese attitudes towards the Okinawa problem during the past two decades, we can hardly afford to neglect the role taken by Japanese newspapers. With large circulation and high quality, Japanese newspapers are important in shaping opinion in the country. Although the formation of public opinion is a complicated process which cannot be attributed to one factor, the activities of the press are undoubtedly important. It can be legitimately claimed that public opinion, or the opinion of the reading public, on an issue is inevitably and substantially conditioned by the image presented by the press. Its impact, direct or indirect, on public policy is also important.

For this reason we shall analyse the treatment of the Okinawa problem in the Japanese press, especially in the *Asahi Shimbun.* The *Asahi* is chosen for three reasons: it has one of the largest daily circulations in Japan today; it is regarded by observers as a 'prestige' paper; it played, as will be explained later in this chapter, an important role in the formation of the Okinawan issue.[1] Although this exclusive attention to one paper may cause some distortion, there is good reason to believe that the fundamental pattern of the press activities in Japan relating to the Okinawa problem is well represented by the *Asahi*.[2] What is more, the disadvantage, if any, will be compensated for by the advantages of continuous observation over a considerable period of time.

If one looks at Fig. 3 which shows the annual number of newspaper accounts on Okinawa in the *Asahi Shimbun* in the first two decades of the post-war period, one can easily observe a substantial increase of information on Okinawa.[3] This general pattern can be divided into three parts: the first phase covers the period 1947–54; the second, 1955–8; the third, 1959–65.[4]

150

The first phase is characterized by a conspicuous paucity of information of any kind on Okinawa. There was practically no news either on the local situation or on Japanese thinking on Okinawa. For example, of the whole 84 items counted in the period between June 1947 and December 1950, 72 items (86 per cent) were news stories reporting the Allied Powers' policy towards Okinawa; only 12 items (14 per cent) were concerned with the activities of the people and the government on mainland Japan or in Okinawa itself. This period was also characterized by a heavy reliance on foreign news services; it was only in 1951 that Japanese sources outweighed foreign ones in the Japanese press concerning Okinawa. A small increase in 1951 and again in 1953 were caused by the increase of press reports on the Japanese Peace Treaty and the Amami Agreement respectively. Also important was the fact

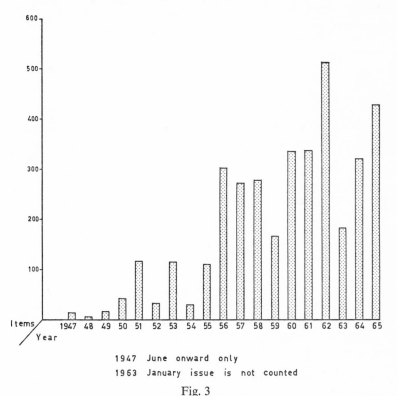

1947   June onward only
1963   January issue is not counted

Fig. 3

Annual numbers of accounts concerning Okinawa, *Asahi*, 1947–65 that there were hardly any accounts on the general conditions of the inhabitants in Okinawa. The earliest example of a first-hand account of Okinawa appeared only in 1949 and, in spite of a relative improvement in 1953 (due to the return of Amami-Ōshima), the news coverage on the local conditions of Okinawa in the *Asahi Shimbun* remained very poor throughout this period.

One of the reasons for this inactivity was the almost complete destruction of communications between Japan and Okinawa. For example, sea-mail services were opened between Japan and Okinawa in September 1946 but were only intermittent because of the poor shipping service. Airmail services to Okinawa from overseas (including Japan) started in November 1947 and from Okinawa in March 1948. Wireless communication between Naha (Okinawa) and Fukuoka (Kyūshū) *via* Naze (Amami-Ōshima) began in January 1950, and direct communication between Naha and Fukuoka was established in August of that year. A liner entered service between Okinawa and Japan in February 1950. After September of that year seven liners of five Japanese shipping companies were commissioned. The first large consignment of Japanese monthly periodicals arrived in Okinawa in October 1949, that of Japanese daily papers in April 1950.[5]

To this physical interruption were added various restrictions imposed on free exchange of people and ideas for political or administrative reasons. Travel to or from Okinawa was strictly limited to 'repatriation' from Okinawa to Japan and *vice versa*. It was only in March 1949 that the first passport was issued for a Japanese citizen to go to Okinawa. The ban on travel to Japan by Okinawans acting in an official capacity was removed on 15 August 1949.[6] Although it is hard to find specific provisions for that purpose in the Occupation's press code, it would be reasonable to say that if the Japanese press had been outspoken on that subject the Occupation authorities would have extended their censorship to such press activities.[7]

No matter what the reasons might have been, there is no sign that the Japanese press of that time was prepared to follow events in and about Okinawa with intense and continuous interest. Arguments and activities for Okinawa were conducted by a very limited number of people; they attracted little attention from the press or the man-in-the-street. Even in 1951 when the Japanese Peace Treaty formed the subject of newspaper articles, only three editorials of the *Asahi Shimbun* made a passing reference to Okinawa and Ogasawara, and that not in critical terms.[8] In that same year only

one letter to the editor expressed dissatisfaction with the disposal
of these territories in the Peace Treaty while approving the spirit
of the Treaty itself.[9] Immediately after the signature of the Peace
Treaty 6 per cent of the people who were interviewed mentioned
the proposal of trusteeship for Okinawa and Ogasawara as being the
point on which they felt unhappy.[10] Thus we can conclude that the
Japanese press of the time was very reserved on such 'dangerous'
topics as Okinawa.

For the first few years after the Japanese Peace Treaty came into
effect the situation remained fundamentally unchanged, although
the movement for the return of Amami-Ōshima came to receive
slightly more treatment in the press.

Things underwent a drastic change in 1955–6. Early in 1955
the *Asahi Shimbun* devoted a large space to a document prepared
by the Japan Civil Liberties Union, which criticized the United
States administration in Okinawa. The charges brought forward
against the U.S. Forces in Okinawa ranged from an unfair land
procurement programme, wage discrimination against Okinawan
labourers (*vis-à-vis* American, Filipino and Japanese labourers)
and other civil rights violations.[11] In many ways this was the most
important single event in the history of press activities concerning
Okinawa. This was the first time that the civil administration in
Okinawa had received a comprehensive treatment in a Japanese
newspaper, or, with a few minor exceptions, in any kind of publication in Japanese.[12]

The *Asahi*'s report found a wide response in Japan, Okinawa
and, to a lesser extent, in the United States. On the following day
the *Asahi Shimbun* set forth its editorial views on the Okinawa
problem for the first time, urging the Japanese government to
demand that the United States improve the civil administration in
Okinawa. Fifteen people, including three who wrote letters to the
editor, expressed their opinions on the matter in that newspaper
during the same month; all were very critical of the American
policy in Okinawa. In the Japanese Diet four Socialist Members
took up the matter and questioned the government, referring to the
Union's report cited in the *Asahi Shimbun*. This made the government decide to 'gather information' on the local conditions through
its agencies.[13]

In Okinawa itself the repercussions were also profound. Both of
the important local newspapers, the *Okinawa Taimusu* and the
Ryūkyū Shimpō immediately devoted space to the Union's report.
Officials of the Government of the Ryukyu Islands stated, in reply

to questions put forward in the Legislature, that the publication of the report was significant because it brought the Okinawa problem before the general public in Japan.[14]

Reaction in Washington was unfavourable.[15] The New York press was indifferent.[16] It is significant, however, that the U.S. Army (Far East), which was directly responsible for the administration of Okinawa, was obliged to defend itself before the Japanese public. They blamed the Japan Civil Liberties Union for preparing the report, not on the basis of a field survey, but on 'hearsay, rumours, incorrect information and prejudice', and denied that any serious issue existed in Okinawa.[17]

An important result of these events is that the Okinawa problem came to command the attention of the general public. For example, about this time 75 per cent of the *Asahi Shimbun* readers who were asked if they knew about the civil rights problem in Okinawa (as it was called at that time) gave affirmative answers. The same survey revealed that only 50 per cent of the *Mainichi Shimbun* readers knew about the same issue. The difference is apparently due to the different treatment of that subject in the *Asahi* and the *Mainichi*.[18]

This event marked the second phase of the Okinawa problem in the Japanese press, 1955–8. This period saw a great improvement in the press activities on Okinawa in many ways. The flow of information on Okinawa increased considerably, with the year 1956 as its peak. There was also a steady increase of first-hand reports from Okinawa, because a local office of a Japanese news agency, *Kyōdō* was opened; correspondents of the *Asahi Shimbun* were occasionally sent to Naha also.[19]

The main theme of the newspaper accounts on Okinawa during these four years was the land problem, which claimed about 40 per cent of the items recorded. Senaga's success in the mayoral election of Naha and its aftermath came next. The strengthening of American military, especially missile, bases in Okinawa was another important topic. These three happenings in Okinawa, particularly the land conflict, supplied a considerable amount of material to the *Asahi Shimbun*'s reading public (Table 11).

In many ways the year 1956 marked the peak of Japanese public concern with the Okinawa problem. The *Asahi Shimbun* treated it as front-page news twenty-five times and discussed the matter editorially eight times in that year (Table 12). It should be recalled that in this year various groups and associations started their activities for the return of Okinawa. It is not surprising, therefore,

154

that 80 per cent of a national sample were aware of the land problem in Okinawa in an opinion poll conducted in mid–1956.[20]

The land problem

To assess the role which the land problem played in the growth of Japanese public concern with Okinawa, we should note its treatment in the press. The land problem was, needless to say, basically an economic problem which involved landowners in Okinawa.

Table 11
NUMBER OF NEWSPAPER ACCOUNTS ON OKINAWA
IN THE *ASAHI SHIMBUN*, BY TOPICS, 1955–8

	Land problem	Senaga affair	Military bases	Russo-Japanese talks*	Others	Total
1955	72	0	8	1	29	110
1956	194	9	6	34	61	304
1957	48	59	14	0	148	269
1958	68	44	10	0	155	277
Total	382	112	38	35	393	960
Percentage	39.8	11.7	3.9	3.6	41.0	100

*In connection with the Russo-Japanese territorial negotiation, Secretary Dulles hinted at American intention to acquire Okinawa permanently.

Table 12
NUMBER OF TOP NEWS ITEMS, EDITORIALS AND
LETTERS TO THE EDITOR IN THE *ASAHI SHIMBUN*
CONCERNING OKINAWA, 1955-65

Year	Top news items*	Editorials†	Letters to the editor‡
1955	—	6	7
1956	25	8	27
1957	9	3	7
1958	8	11	6
1959	1	4	7
1960	6	4	10
1961	3	1	8
1962	15	9	3
1963	—	5	1
1964	3	12	4
1965	19	18	13

*In Japanese newspapers the most important news items are usually printed on the front page and next to the title of the paper.
†Including the column *'tensei jingo'*.
‡Including articles contributed by persons other than the editorial staff.

Because of the number directly involved and also because of emotional implications, it easily became a political problem with which virtually all people in Okinawa were concerned. In the earlier stages the Japanese press played a very small role. The *Asahi Shimbun* referred to it only a few times before the end of 1954. As pointed out above, it was taken up by lawyers, both in the United States and in Japan, who were concerned with the vindication of human rights; as such, the matter received publicity for the first time through the *Asahi Shimbun* early in 1955. At this stage the problem was discussed primarily from the viewpoint of universal values, such as fundamental human rights, and Japan's concern with the matter was justified in that light.[21]

As time proceeded such universal symbols were quickly replaced by nationalistic symbols such as 'fatherland Japan', 'the fate of the Japanese people as a whole', 'our compatriots in Okinawa under foreign control' and the like.[22] An argument used frequently in the press of the time was that the proposed lump-sum payment system would give the United States fee title (which was regarded as being very similar to absolute ownership) to the lands in question. This would threaten the territorial integrity of Japan because, it was argued, the United States might refuse to transfer those lands to their former owners when she transferred administrative power over the island to Japan.[23] Thus the struggle against the American land policy in Okinawa became a struggle to preserve the national integrity of Japan—the *land* problem of Okinawa was identified with the *territorial* problem of Japan. 'What really matters', the *Asahi Shimbun* argued, 'is not the economic but the national problem'.[24]

Public debates over the Okinawan issue in 1956 were intensified by other factors. The release of the Price Report on the Okinawan land problem coincided with the election campaign for the House of Councillors in Japan; this provided the Opposition with a weapon against the government policy towards the United States.

More important was the fact that the Soviet-Japanese talks for resumption of diplomatic relations between the two countries were under way at that time. Both the Conservatives and the Opposition were urging the government to take a strong line with the Soviet Union on the territorial matters for Chishima and Karafuto. In order to lead the negotiations with the Soviet Union on these matters in a direction favourable to Japan, it was argued, a more tolerant attitude on the part of the United States towards Okinawa and Ogasawara was desirable. Contrary to this desire, the Japanese government was faced with a decisive and non-conciliatory policy

156

on the part of the United States regarding Okinawa. This situation made some elements in the Conservative Party discontented with the American position in Okinawa.[25]

The situation was further complicated when Secretary of State Dulles was reported to have said that the United States would be able to claim the permanent retention of Okinawa on the grounds of Article 26 of the Japanese Peace Treaty if Japan made concessions to the Soviet Union concerning Chishima. The Japanese were puzzled about Dulles's reasons for making that statement. Some, like the former Foreign Minister Okazaki Katsuo, defended Dulles by saying that his real intention was to back Japan against the Soviet Union on the territorial dispute. Others, like Professor Yokota Kisaburō, argued that Dulles's interpretation was wrong because the Peace Treaty had provided for the transfer of Chishima to the Soviet Union. The *Asahi* expressed editorially its surprise at Dulles's statement.[26] Whatever his real intention might have been, it was the worst time and the worst thing to say to the Japanese public which had been suspicious enough already about the American position on Okinawa.

The Senaga affair

The Senaga affair added another aspect to the Okinawan issue. In late 1956 Senaga Kamejirō, head of the Okinawa People's Party (which the Americans regarded as a pro-Communist party), won the Naha mayoral election. This was a damaging blow to United States prestige in Okinawa. *The Times* expressed the fear that Okinawa might become a Cyprus in the Far East, calling the Okinawan situation 'a slight case of "colonialism" '.[27] For about two years after the emergence of Senaga as Mayor, Okinawan politics was a series of bitter fights between Senaga and *Minren* (Council for Vindication of Democracy) on the one hand and the anti-Senaga group (League for Reconstruction of Municipal Administration of Naha) and the U.S. Civil Administration on the other. The measures taken by the latter to oust Senaga from his office included suspension of payment to the city by the Ryukyu Bank (which was under U.S. control) and freezing of deposits.[28] However, Senaga managed to keep his post until the High Commissioner, General Moore, appeared and issued ordinances to amend the Local Government Act and the Local Election Act. One reduced the quorum for a non-confidence bill in the Mayor from two-thirds to a simple majority which enabled the city assembly to dismiss him; the second prevented him from standing for future elections.

The U.S. Civil Administration suffered another setback when Naha elected a pro-Senaga candidate, Kaneshi Saichi, as Senaga's successor in January 1958. This happened in spite of the merger of an adjacent district called Mawashi with the capital to form 'Greater Naha', the measure taken apparently to facilitate the anti-Senaga group to gain victory at the coming election. The tide of affairs began to turn, however, in favour of the United States about the middle of that year, largely because of a split between the newly elected Mayor and the *Minren* (which was under the leadership of Senaga). On the other hand a gradual *rapprochement* between Kaneshi and the U.S. Civil Administration ended the freezing of the city's deposits in January 1959.

The developments of this story were well covered in the Japanese press, especially by magazines like *Sekai*. Various groups and the press, not to mention the Opposition, united in opposing the acts of the U.S. Civil Administration as 'undemocratic'. The *Asahi Shimbun* bitterly criticized the United States, using the words, 'colonial rule', 'undemocratic methods', etc. It also argued 'it would not be happy for both the United States and Japan to see Okinawa becoming the Cyprus in Asia'.[29] This was a severe blow to the Americans who were inclined to talk about the 'show-case for Western democracy' in Okinawa.[30]

During the period from 1955 to 1958 the *Asahi Shimbun* expressed itself frequently and frankly on the Okinawa problem. Almost all opinions expressed in the newspaper were unfavourable to the United States. More important is the fact that the immediate target of their criticism was the lack of concern and the weak attitude of the Japanese government. 'It seems that our Government is always inclined to avoid facing the Okinawa problem squarely and concerns itself very little with the matter', is one comment, typical of many.[31] Another *Asahi* columnist criticized the weak attitude of the Hatoyama administration as compared with that of the Greek government 'which has taken up the problem of Greek Cypriots as its own concern in spite of the fact that it has no legal basis to do so.'[32] Letters to the editor of the *Asahi Shimbun* in June and July of 1956 focused on this subject and almost unanimously disapproved of the position of the Hatoyama Cabinet.

Kishi, who succeeded Hatoyama as Prime Minister after an interval of two months of Ishibashi administration (in which Kishi served as Foreign Minister), was kept under strong pressure by public opinion on the Okinawan issue. Strong statements by Kishi on the Okinawa problem in the earlier days of his administration were to some extent caused by this pressure,[33] which was particularly forceful when he visited President Eisenhower in mid-1957. Surveys carried out shortly after the release of the Kishi-Eisenhower joint communiqué of July 1957 showed that 70–80 per cent of the Japanese people who were interviewed strongly supported Kishi's demand to the United States for the return of Okinawa.[34]

With the settlement of the land issue in Okinawa in mid–1958 as a turning point, the activities of the Japanese press on Okinawa entered the third phase; this is characterized by continuous interest and a moderate attitude. The volume of information greatly increased, but much of it was about ordinary rather than extraordinary events. The reading public was kept informed about everyday life in Okinawa by news from permanent correspondents stationed at Naha.[35] It should be pointed out here that the *Asahi Shimbun*, which had led the formulation of the Okinawan issue among the Japanese public, now became one of the more moderate newspapers on this issue.

The calmness of the Japanese press (or of the *Asahi Shimbun*) was illustrated by its mood over two events: the crash by a U.S. plane into an Okinawan school and the enactment of a new criminal law by USCAR in 1959. On 30 June 1959 an American jet fighter, F–100, crashed into a primary school building in Ishikawa city, Okinawa, killing 17 and injuring some 120, most of them children. A *Washington Post* editorial feared that this accident might resuscitate the anti-American feeling in Japan and in Okinawa which the United States had only recently managed to quieten.[36] The U.S. State Department showed a special consideration for Japanese feeling about the incident by publicly expressing deep sympathy for the victims.[37] The Japanese press, however, refrained from emotionalism in reporting the event, although an *Asahi* columnist suggested a likely effect of this incident would be Japanese hostility to the American bases in Japan.[38]

The calmness of the *Asahi Shimbun* in this period was more clearly illustrated by its position on the new criminal law. The earliest report on this subject in the *Asahi Shimbun* was in favour of the proposed amendment, describing it as being 'in the interests of the protection of the accused'.[39] Later the severe penal provisions against espionage were emphasized; some argued that they could affect freedom of every kind of activity relating to Japan, including the press activities of Japanese reporters in Okinawa (not to mention the movement for the return of Okinawa to Japan). An interesting fact is that the Okinawan public responded at first favourably or indifferently to this enactment.[40] In Japan, however, the Opposition promptly took up the matter and launched a vigorous campaign against it. Some of the Japanese press also were hostile towards it.[41] Okinawan opinion gradually followed the trend of opinion on the Japanese mainland. In these circumstances the *Asahi Shimbun* was silent until 3 September of that year when its editorial echoed the view of Roger N. Baldwin (chairman of the American Civil Liberties Union) that civil liberty in Okinawa tended to be interpreted narrowly in the interests of security considerations for the American military bases.[42] The *Asahi Shimbun*, however, made no protest against the government's adoption of the view of its Minister of Justice, Ino; he said that the new criminal law was not oppressive and that there was therefore no need for the Japanese government to take up the matter with the United States.

It may be that this change of tone was due to a change in the editorial policy of the *Asahi Shimbun* but, in more general terms, it can be explained by the Japanese public's recognition that the complexity of the Okinawa problem required a sober and patient approach. The fact that the Japanese and the American governments had established a *modus vivendi* about Okinawa, especially in relation to the economic and social advancement of its inhabitants, contributed also to the calmness. This is not to say, of course, that the government acquired either wide freedom of action on Okinawa *vis-à-vis* the press or public opinion, especially when it came to the connection of Okinawan bases with Japan's security. This was shown by the public reaction to Kishi's proposal to include Okinawa and Ogasawara in a joint defence area in a new U.S.-Japan security treaty in 1958–60.

When Kishi's proposal that the U.S.-Japan Security Treaty should be revised on the principle of 'mutual defence' and that the defence area under the new arrangement should be extended to Okinawa and Ogasawara, the *Asahi Shimbun* objected strongly.[43] Although some important newspapers sided with Kishi on this matter, the general press reaction was adverse[44] which, together with fierce objections from dissenters within the ruling Party as well as from the Opposition, forced Kishi to abandon his original plan.

The policy originated in the Kishi Cabinet and developed fully in the Kennedy-Ikeda era of furthering the socio-economic welfare of the Okinawan people in preparation for the eventual return of Okinawa to Japan. The response of press and public was favourable, although some were afraid that it might be used to maintain the *status quo* in Okinawa.[45] The press was irritated by the inflexible policy of High Commissioner Caraway and the slowness with which the United States would carry out Kennedy's new Okinawa policy as seen, especially, in the protracted negotiations on the setting-up of U.S.-Japan consultative committees on Okinawa.[46] In

Table 13

THE TREATMENT OF OKINAWA IN JAPANESE PRESS:
1956 AND 1962 COMPARED

	1956	*1962*
Main theme	land issue	financial aid
Issue initiator	voluntary associations and the press	the government
General tone of the press	excited and emotional	calm and judicious
Trend of opinion of the press	highly critical of the position of the Japanese government; hostile to the U.S.	encouraging U.S.-Japan partnership on Okinawa, with a moderate criticism of the U.S.
Front-page top news	25	15
Editorials and columns	8	9
Letters to the editor	27	3
Number of whole items	304	517
	Opinion polls per cent	
Respondents who knew of Okinawan issues	80[a] 40[b]	72[d] 40[e]
Respondents who agreed that Japan should request Okinawa's return	70[c]	66[f]

[a]Land issue; Newspaper Survey Institute, July 1956.
[b]Price Report; ibid.
[c]Eisenhower-Kishi communiqué; *Yomiuri*, 16 September 1957. (A comparable survey for 1956 is unavailable.)
[d]The reversion movement of the Okinawan people; Cabinet Investigation Room, March 1962.
[e]Kennedy Policy; ibid., May 1962.
[f]Kennedy-Ikeda communiqué; ibid., March 1962.

general, however, the Japanese press tended to believe in a slow and steady approach on Okinawa. In many ways there is a contrast between the situation in 1956 and that in 1962, which constitute the peaks of the second and third phases of press activities concerning Okinawa. This contrast is summarized in Table 13.

We have seen the mood and activity of the Japanese press concerning the Okinawa question, which was energetic and continuous, at least in the second and third phases. What then is the role of the press in the formulation of Japanese attitudes towards the matter? The question can be divided into two: the effect of the mass media on the general public and its effect on government policy.

It may be misleading simply to say that Japanese opinion in favour of the return of Okinawa grew from 6 per cent in 1951 to 70 per cent in 1957 or to 66 per cent in 1962,[47] but it is fair to assume that the sympathy of the general public for the cause of the return of Okinawa to Japan considerably increased. This is not a change of attitude if one means by that a change from one attitude (objection to the return of Okinawa to Japan) to another (support for that cause). It is better to call it an intensification of an existing opinion. Many complicated factors worked, of course, for this intensification. Although it is very difficult to identify the exact role of the press, it was certainly a major factor in the making of Japanese opinion on Okinawa.

Two reasons, among others, accounted for this. First, Okinawa is, like other foreign policy issues, a subject of which most people have no personal experience and about which they have no other source of information (at least this was the case in the first decade of the post-war period). Nobody would deny the great role played by the press in disseminating information about Okinawa and in making people aware of the issue. The second, but no less important, reason is that Okinawa is the kind of problem which easily appeals to the nationalistic feeling of the Japanese people. Memory of the time when Okinawa was a prefecture of Japan; memory of the more recent and more tragic history of the Okinawan battle; a similar but fortunately a shorter experience of life under the control of the Occupation forces; the existence of American bases which are still significant in Japan and which are inevitably associated with those in Okinawa; and finally a sort of guilt towards the ill-fated 'compatriots': all these make up the psychological texture of the Japanese people when reading information about Okinawa. In this situation Okinawa assumes a symbolic meaning in the public image of U.S.-Japanese relations.

The growth of public concern itself, however, does not guide policy-makers. There is a consensus of opinion in Japan about the return of Okinawa to Japan and in that sense Okinawa does not present a choice to Japanese political leaders. The real alternative lies between the way in which this particular cause is related to other objectives of national importance, such as the alliance with the United States or Japan's defence policy. It is this that produces the situation where a debate on security issues is bound to bring up the Okinawa problem. In the past the Japanese government put this question to the public on two occasions. First it was presented as a proposal to increase significantly Japan's responsibility for regional defence so that Japan could persuade the United States to loosen its control over Okinawa. The general reaction was unfavourable. The second was as a proposed policy to promote the social and economic welfare of the Okinawan people in co-operation with the United States, while avoiding the problem of military bases. The public response to this was, if not positive support, at least acquiescence. One thing is common in both cases: the public was conservative, not in the sense that they favoured the Conservative Party's policy, but in the sense that they did not want to change the existing order drastically in either direction. They did not want a radical departure from the policy of non-involvement in international conflicts of a military kind. They believed in, or at least they did not question seriously, the argument that the Japanese and the United States governments could solve the Okinawa problem without destroying or weakening their alliance.

The slow and steady approach was apparently the consensus of the general public and of the press about Okinawa. This was, however, based on two assumptions: that reliance on the deterrent power of the United States for maintaining international peace in the Far East, coupled with a modest 'self-defence' force, would continue to be the best policy for Japan; and that the United States would eventually return Okinawa to Japan and the governments of the two countries were prepared to proceed to that goal even if the pace might not be very quick.

The trend of Japanese public opinion in recent years appears to show that the public are exhausting their patience on the latter condition. This is partly a 'natural' consequence of the prolonged occupation of the island by the United States military, which has now lasted almost a quarter of a century. Another, and perhaps a more important, reason for the recent intensification of public debate on Okinawa is the fact that some political leaders now see the two conditions as incompatible. The Japanese government is placed in a dilemma: the pressure from within for an early return of Okinawa to Japan has been mounting, but it is difficult to persuade the United States to return the island to Japanese control without making a substantial change in the country's defence policy, which in turn might arouse a serious objection at home. This indecisiveness on the part of the government seems to support the Opposition's contention that a solution to the Okinawa problem is impossible within the framework of the U.S.-Japan alliance and that a 'real' solution must be sought in Japan's efforts to end the alliance and, in so doing, to ease the international tension. In order to refute this leftist contention, the Conservatives, or at least some militant elements among them, have begun to view it as their duty to 'help' the Japanese people come out of the 'sinister' influences of the leftist Opposition as well as of the 'irresponsible' mass media in their thinking about problems of collective defence for the 'free world'.[48]

The Japanese press in general is typically uncommitted to either of these two extreme views. It is a general characteristic of the Japanese press to be sceptical about any drastic change in the existing order. But any attempt by the government to use the Okinawa problem to launch a new, bolder military policy will probably be severely criticized by the press. The power of the press to restrain the government may not be very great by itself, but it would be surely a formidable task for the government to combat the combined force of the press, the Opposition and the general public.

Conclusion: An Intra-alliance Conflict[1]

In his speech at a National Press Club luncheon in Washington after the conference with President Nixon in November 1969, Prime Minister Satō stated that the greatest result of their conference was the settlement of the Okinawa problem. This created, he claimed, a new formula for the solution of an international conflict: a territorial problem arising from war was solved by friendly negotiations in an almost unprecedented way.

One precedent is provided by the Saar problem (1945–55).[2] It was similar to the Okinawa problem in that both present a conflict of interests within an alliance system. But why was it that France and Germany succeeded in solving the Saar conflict within ten years of the war, whereas it took nearly a quarter of a century for the United States and Japan to arrive at a solution?

The first point concerns the relationship between the allies. The two cases are similar in that both originated directly from the war and became issues when attempts were made to transform war-time hostilities into alliance. In both cases, there was a change in the relative strength of the victors and the vanquished; the latter progressed from enemy, to ally, to an increasingly important member of a new alliance. In this sense, the Saar (or Okinawa) is a measure of the 'maturity' of the new alliance on the one hand and the re-emergence of the defeated nation on the other. Despite this similarity, however, there is an important difference between the Franco-German and the U.S.-Japan relationship: the former consists of two countries of nearly equal strength; the latter, of a greater and a lesser power. This means that the defeated country, in each case, possesses differing degrees of diplomatic leverage over its new partner.

The second aspect is related to the regional international environment in which friction between the allies developed. More concretely, the European-Atlantic Community, as a concept as well as a diplomatic entity, was significant in the solution of the Saar conflict, whereas nothing like an Asiatic-Pacific Community really exists. This difference affects the role of third parties and the way in which the conflict is solved in each case. The United States and Great Britain, for example, initially supported the French view that the Saar should be economically united with France and politically separated from Germany, but their attitude gradually shifted from firm support to increasingly marked reserve. Some European organizations such as the Council of Europe also worked for a *rapprochment* between France and Germany. The basic concern of third parties was to get rid of the Saar barrier to the ratification of the European Defence Community (signed in May 1952) and the Paris Agreement (signed in October 1954). Although throughout the dispute the idea of making the Saar 'European' suggested itself to some of those involved as a possible compromise, the final settlement was along nationalistic lines; that is, the return of the Saar to Germany.

In Okinawa, however, the situation was quite different. There were no moderators acting from a broader view of the problem. (The sole exception to this was India, who refused to participate in the San Francisco Peace Conference on the grounds, among others, that the proposed arrangements concerning Okinawa in the Peace Treaty would become a source of dissatisfaction to large sections of the Japanese people and might consequently give rise to dispute and conflict in the Far East.) Far from assuming the role of mediators, some other countries in the Pacific, harbouring deep mistrust of a militaristic Japan, fully supported the United States. Even after the Peace Treaty came into effect some countries continued to try to restrain the United States from relinquishing her rights in Okinawa.[3] In fact, those governments which were heavily dependent on the United States for their national defence had no reason to prefer withdrawal of the United States military from Okinawa. Neither did they have influence to urge the United States government to change its attitude towards Okinawa.

This brings us to the next point of comparison which is the differences in the nature of the interests involved. The principal interest of France in the Saar lay in the hope that its incorporation would contribute to the economic strength of France. The United States' interest in Okinawa has been based entirely upon security. This vitally influenced the Okinawa problem in two ways.

First, it affected the position taken by third parties who opposed the U.S.-Japan alliance. It is only natural that both the Soviet Union and the People's Republic of China should have repeatedly voiced strong opposition to the presence of the United States in Okinawa, claiming to support the desires of the Japanese people for the return of the island to Japan. The matter was further complicated by the fact that both the United States and the Soviet Union (which occupies Habomai, Shikaton and Chishima islands) were directly involved in a territorial dispute with Japan and the one dispute could easily become linked with the other in international power politics. This was demonstrated in 1957 when Dulles intervened in the Soviet-Japanese negotiations for the restoration of diplomatic relations between the two countries, saying that Japan's concession to the Soviet claim over the southern part of the Chishima islands would entail the loss of her residual sovereignty over Okinawa. China at that time concentrated her attack upon the United States and, by so doing, tacitly supported the Soviet position on the ex-Japanese islands. With the Sino-Soviet split, however, China increasingly came up to support Japan in the territorial dispute *vis-à-vis* the Soviet Union.[4]

Secondly, the deployment of American forces in Okinawa highlighted a difference between the American and Japanese attitudes towards the alliance and especially towards the People's Republic of China which was obviously the principal preoccupation of the alliance. While the United States emphasized the mobility and flexibility of its military strength, always watching the Communist Chinese threat as a whole, Japan preferred that the movement from Japan of U.S. armed forces stationed in Japan under the Treaty should be limited to the vicinity of Japan itself. Otherwise, many Japanese feared, Japan could become involved in hostilities due to American action over which Japan had no control and which were unconnected with Japan's security. That was why Japan tried (with success) to obtain a veto over such movement in the negotiations for the revision of the U.S.-Japan Security Treaty in 1960. One of the methods adopted by the United States and Japan to fill this gap in their alliance system was to allow the United States to use without any restrictions military facilities on Okinawa, while Japan reserved the right to get the island back in the future.

Despite such legal pretension to Japanese innocence about the American action in Okinawa, Okinawa was to be a hot issue in Japanese politics because after all it was impossible to insulate Okinawa from Japanese influence. Here lies another sharp contrast between the Saar and Okinawa. The Saarlanders are a border people between France and Germany; Okinawa is not in any sense a border between the United States and Japan. Had conflict over Okinawa developed between Japan and China, we would have had a somewhat similar situation to that of the Saar. In fact, however, the two countries involved in the Okinawa problem were quite unlike each other in their historical, ethnic and cultural relations with Okinawa. The Okinawan people, as did the Saarlanders, took an ambivalent attitude towards their defeated and seemingly hopeless 'fatherland' for a brief period after the war. The belief that the Okinawan people were an independent ethnic entity which had been exploited by Japanese colonialism apparently contributed to some extent to their attitude in that period. Such ambivalence had, however, disappeared by the time of the conclusion of the Japanese Peace Treaty. After that there were virtually no political activities in Okinawa aimed at political independence or at association with the United States. To all political groups in Okinawa the question was not whether return to Japan was desirable but how soon and in what manner that aim could be realized.

One thing which emerges from the above comparison is the fact that the Okinawa problem was more entangled with the management of the U.S.-Japan alliance than the Saar was with the Western alliance in Europe. The former was, so to speak, a conflict built into the alliance system, whereas the latter constituted an obstacle to the making of the alliance. One was central, the other peripheral to the question of alliance. Solution of the Okinawa problem was to require modification of the alliance in one way or another. This was the basic reason why the United States and Japan took so many years to come to a solution.

The history of the Okinawa problem provides additional evidence that alliance is by no means frictionless. Although the American and Japanese governments managed to maintain their alliance system, they were often slow to adapt the institutional arrangements to the changed reality in the distribution of power in the alliance. Such slow adaptation was due to the fixed image of the relationship between the United States and Japan as it was formed at the time when they originally concluded the alliance. Okinawa remained for a long period as a visible symbol of the unequal status of the two partners.

The solution of the Okinawa problem was also delayed by the fact that there was always a great difference in the importance attached to the problem in the respective countries. This is in fact another expression of the 'unequal' arrangement between them. To the United States, alliance with Japan was at best one among many other similar arrangements. To Japan, however, an American alliance was the cornerstone of her entire foreign policy. This imbalance was likely to lead to a one-way international communication, making the lesser partner oversensitive to its greater partner's moves, and the latter indifferent to its partner's opinions. For example, the United States government might have been moved by pressure of American textile interests against Japan's opinion for an early settlement of the Okinawa conflict.

The solution of the Okinawa problem signifies the recognition by the United States of the rising status of Japan. It could possibly have a favourable effect on the stability of the U.S.-Japan alliance. It must be remembered at the same time, however, that its actual effects on the future American-Japanese relationship are subject to detailed arrangements to be worked out between the two governments concerning the Okinawan bases. Now that the alliance is going to be modified so that Japan can play a greater role, its successful management will require that the two partners display a deeper insight into and a more flexible attitude towards each other's problems. A stronger Japan is also likely to arouse a more vigorous response from third parties, friendly or hostile, to the alliance. All this seems to suggest an eventful future for the U.S.-Japan alliance.

Notes

1 Historical Background

[1] Four per cent of the Okinawan sample (and 2 per cent of the Japanese) disagreed with the reversion, and 2 per cent of each sample gave ambiguous answers, while 9 per cent (and 11 per cent) did not answer. The surveys were conducted in Okinawa on 9-11 September and in Japan on 12-13 September 1967. The results were published in *Asahi*, 17 October 1967. See also Asahi Shimbunsha, *Okinawa henkan*, p. 268ff.

[2] See, e.g. Hattori Shirō (tr. Mauer Thorpe), 'A Glottochronological Study of Three Okinawan Dialects', *International Journal of American Linguistics*, vol. 27 (1961), pp. 52-62; Komatsu Isao, *The Japanese People: Origins of the People and the Language*, p. 60.

[3] See, among others, various articles contributed to the journal *Minzokugaku Kenkyū*, vol. 15, no. 2 (1950) (special issue on Okinawan studies).

[4] According to the Sui History, a Chinese expedition sent out by the Emperor in search of a legendary Land of Happy Immortals reached islands in the Eastern Sea, which the Chinese called Liu Ch'iu (Ryukyu in Japanese pronunciation). Whether this was today's Ryukyus is open to question. A more recent and more credible instance of the Chinese expedition to the Ryukyus was the one undertaken by the Yuan Dynasty after its failure to persuade the Ryukyuans to participate in the projected invasion of Japan. Neither of these expeditions had any lasting effect on Okinawan history.

[5] For the Chinese tributary system in general, and the Ryukyus' place therein, see J. K. Fairbank and S. Y. Teng, 'On the Ch'ing Tributary System', *Harvard Journal of Asiatic Studies*, vol. 6, no. 2 (June 1941), pp. 135-246; Ta-tuan Ch'en, 'Investiture of Liu-ch'iu Kings in the Ch'ing Period' in J. K. Fairbank (ed.), *The Chinese World Order*, pp. 135-64. For the Ryukyuan commercial activities in Southeast Asia in this period, see S. Sakamaki, 'Ryukyu and Southeast Asia', *Journal of Asian Studies*, vol. 23, no. 3 (May 1964), pp. 383-9.

[6] For the Satsuma-Ryukyu relations during the Tokugawa period see, for instance, Robert K. Sakai, 'The Satsuma-Ryukyu Trade and the Tokugawa Seclusion Policy' *Journal of Asian Studies*, vol. 23, no. 3 (May 1964), pp. 391-403. Also the same author's 'The Ryukyu (Liu-ch'iu) Islands as a Fief of Satsuma' in Fairbank, op. cit., pp. 112-34.

[7] Apart from earlier and sporadic examples of the European arrivals in the Ryukyus, including the alleged first European visit made by a Portuguese adventurer, F. M. Pinto, circa 1542, more regular contacts began in the early nineteenth century. The first official attempt by the British to make contact with the Ryukyuans was in 1816. For this and other examples of

Western contact with the Ryukyus before Perry, see G. H. Kerr, *Okinawa: The History of An Island People*, pp. 249-96. Kerr's is the most systematic and comprehensive history of Okinawa so far written in a Western language.

[8] According to an American author, about one-fifth of Perry's 600-page *Narrative* was devoted to a description of the government and the people of the Ryukyus. Cf. R. Braibanti, 'The Ryukyu Islands: Pawn of the Pacific', *American Political Science Review*, vol. 48, no. 4 (December 1954), p. 973.

[9] Text of the Peking agreement in the Maritime Customs (comp.), *Treaties, Conventions, etc., between China and Foreign States*, vol. 2, pp. 585-7.

[10] The Sino-Japanese controversy over the Ryukyus has not been fully treated in a Western language, but consult T. F. Tsiang, 'Sino-Japanese Diplomatic Relations, 1870-1894', *Chinese Social and Political Science Review*, vol. 17, no. 1 (April 1933), pp. 34-53; Sophia S. H. Yen, *Taiwan in China's Foreign Relations, 1836-1874*, especially pp. 244-84.

[11] In his book *China's Destiny*, first published in 1943, Chiang Kai-shek mentioned 'the memory of the disastrous loss of Ryukyu, Hong Kong, Formosa, the Pescadores, Annam, Burma, and Korea'. It is interesting to note that Mao Tse-tung also wrote in 1939: 'In defeating China in war, the imperialistic powers had taken away many Chinese dependent states and a part of her territories. Japan took Korea, Taiwan, the Ryukyu Islands, the Pescadores, Port Arthur; England seized Burma, Bhutan, Nepal and Hong Kong; France occupied Annam; and even an insignificant country like Portugal took Macao'. See Mao Tse-tung, 'The Chinese Revolution and the Chinese Communist Party', the English version of which appeared in the *China Digest*, Hong Kong, 22 March 1949; reproduced in U.S. Consulate General, Hong Kong, *Current Background*, no. 135, 10 November 1951. Such names as the Ryukyus, Korea and Annam are omitted from its official English version in *Selected Works of Mao Tse-tung*.

[12] For the impact of the Sino-Japanese war on Okinawan thinking, see an excellent study by Professor Ōta Masahide in his *Okinawa no minshūishiki*, especially pp. 116-26.

[13] Figures from Higa Shunchō *et al.*, *Okinawa*, p. 137.

[14] Ōta Chōfu, *Okinawa kensei gojūnen*, p. 192.

[15] One Japanese writer argues that the social prejudice against the Okinawans is one of the 'three deadly sins' that modern Japanese have committed; the other two are discrimination against the Koreans and prejudice against *eta* or 'outcasts'. Fujishima Udai, *Nihon no minzokuundō*, pp. 28-34.

[16] According to one authority, for the period from 1899 to 1938, a total of 72,789 Okinawans emigrated of which 20,118 went to Hawaii, 16,426 to the Philippines, 14,830 to Brazil, 11,311 to Peru, 2,754 to Argentina and so forth. Asato En, *Okinawa kaiyō hattenshi*, Appendix.

[17] The film *Himeyuri no tō* (produced by Makino Mitsuo, directed by Imai Shō) was released in 1953. It was founded on a novel under the same title written by the Okinawan writer, Ishino Keiichirō.

[18] See Ōya Sōichi, 'Chūsei, amarinimo chūsei,' *Bungei Shunjū*, September 1959, pp. 62-71. For a criticism on this, see, e.g., Fujishima Udai, op. cit., pp. 177-82.

[19] For the concept of 'marginal nationalism', see L. L. Snyder, *The Meaning of Nationalism*, p. 124.

[20] *Uruma Shimpō*, 24 April 1946. This newspaper, which first appeared in post-war Okinawa and is the forerunner of today's *Ryūkyū Shimpō*, is described by an authority as virtually the mouth-piece of the American military government. See, for this, Ōta Masahide and Tsujimura Akira, *Okinawa no genron: shimbun to hōsō*, pp. 25-6.

[21] *Uruma Shimpō*, 1 August 1947.

171

[22] Before the establishment of a central Ryukyuan-wide government in April 1952, the American military government permitted the four major island groups (Okinawa, Amami, Yaeyama and Miyako *Guntō*) to elect their own governors and Assemblymen in September-October 1951. For a systematic account of the change of Okinawa governmental structure in the early postwar period, see Higa Mikio, *Politics and Parties in Postwar Okinawa*, pp. 24-5.

[23] Okinawa Shi-chō-son-chō-kai (comp.), *Chi hō jichi shichi shūnen kinenshi*, p. 60.

[24] Proceedings of the meetings of the Okinawa *Guntō* Assembly and text of resolution in Nampō Dōhō Engōkai (comp.), *Okinawa mondai kihon shiryōshū*, pp. 1009-26.

[25] The following analysis of the Okinawan opinion is based largely on editorials of the *Uruma Shimpō*, 27 January, 2 February, 8, 9 April and of the *Okinawa Taimusu*, 3, 4, 17 February and 1 May 1951. Both of these papers gave a large space to contributions on this subject from various people. Some of these opinions are included in Ikema Toshihide (ed.), *Ryūkyū kizokuron*.

[26] American authorities in Okinawa attributed the dissolution of the Republican Party to 'the unpopular platform it had been sponsoring—that of advocating Ryūkyū independence'. USCAR, *Civil Affairs Activities in the Ryukyu Islands*, vol. 1, no. 1, p. 125.

[27] These election results are concerned only with the former Okinawa *Guntō* district, since Ryukyuan-wide political parties were yet to be formed and it is impossible to show distribution of seats (thirty-one in all) in a meaningful way. See, for further details, *Okinawa Nenkan*, 1959, pp. 69-70.

[28] Ryūkyū Seifu (comp.), *Ryūkyū shiryō*, vol. 2, pp. 102-10.

[29] For example, the Ryukyu Democratic Party's new platform adopted in January 1954 failed to mention 'the return to Japan' and instead stated: 'We will trust the American goodwill and policy of world peace and secure the prosperity of the inhabitants through the expansion of autonomy'. English translation is taken from Higa Mikio, op. cit., p. 38.

[30] Quoted in *Okinawa Taimusu*, 3 February 1951.

[31] The *Asahi* survey shows that quite a high percentage of the Okinawan people (18 per cent) are inclined to attribute the delay of their return to Japan to 'weak-kneed diplomacy of the Japanese government', while others attribute it to 'the existence of American bases' (12 per cent), 'divided opinions among the Okinawans themselves' (12 per cent), 'the reluctance on the part of the United States to do so' (11 per cent), 'the war in Vietnam' (9 per cent), and so forth. Another survey conducted by the *Ryūkyū Shimpō* in December 1967 presents a rather different picture. The largest group (32 per cent) gave as the most important reason for the delay of the return of Okinawa 'the existence of the American bases', followed by other groups which mentioned 'the Vietnam war' (10.6 per cent), and the 'subservient attitude of the Japanese government towards the United States' (9.9 per cent). Ryūkyū Shimpōsha, *Okinawa no seron: dai nikai zenryū seron chōsa*, p. 5.

2 Genesis (1945-52)

[1] The term 'Nansei shotō' (lit. south-western islands) was first used in the Japanese Peace Treaty as one designating generally those former Japanese islands south of latitude 29° N. which were to be placed under American control in compliance with its provisions. Before that, although the same term had been used to designate those islands south of Kyūshū which were to be removed from Japanese administration, its exact geographical scope remained ambiguous. A proclamation issued by the U.S.

Navy on 26 November 1945 was the earliest attempt, as far as ascertained, made by the United States authorities to determine its boundary. It declared 'Nansei shotō south of 30° N. latitude and its adjacent waters' to be outside the Japanese control. This boundary was confirmed by the SCAP Memorandum of 29 January 1946 (see note 16 below) and maintained until the Peace Treaty came into effect. The term 'Nampō shotō' (lit. southern islands) was likewise created by the Americans to designate the Bonin and its neighbouring islands.

[2] U.S. Department of State, *Conference for the Conclusion and Signature of the Treaty of Peace with Japan, San Francisco, California, 4-8 September 1951, Record of Proceedings*, p. 78 (hereafter cited as *Treaty of Peace with Japan: Proceedings*).

[3] Roosevelt-Chiang Dinner Meeting, 23 November 1943, Cairo, reproduced in U.S. Department of State, *Foreign Relations of the United States: The Conferences at Cairo and Teheran 1943*, pp. 322-5.

[4] Ibid., pp. 868-70. The report was made at a meeting held on 12 January 1944.

[5] For an official account of the Okinawa campaign, see U.S. Department of Army, Historical Division, *United States Army in World War II, The War in the Pacific, Okinawa: The Last Battle*.

[6] Ibid., pp. 419-20.

[7] For the U.S. Navy's opinion in the immediate post-war period about overseas bases, see, for example, a statement of Assistant Secretary of the Navy H. S. Hensel on what the Navy regarded as the 'absolute minimum' number of bases required in the Pacific, whose list included Okinawa and Iwō-jima among others. Quoted in *New York Times*, 6 September 1945. For naval history which constituted a background of the American thinking of the problem of overseas bases, see E. S. Pomeroy, 'The Problem of American Overseas Bases: Some Reflections on Naval History', *U.S. Naval Institute Proceedings*, no. 532 (1947), pp. 689-700; and A. E. Sokol, *Sea Power in the Nuclear Age*, pp. 161-78.

[8] For the difference of opinion between the Department of State and military services on this question, see H. Baldwin, 'U.S. Military Urge Isle Annexations', *New York Times*, 3 February 1946; J. Maki, 'U.S. Strategic Area or U.N. Trusteeship', *Far Eastern Survey*, 13 August 1947, pp. 175-8.

[9] An example of the latter's opinion is found in E. Lattimore, 'Pacific Ocean or American Lake?', *Far Eastern Survey*, 7 November 1945, pp. 313-16.

[10] See Baldwin, op. cit.

[11] This is based on an account given by the then Secretary of State James F. Byrnes, *Speaking Frankly*, pp. 219-20.

[12] U.S. Department of Army, op. cit., pp. 34-5. It is not known what effects the American propaganda had on the relations between the Japanese Army and the local population. An Okinawan writer who was at that time in the service of the Okinawa Prefectural Office relates that the Japanese Army drew the attention of the Prefectural Office to a rumour that some Okinawans were collaborating with the Americans. The ill-feeling created by this incident, he says, persisted between the military and civilians despite a refutation of the allegation by the latter. Urazaki Jun, *Kieta Okinawa-Ken*, p. 122.

[13] A recent example of the remnants of this thinking is found in a report of the House of Representatives Armed Services Committee in 1962 which said, 'While it is true that Okinawa was part of Japan, and Japan was an enemy of the United States, the Okinawan people themselves were not, as a group, enemies of the United States and both practically and psychologically somewhat dissociated from participation in the military actions taken by Japan against the United States. Perhaps it would not be far from the truth to say that the Okinawan people were innocent victims in the war between the United States and Japan.' U.S. House of Representatives,

Committee on Armed Services, *Report, Amending the Act Providing for Promotion of Economic and Social Development in the Ryukyu Islands* (1962), p. 12.

[14] The present writer has never seen these terms. They were referred by F. H. Stires, 'The Ryukyus: An American dependency—An analysis of the military and civil administrations of the Ryukyu Islands, 1945-58' (unpubl. Ph.D. dissertation, Georgetown University, 1960), p. 38.

[15] For details of institutional developments of American military government in the Ryukyus, see ibid., pp. 25-43.

[16] SCAPIN (SCAP Memorandum to the Japanese government) 677, 'Governmental and Administrative Separation of Certain Outlying Areas from Japan', 29 January 1946. The areas which were removed from Japanese administration by the same directive included Okinawa, Ogasawara, Chishima (including Habomai and Shikotan) and Takeshima, the last of which is now claimed by the Republic of Korea.

[17] Ibid.

[18] In May 1950 the Soviet representative for the Allied Council for Japan required an official explanation about the American administration in Okinawa, accusing the United States of violating the basic policies concerning the Japanese Occupation, in relation to a statement made before Congress on 4 April 1950 by the U.S. Undersecretary for the Army, Tracy S. Voorhees, to the effect that the United States would retain military forces for an indefinite period on Okinawa. General MacArthur refused the Soviet request, maintaining that neither the Allied Council nor the Far Eastern Commission had the right to require a report about Okinawan affairs (*Asahi*, 4, 5 May 1950).

[19] For the severance of communications between Okinawa and Japan in the early post-war period, see chapter 10.

[20] For instance, repatriation of Okinawans was treated in a similar way to that of Koreans and Formosans.

[21] Quoted in U.S. Department of State, *Bulletin*, 23 January 1950, pp. 115-18.

[22] See F. Gibney, 'Okinawa: Forgotten Island', *Time*, 28 November 1949, p. 20. In the previous year, Congress had rejected an appropriation bill for the construction of military installations in Okinawa, while it voted for a sum for similar purposes in the Philippines, Guam and the Marianas. See an Associated Press dispatch from Washington dated 28 April 1948, quoted in *Uruma Shimpō*, 7 May 1948.

[23] For example, Secretary of the Army Kenneth C. Royall made unofficial statements at a press conference after visiting U.S. Army installations in Japan and Okinawa in February 1949 and said that it would not be worth while holding American troops in Japan in case of war with the Soviet Union. An assumption of his argument was, however, that American forces should be maintained in Okinawa and the Philippines. These statements gave rise to much discussion. For Royall's statements see *New York Times*, 14, 26 February 1949. Also F. Dunn, *Peace-Making and the Settlement with Japan*, pp. 78-9, 191, and E. J. Lewe Van Aduard, *Japan: From Surrender to Peace*, pp. 102, 109.

[24] The number was reduced to twenty-nine when Amami-Ōshima was transferred to Japanese administration in 1953, and increased again to thirty-two in 1965.

[25] Dunn, op. cit., p. 108.

[26] Ibid.

[27] According to Nishimura Kumao, who was at that time head of the Treaty Bureau of the *Gaimushō* and helped Yoshida in negotiations with Dulles about the problem of a peace treaty, Dulles told the Japanese negotiators that he had come to see them not to conduct 'negotiations' but to hold 'consultations'. Nishimura, 'San Furanshisuko no omoide', *Chūō Kōron* (May 1957), p. 74.

[28] During the first tenure of Yoshida's premiership in 1946, *Gaimushō* officials prepared volumes of materials reflecting Japanese viewpoints on various matters (including territorial questions) which might arise in a future peace settlement for submission to the Allied powers. This fact was not, however, made public at that time. These documents are still not available for academic purposes. Yoshida Shigeru, *Kaisō jūnen*, vol. 3, pp. 25-6.

[29] *Asahi*, 7 June 1947.

[30] Ibid., 8 June 1947.

[31] Ibid., 10 June 1947. MacArthur told American newspapermen that the Ryukyus were a natural frontier of his country, adding that the Japanese had no objection to American occupation of the islands since the Ryukyuans were not Japanese. See a United Press dispatch from Tokyo, quoted in *Uruma Shimpō*, 4 July 1947.

[32] *Asahi*, 9 June 1947. Shortly afterwards Chang Chung, president of the Executive Yuan, made a formal statement that China would demand restoration of her sovereignty over the Ryukyus (ibid., 20 October 1947). The domestic reaction to Ashida's statement is discussed below.

[33] A document prepared about this time by *Gaimushō* officials in the light of the recently concluded Italian Peace Treaty included, according to an American journalist who obtained a copy of it, the following passage: 'Japan has little hope of recovering the Kuriles and Okinawa. But Japan will press for recovery at least in the form of mandate rule on the basis of contention that these areas were not originally obtained through aggression'. G. Walker, 'Peace: Japanese Style—"Treaty Bureau" lets out "secret" version of what would be acceptable', *Christian Science Monitor* (Weekly Magazine Section), 24 January 1948, p. 2. See also Nishimura Kumao, 'Okinawa kizoku no kimaru made', *Asahi Jānaru*, 21 June 1959, pp. 19-20.

[34] See details in chapter 8.

[35] Nishimura, op. cit. His is the most authoritative account so far available of the inside story of the Yoshida-Dulles negotiations over Okinawa.

[36] Ibid.

[37] See Dulles's explanation in his address before a luncheon held by the Japan Chamber of Commerce and Industry and the American Chamber of Commerce in Japan on 14 December 1951. *Asahi*, 14 (evening) December 1951.

[38] Nishimura, op. cit.

[39] For the British attitude see Dunn, op. cit., pp. 137-8.

[40] U.S. Department of State, *Bulletin*, 23 July 1951, pp. 132-8.

[41] Nishimura, op. cit.

[42] Quoted in *Asahi*, 6 August 1951.

[43] See ibid., 7 August 1951.

[44] One political commentator wrote that the United States government issued a protest and warning against the statements of Iguchi and consequently he was punished for the 'leakage of diplomatic secrecy'. Mori Shōzō, *Sengo fūunroku*, pp. 234-6.

[45] Yoshida Shigeru (Prime Minister), House of Representatives, 18 August 1951.

[46] U.S. Department of State, *Treaty of Peace with Japan: Proceedings*, pp. 78, 93.

[47] U.S. Senate, Committee on Foreign Relations, *Hearings, Japanese Peace Treaty and Other Treaties Relating to Security in the Pacific* (1952), pp. 51-2.

[48] For MacArthur's position on Japan's post-Treaty security and Okinawa, see Dunn, op. cit., pp. 54-6.

[49] Evidence of Okazaki Katsuo (Permanent Undersecretary for Foreign Affairs at the time of Yoshida's first Cabinet and of the Katayama Cabinet) before the Commission on the Constitution, 6 May 1959. Kempō Chōsakai, *Kempō Chōsakai dai 30-kai sōkai gijiroku*, pp. 3-4.

[50] For example, Nishimura predicted this possibility. His contention was based on an assumption that the strategic significance of Japanese bases had tremendously increased because of the outbreak of the Korean war. Quoted in *Asahi*, 30 August 1950. See also his article in *Asahi Jānaru*, 21 June 1959, p. 21.

[51] See N. D. Harper, 'Australia and the Peace Settlement with Japan', in Australian Institute of International Affairs, *Australian Papers for Eleventh Conference of Institute of Pacific Relations, Lucknow, 3-15 October 1950*, no. 3, pp. 21, 30.

[52] An example of this opinion was provided by a statement made by a Republican Congressman, W. H. Judd, in January 1952, quoted in 'The United States, Japan and the Ryukyu Islands', *World Today* (August 1952), pp. 352-60.

[53] Nishimura Kumao, 'Ampojōyaku kaitei no rekishi', *Kokusaihō Gaikō Zasshi*, July 1960, pp. 11-13.

[54] A straightforward opinion on this point by an American politician is seen in the following passage written by the unsuccessful Republican candidate for the Presidential election in 1948: 'It is not quite clear who legally owns the Ryukyus now but possession is nine points of the law. We possess them and I hope we never leave them'. T. E. Dewey, *Journey to the Far East*, p. 92.

3   Evolution (1952-8)

[1] Quoted in *Ryūkyū Shimpō*, 3 April 1952.

[2] Ibid. The American policy made no mention of a date for such an election, but evidence shows that the American authorities intended to change the Okinawan administration into an indirect rule under a popularly elected government with the veto of the American governor, not in the distant future, probably within a year after the inauguration of the GRI. See Miyasato Seigen, *Amerika no Okinawa tōchi*, pp. 45-6.

[3] See Ryūkyū Seifu, *Ryūkyū shiryō*, vol. 7, pp. 14-17, 52-3.

[4] For a discussion of some legal aspects of these agreements, see Irie Keishirō, 'Okinawashotō no hōtekichii', *Kokusaihō Gaikō Zasshi* (April 1955), p. 81.

[5] See R. Murphy, *Diplomat Among Warriors*, pp. 421-2. Also Nakayoshi Yoshimitsu, *Okinawa sokokufukki undōki*, p. 37.

[6] See, e.g., J. W. Ballantine, 'The Future of the Ryukyus'. *Foreign Affairs* (July 1953), pp. 663-4; D. G. Haring, 'Amami-Gunto: Forgotten Islands', *Far Eastern Survey*, 19 November 1952, pp. 170-2; and R. Braibanti, 'The Outlook for the Ryukyus', ibid., 12 June 1953, pp. 73-9. These writers advocated an immediate return of the Amami islands to Japan as a desirable step for diplomatic reasons.

[7] *Asahi*, 27 September and 1 October (evening), 1952.

[8] Text in *Kokusaihō Gaikō Zasshi*, April 1955, pp. 246-57.

[9] Okazaki Katsuo (Minister of Foreign Affairs), House of Councillors, 24 December 1953. For examples of the press comments on Dulles's statement in August on the return of the Amami islands, see *Asahi*, 11 August 1953 (editorial) and 12 August (the column 'tensei jingo').

[10] U.S. Department of State, *Bulletin*, 2 January 1954, p. 17.

[11] J. F. Dulles, 'Policy for Security and Peace', *Foreign Affairs*, vol. 32, no. 3 (April 1954), p. 360.

[12] Ryūkyū Seifu, *Ryūkyū shiryō*, vol. 1, pp. 378-9. See also *Okinawa Taimusu*, 11 January 1954.

[13] *Okinawa Taimusu*, 19 February 1954. It should be added here that the Council was not opposed to the retention of Okinawan bases by the

United States. See a letter from the Council to General Ogden, Deputy Governor of USCAR, on 10 February 1954, reproduced in Nampō Dōhō Engokai, *Okinawa mondai kihon shiryōshū*, pp. 1153-4.

[14] Civil Administration Ordinance no. 95, Election Law for the Chief Executive of the Government of the Ryukyu Islands' (9 January 1954).

[15] The statement by Major-General David A. Ogden, Deputy Governor, at a press conference held on 14 April 1954, quoted in *Ryūkyū Shimpō*, 15 April 1954; the letter from General John E. Hull, Governor of the Ryukyu Islands, to Speaker Taira Kōichi of 14 June 1954, quoted in *Okinawa Taimusu*, 22 June 1954.

[16] For a concise account of the American military land policy, see Higa Mikio, *Politics and Parties in Postwar Okinawa*, pp. 40-56.

[17] This figure is especially impressive when one remembers that the total area of Okinawa *Guntō* (on which most of the military facilities are located) is only about 348,000 acres, of which only about 28 per cent is arable. In other words, some 12 per cent of the total area of Okinawa *Guntō* was utilized by U.S. Forces. This included about 16,000 acres of farmland, or nearly 20 per cent of the total arable land of the Okinawa island. The number of landowners affected by the American military land policy came to about 50,000, which meant almost 35 per cent of the total households on the Okinawa island. See Ryūkyū Seifu, *Ryūkyū yōran*, 1955, pp. 8-10, and USCAR, *Ryukyu Islands Fact Book*, p. 130.

[18] The United States' military land policy in Okinawa was set out in the following three ordinances of USCAR: Civil Administration Ordinance no. 91, 'Authority to Contract', 1 November 1952; Civil Administration Ordinance no. 109, 'Land Acquisition Procedure', 3 April 1953; and Civil Administration Proclamation no. 26, 'Compensation for Use of Real Estate within Military Areas', 5 December 1953.

[19] This solution was suggested in a report prepared by a special study mission of the U.S. House of Representatives Committee on Foreign Affairs, which paid a visit to Okinawa in November 1953. See U.S. House of Representatives, Committee on Foreign Affairs, *Report of Special Study Mission to Southeast Asia and the Pacific*, Committee Print, 29 January 1954, pp. 90-1.

[20] Nampō Dōhō Engokai (comp.), *Okinawa kankei shiryō*, pp. 30-1.

[21] U.S. House of Representatives, Committee on Armed Services, *Hearings, Military Public Works, on H.R. 5700*, 1955, pp. 3816-44, 3929-32.

[22] U.S. House of Representatives, Committee on Armed Services, *Report of a Special Subcommittee, Following an Inspection Tour, October 14 to November 23, 1955*, 1956, pp. 7651-67.

[23] U.S. Department of State, *Bulletin*, 8 July 1957, p. 52.

[24] For further details, see, e.g., A. Wantanabe, 'Okinawa in United States Strategy', *Australia's Neighbours*, 4th series, nos. 8-9 (September-October 1963), pp. 6-8. See an Associated Press dispatch from Washington reporting the Defense Department announcement, quoted in *Asahi*, 30 (evening) May 1957.

[25] U.S. Department of State, *Bulletin*, 8 July 1957, pp. 55-8.

[26] USCAR, *Address of Lt-Gen. James E. Moore, High Commissioner of the Ryukyu Islands, to the First Session of the Fourth Legislature of the GRI*, 11 April 1958, pp. 8-9.

[27] U.S. Department of State, *Bulletin*, 5 May 1958, p. 723.

[28] USCAR, *Civil Affairs Activities in the Ryukyu Islands*, vol. 7, no. 1 (October 1958 to March 1959), pp. 22-4.

[29] A high-ranking USCAR officer remarked in his reminiscences: 'I believe that the period from June 1956 to the middle of 1958 was the most trying peacetime in my thirty-five years in the Army. We had innumerable elections, tragedies, typhoons, budget cuts, recessions . . . However, that which could be replaced or repaired was replaced and out of this all has come a unity and spirit of cooperation unknown prior to 1956'. USCAR, *Text of*

Notes of Gen. Burger's Reminiscences before Golden Gate Club, 28 April 1959, p. 4.
[30] Details of the Senaga affair are discussed in chapter 11.

4 Towards U.S.-Japan Partnership (1958-65)

[1] Kishi Nobusuke, 'Tobei o mae ni shite' (an interview between Kishi and a member of the editorial staff of the *Nihon Keizai Shimbun*), *Chūō Kōron*, May 1957, pp. 124-32.
[2] Quoted in *Asahi*, 6 (evening), 15 August 1957.
[3] For a brief discussion of the activities of the U.S.-Japan Committee on Security Problems see Asahi Shimbunsha, *Nichi-Bei anzenhoshō jōyaku no shōten* (Asahi shimin kyōshitsu: Nihon no anzenhoshō, vol. 10), pp. 51-4.
[4] U.S. Department of State, *Bulletin*, 6 October 1958, pp. 532-3.
[5] See *Gaimushō*'s views as reported in *Asahi*, 6 October 1958.
[6] U.S. Department of State, op. cit.
[7] Fujiyama Aiichirō (Minister of Foreign Affairs), House of Representatives, 30 September 1958.
[8] This figure was taken from Gaimushō, *Okinawa binran*, p. 28. *Okinawa Nenkan*, 1960, p. 118, put the figure at 10 million yen. Both differed from the figure shown in Table 2, i.e. 12.3 million yen. I am unable to explain the difference, but one possible explanation is that the first figure includes not only the sum for technical assistance in the strict sense but also some other expenditures such as the Japanese government contribution to the teachers' training programme in Okinawa.
[9] An outline of the plan is given in USCAR, *Civil Administration of the Ryukyu Islands*, vol. 9, no. 1 (October 1960 to March 1961), pp. 75-8.
[10] High Commissioner Ordinance no . 11, 'Foreign Investment', 12 September 1958; no. 12, 'Foreign Trade in the Ryukyu Islands', 12 September 1958; and no. 14, 'Conversion of Currency,' 15 September 1958.
[11] The main reasons for the objection were: that the currency conversion would bring about a rise in prices; that the lack of its own currency would render it impossible for the Government of the Ryukyu Islands to pursue an independent monetary policy; that the Ryukyuan economy would be thereby linked closely with the American economy; and that the United States aimed at separating the Ryukyus from Japan not only politically but also economically. See *Okinawa Nenkan*, 1959, p. 95. For an argument in favour of the American policy, see Takaramura Nobuo (President of the Ryukyu Development Loan Corporation), 'Doru kirikae no keii to eikyō', *Okinawa Taimusu*, 27 to 30 August 1958.
[12] The annual growth rates of the Okinawan national income for the financial years 1959-60 and 1960-1 were 13.6 per cent and 19.1 per cent respectively, whereas comparable figures for the preceding four years were between 6.6 per cent and 8.0 per cent. The per capita national income increased from $149 in 1955 to $173 in 1958 and then to $237 in 1961. These figures are taken from USCAR, *Ryukyu Islands Fact Book*, pp. 52-3. For a brief discussion of the Okinawan economy after currency conversion, see 'Okinawa keizai no tembō', *Chōsa Geppō* (Naikaku Chōsashitsu), May 1960, pp. 58-75. See also Yamashiro Shinkō, 'Ryūkyū ni okeru gaishidōnyū' in Ryūkyū Daigaku Keizai Kenkyūjo, *Ryūkyū keizai no kenkyū*, pp. 56-86; Yamazato Shōkō, 'Ryūkyū keizai to nōgyō', ibid., pp. 87-114.
[13] USCAR, *Civil Administration of the Ryukyu Islands*, vol. 9, no. 1 (October 1960 to March 1961), p. 30.
[14] Ōta's idea of 'step-by-step return to Japan' was elaborated in the OLDP's booklet, *Sokoku e no michi*, which was widely distributed as propaganda

material in the election campaign in November 1960. Its English transla
tion appears in ibid., pp. 253-68.

[15] Public Law 86-629 Providing for Promotion of Economic and Social
Development in the Ryukyu Islands, known as the Price Act because the
bill for its legislation was introduced by Congressman Price who once
headed a special subcommittee of the House of Representatives Armed
Services Committee to investigate the land problem in Okinawa in 1955.
The original bill was designed to provide for a grant of an amount equal
to the U.S. Federal taxes withheld at the source during the fiscal year from
persons stationed or employed in the Ryukyu Islands, and not to exceed $6
million in any fiscal year, to the High Commissioner of the Ryukyu Islands.
It included also the provision for carry-over of the unobliged balances
thereof to a total of $6 million. Thus, it is conceivable that in any one year
as much as $12 million might have been available for these purposes.
(Similar legislation had been enacted by the Congress with respect to the
Virgin Islands, Guam, the Philippines and Puerto Rico.) The bill was,
however, shelved in 1959 and passed in the following year but only after
the deletion of the provision for the automatic grant of $6 million annually,
and of the provision for the carry-over of unobliged balances. In actual
practice, therefore, the $6 million became interpreted as a ceiling. See U.S.
House of Representatives, Committee on Armed Services, *Report to
Accompany H.R. 10937, Amending the Act Providing for Promotion of
Economic and Social Development in the Ryukyu Islands*, 1962, pp. 14-15.

[16] Statement of General Armistead D. Mead, Chief of the Civil Affairs
Division of the Army, text in U.S. House of Representatives, Committee
on Armed Services, Subcommittee no. 3, *Consideration of H.R. 1157 to
Provide for Promotion of Economic and Social Development in the
Ryukyu Islands*, 1960, p. 3887.

[17] Senator Daniel K. Inouye from Hawaii, one of the sponsors of the Price
Bill, said: 'There is no doubt that Okinawa is very important to the United
States from a military standpoint. I, therefore, respectfully contend that if
the United States is to remain in the Ryukyu Islands for a considerable
length of time, we should indicate such intention by demonstrations of
brotherly assistance. In this troubled world, I believe, it would be very
important to psychologically prepare the inhabitants of the Ryukyu Islands
for this long siege. We should demonstrate with activities such as will make
the inhabitants want to have our troops remain on the islands.' Ibid.,
p. 3879.

[18] For example, Fujieda Sensuke, Director-General of the *Sōrifu* of the Ikeda
Cabinet, stated during his visit to Okinawa that it was an important policy
of the Ikeda Cabinet to assist the development of 'under-developed areas'
and that the aid programme to Okinawa was to be approached from that
angle. *Asahi*, 27 December 1960.

[19] See, e.g., *Asahi*, 29 July, 2 (evening), 6 August 1960.

[20] There is evidence to show that J. F. Kennedy had had considerable interest
in the Okinawa problem before he became President. In reply to a petition
advanced from the *Okinawashotō Sokokufukki Kiseikai* (for which see
chapter 10) to all the members of the Senate Foreign Relations Committee
for a prompt return of Okinawa to Japan, Senator Kennedy showed his
sympathy to the petitioner, saying that this grave and unsettled problem
of Okinawa was well worth the deep concern of the leaders of both the
United States and Japan. More than ten members of the Committee
responded to the petition; among them were Senators J. W. Fulbright, John
Sparkman, Hubert Humphrey and Everett K. Dirksen. See Nakayoshi
Yoshimitsu, *Okinawa sokokufukki undōki*, pp. 72-4.

[21] See Civil Administrator J. G. Ondrick's remarks at his interview with
members of the Okinawa Liberal Democratic Party, reported in *Okinawa
Taimusu*, 11 (evening) March 1961.

[22] See High Commissioner P. W. Caraway's remarks at his interview with Nagamine Akio, Speaker of the Ryukyuan Legislature, reported in ibid., 25 April 1961.

[23] Ibid., 28 March 1961.

[24] *Asahi*, 3 May 1961.

[25] Reported in ibid., 6 (evening) June 1961.

[26] See testimony of W. P. Bundy, Deputy Assistant Secretary of Defense for International Security Affairs, in U.S. House of Representatives, Committee on Armed Services, Subcommittee no. 2, *Consideration of H.R. 10937, to Amend the Act Providing for the Economic and Social Development of the Ryukyu Islands*, 1962, p. 5210. In mid-May 1962, some 6,000 U.S. troops, 2,800 of which were Marines of the Third Division usually stationed in Okinawa, were sent to Thailand to be ready for any eventuality in Laos. For this see the *Times of Viet Nam*, 19 May 1962; the *Bangkok Post*, 28 May 1962; and the *Straits Times*, 3 July 1962.

[27] *Asahi*, 20 (evening) February 1961.

[28] F. G. McGuire, 'Calculated Risk—Mace B bases readied on Okinawa', *Missiles and Rockets*, 13 March 1961.

[29] According to Miyazawa Kiichi, a close friend of Ikeda who was present at every meeting between Ikeda and Kennedy during the former's stay in Washington in June 1961, Ikeda attached the greatest importance to the Okinawa problem on that occasion. Miyazawa Kiichi, 'Nichi-Bei kankei e no teigen', *Sekai*, January 1966, p. 82.

[30] U.S. Department of State, *Bulletin*, 10 July 1961, p. 57.

[31] One observer described the immediate reaction of the Defense experts who were present at the meeting to Kennedy's decision on this question as being a frown at 'an imprudent judgment of a young President'. Miyazawa, op. cit.

[32] See *New York Times*, 4 September 1961. Some people believed that Kennedy's decision to dispatch an investigating team to Okinawa was made at the request of High Commissioner Caraway. Caraway denied this, however, describing the decision as 'an outgrowth of those various talks that have been taking place in Washington between the President and the Prime Minister.' See USCAR, *Press Conference of the High Commissioner, Paul W. Caraway*, 7 September 1961, p. 1.

[33] See Robert Kennedy's remarks at the press conference which was held before he left Japan, reported in *Asahi*, 7 February 1962.

[34] Text in Sōrifu, *Tokubetsu chiiki kankei hōreishū* (part 1), December 1965, pp. 51-68. See also *New York Times*, 20 March 1962, p. 8.

[35] U.S. Senate, Committee on Armed Services, *Report No. 2103, Amending the Act Providing for Promotion of Economic and Social Development in the Ryukyu Islands*, 1962, pp. 1-9.

[36] U.S. House of Representatives, Committee on Appropriations, *Hearings before Subcommittees, Foreign Operations for 1963*, 1962.

[37] General Caraway was the most controversial personality among the successive American Governors and High Commissioners of the Ryukyu Islands. The public image of Caraway as being austere makes a good contrast with that of his immediate predecessor General Booth. The press comments on the political approach of High Commissioner Caraway were unanimous in pointing out his inflexibility. See, e.g., 'Shinseisaku ichi-nen no Okinawa', *Asahi*, 20, 21 March 1963; 'Okinawa no jichiken kakudai sezu', *Mainichi*, 20 (evening) March 1964; 'Kyarawei-jidai no sokuseiki', *Yomiuri*, 27 April to 7 (evening) May 1964; and 'Dissension in Okinawa— U.S. Military, Ryukyuans at odds over autonomy issue', *Japan Times*, 28 June 1964.

[38] USCAR, *Briefing by High Commissioner Paul W. Caraway of the Ryukyu Islands to Members of News Media*, 28 February 1962, pp. 3, 17.

[39] See remarks by Kodaira Hisao, Director-General of the *Sōrifu*, at the conclusion of his official visit to Okinawa, quoted in *Asahi*, 1 (evening) December 1961. For the High Commissioner's response, see USCAR, *Press Conference of the High Commissioner Paul W. Caraway*, 7 December 1961, p. 3.

[40] USCAR, *News Release*, 63-81, 6 March 1963, 'Text of Remarks of High Commissioner Paul W. Caraway at a dinner meeting of the Golden Gate Club, Naha, on 5 March 1963', p. 2.

[41] See, e.g. [Okinawa Liberal Democratic Party], 'Bemmukan hatsugen ni taisuru Jimintō giindan no kenkai', *Okinawa Taimusu*, 7 March 1963 and [Okinawa Socialist Masses Party], 'Bemmukan hatsugen ni taisuru Shadaitō kenkai', ibid., 13 March 1963.

[42] The United States maintained in Okinawa at that time the First Special Forces Group (about 500 strong), some 2,300 paratroopers as well as 19,000 Marines of the Third Division. These were the main components of 'strong and highly mobile forces' to be deployed from American bases in Okinawa. For the military situation in Okinawa in 1960-2, see D. Warner, 'Our Fire Brigade on Okinawa', *Reporter*, 13 October 1960, pp. 37-8, and R. Steiner, 'Build-up in Okinawa', *Newsweek*, 5 March 1962, pp. 28-9.

[43] Text of agreement in U.S. Department of State, *Bulletin*, 11 May 1964, p. 755. A detailed analysis of the Japanese position on the formation of these committees is made in chapter 6.

[44] In testimony to Congress, Assistant Secretary of State U. A. Johnson (a later U.S. Ambassador to Japan) revealed that it was the intention of his government to 'channel that [i.e. Japanese] assistance [to Okinawa] in directions that the Americans would like to see it to go', emphasizing that Japan's role in this respect was not that of a partner but merely that of a supplementary character. See U.S. House of Representatives, Committee on Armed Services, Subcommittee no. 2, *Consideration of H.R. 10937, to Amend the Act Providing for the Economic and Social Development of the Ryukyu Islands*, 1962, p. 5225.

[45] *Mainichi*, 19 April 1964.

[46] For press comments on this problem, see *Asahi*, 25 April 1964; *Tōkyō*, 25 April 1964; *Yomiuri*, 26 April 1964; *Nihon Keizai*, 26 April 1964.

[47] Text of the Johnson-Satō communiqué in U.S. Department of State, *Bulletin*, 1 February 1965, pp. 135-6. See also the United States and the Japanese notes on broadening of the functions of the Consultative Committee on 2 April 1965, in ibid., 19 April 1965, pp. 601-2.

[48] See, e.g., an editorial in *Asahi*, 29 July 1964.

[49] For a detailed analysis of Okinawan politics in the Caraway-Ōta era, see Higa Mikio, 'The Reversion Theme in Current Okinawan Politics', *Asian Survey*, vol. 7, no. 3 (March 1967), pp. 156-8. The Democratic Party was renamed Okinawa Liberal Democratic Party in December 1967.

[50] USCAR, *Press Conference of High Commissioner Albert Watson II*, 1 August 1964, pp. 1-2; 7 January, 1965, pp. 8-9.

[51] Ibid., 7 January 1965, p. 1.

[52] USCAR, *Civil Administration of the Ryukyu Islands*, vol. 14 (1 July 1965 to 30 June 1966), p. 38. The number of USCAR legislations decreased further to sixty-eight by the end of 1966. See USCAR, *News Release*, 66-432, 30 December 1966.

[53] See, e.g., the statement by Uno Sōyū who led the LDP delegation to Okinawa, reported in *Asahi*, 21 September 1965.

[54] USCAR, *Press Conference of High Commissioner Albert Watson II*, 21 October 1965.

[55] Text of the amended Executive Order in U.S. Department of State, *Bulletin*, 10 January 1966, p. 66.

[56] See *Asahi*, 16 January 1965.

⁵⁷ USCAR, *Press Conference of High Commissioner Albert Watson II*, 20
August 1964, p. 5.
⁵⁸ A bill amending the Price Act so as to raise the ceiling of the annual grant-
in-aid to the Ryukyus from the current $12 million to $25 million was
introduced in 1966 but it was shelved. A bill to the same effect was again
introduced in 1967 and this time it was passed but only after being modified
so that the ceiling was $17·5 million annually.
⁵⁹ The transfer of functional authority from USCAR to GRI caused some
confusion. For example, a serious conflict developed in 1966 over two
civil cases—one concerned with the taxability of certain commodities (the
'mackerel' case) and another concerned with the eligibility of a certain
successful candidate for the legislative election (the 'Tomori' case)—when
they involved the validity of USCAR legislation. The High Commissioner
ordered the transfer of these two cases from the GRI Court of Appeals to
the USCAR Civil Court on the ground that the GRI court was not
authorized 'to examine the propriety or legality of any official act of
USCAR'. This decision caused an uproar among the Okinawan people.
For further details, see Higa Mikio, op. cit., pp. 162-4.
⁶⁰ *Asahi*, 30 (evening) July 1965. The use of the Okinawan base by B-52s at
this time was temporary; it was necessitated, according to the American
explanation, by the weather conditions. Permanent use of the Okinawan
base by a squadron of B-52 bombers began in 1968.
⁶¹ An address by the High Commissioner Albert Watson II to members of the
United Okinawan Federation of Hawaii, 14 April 1965, Honolulu, Hawaii.
USCAR, *News Release*, 65-105, 26 March 1965.
⁶² USCAR, *Transcript of Questions and Answers at Meeting of Members of
the Japan Newspaper Publishers and Editors Association with High Commissioner Albert Watson II*, 21 January 1965.

5 The '1970 Problem'

¹ Paul M. A. Lineberger, 'America's Okinawa policy', *World Affairs*, vol. 126
(Summer 1963), pp. 85-91.
² U.S. House of Representatives, Armed Services Committee, Subcommittee
no. 3, *Hearings on H.R. 4903 to Amend Act Providing for Economic and
Social Development in the Ryukyu Islands*, 1967, p. 5146.
³ An English version of the Japanese government report on Japan-Okinawa
'ittaika' in *Weekly Okinawa Times*, 3, 10 August 1968. For the response
of the Okinawans to it, see, e.g., *Asahi*, 19 September 1968.
⁴ *Okinawa Taimusu*, 8 February 1965.
⁵ Quoted in *Ryūkyū Shimpō*, 28 January 1965.
⁶ *Okinawa Taimusu*, 9, 10 February 1965.
⁷ A local newspaper reported in April 1965 that the 173rd Airborne Brigade
began training for jungle warfare in mountains in northern Okinawa. On
completion of this training, it was deployed to South Vietnam in May-
August; ibid., 3 April 1965.
⁸ A high-ranking officer of the U.S. Strategic Air Command (SAC) at
Omaha told reporters that Kadena Air Base was one of three operational
bases for B-52s that the United States held in the Western Pacific, the other
two being Andersen Air Force Base in Guam and Ban U-Tapao in Thailand
(*Asahi*, 29 March 1968). An Associated Press dispatch from Saigon (2
July 1968) reported that the U.S. military authorities there made it public
that seventy-five B-52s made fifteen sorties on North Vietnamese military
targets north of the demilitarized zone. Kimura Toshio, Chief Cabinet
Secretary of the Satō government, revealed at a press conference that the
Japanese government's inquiry on this report resulted in a denial by the
U.S. Embassy in Tokyo of such an announcement by the American military

authorities in Saigon (ibid., 3, 4 July 1968). Despite this denial, however, it seems difficult to dispel the suspicion.

[9] Ryūkyū Shimpōsha (ed.), *Kichi Okinawa*, pp. 57-8; Takahashi Minoru, 'Hembōsuru kichi Okinawa', *Sekai*, May 1967, p. 97.

[10] For the role played by the Okinawan bases in the Vietnam war, see, besides those quoted above, Asahi Shimbun Anzenhoshōmondai Chōsakai, *Amerika senryakuka no Okinawa*, pp. 11-24.

[11] U.S. House of Representatives, Armed Services Committee, Subcommittee no. 3, *Hearings on H.R. 12617 to Amend Act Providing for Economic and Social Development in the Ryukyu Islands*, 23 March 1966.

[12] *Pacific Stars & Stripes*, 10 December 1965.

[13] High Commissioner F. T. Unger's speech at a luncheon meeting of the American Chamber of Commerce in Okinawa on 16 August 1968, quoted in *Weekly Okinawa Times*, 24 August 1968.

[14] Figures from the statistics submitted by the GRI Police at the request of the Ryukyuan Legislature Special Committee on Matters Related to the U.S. Forces, 26 January 1967, cited in Nihon Bengoshi Rengōkai, 'Okinawa hōkokusho', *Hōritsu Jihō*, March 1968 (special number on Okinawa), p. 127.

[15] For the commotion caused by the accident among the local population, see, e.g. editorial in *Weekly Okinawa Times*, 23 November 1968.

[16] Ryūkyū Shimpōsha, *Okinawa no seron: dai ikkai zenryū seron chōsa*, p. 26.

[17] Ryūkyū Shimpōsha, *Okinawa no seron: dai sankai zenryū seron chōsa*, p. 44. A survey made by the *Fukki Mondai Kenkyūkai*, Study Committee of Problems Related to the Reversion of Okinawa (an independent committee consisting of various civic leaders), in May 1968 resulted in similar findings: 84.5 per cent of the respondents answered that they felt their safety was endangered by the existence of the American bases in Okinawa (48.8 per cent expressed grave apprehension and 38.7 per cent mild), while only 10.3 per cent differed, in various degrees of intensity, from the view that the military bases were a source of feelings of insecurity; the remaining 5.3 per cent were ambiguous. See Fukki Mondai Kenkyūkai, *Zenryū kyōtsū seron chōsa*, p. 15.

[18] Ryūkyū Shimpōsha, *Okinawa no seron: dai ikkai zenryū seron chōsa*, p. 36.

[19] *Weekly Okinawa Times*, 28 December 1968. The Ryukyu Legislature had passed anti-B-52 resolutions twice before: 30 July 1965 and 10 February 1968.

[20] See, e.g., Yoshida Shikō, 'Nahakō no kobaruto 60', *Sekai,* October 1968, pp. 158-62; *Weekly Okinawa Times*, 10 August, 14 September 1968; *Asahi*, 17 November 1968.

[21] For a discussion of these two incidents, see Professor Miyake Yasuo, 'Hōshanō osen jiken wa nani o monogataru ka', *Sekai*, July 1968, pp. 145-58; 'Kyūdai jettoki tsuiraku jiken no yukue', ibid., August 1968, pp. 231-4.

[22] Saitama and Kanagawa are two Japanese Prefectures where relatively large U.S. military facilities are located. Figures from Ryūkyū Seifu, *Ryūkyū yōran*, 1967, p. 75; information supplied by the Defence Agency of the Japanese government, quoted in *Asahi*, 18 June, 28 July 1968.

[23] This was announced on 1 February 1968 by High Commissioner Unger in his message to the Okinawan Legislature.

[24] *Weekly Okinawa Times*, 16 November 1968. For a detailed analysis of the elections, see Higa Mikio, 'In Retrospect: significance of three major elections', ibid., 21, 28 December 1968.

[25] A draft policy prepared by Funada Naka, Chairman of the LDP Committee on National Security, took this viewpoint. Although announced as Funada's personal view, it is regarded as reflecting the official position of the Party (*Asahi*, 14 June 1968).

26 For the expectation held by some Australian defence planners that Japan will take a more positive role in collective defence in the Western Pacific, see D. C. S. Sissons, 'Australia and Japan', in J. D. B. Miller (ed.), *India, Japan, Australia: Partners in Asia?*, pp. 60-3. Sissons does not regard this school of thought as a very important factor in the making of Australian foreign policy.

27 Among many books and articles written on the '1970 problem', the following are useful guides: Asahi Shimbun Anzenhoshōmondai Chōsakai, *1970-nen no seiji kadai*; Yomiuri Shimbun Kokusaijōsei Chōsakai, *1970-nen*. See also John K. Emmerson, 'Japan: Eye on 1970', *Foreign Affairs*, January 1969, pp. 348-62; Wakaizumi Kei, 'Japan Beyond 1970', ibid., April 1969, pp. 509-20.

28 Tokonami Tokuji, *Okinawa fukki e no shiken: kasanete Okinawa fukki ni tsuite*. See also Tokonami, 'Nihon no anzenhoshō to Okinawa mondai', in Nihon Kokusai Mondai Kenkūjo and Kajima Kenkyūjo (eds), *Nihon no anzenhoshō*, pp. 322-8.

29 Text of the interim report in *Kikan Minami to Kita*, no. 37 (June 1966), pp. 119-20.

30 For the Mori plan, see *Okinawa Nenkan*, 1968, pp. 66-7.

31 For a discussion of the various problems involved in the U.S.-Japan Security Treaty, see Asahi Shimbun Anzenhoshōmondai Chōsakai, *Nichibei ampojōyaku no shōten*.

32 In testimony to Congress, Richard L. Sneider, Country Director for Japan, Bureau of East Asian and Pacific Affairs, Department of State, emphasized the importance of 'differentiating between the return of administrative rights of the island to Japan, which is contemplated, and the return of the base structure which is not contemplated'. U.S. House of Representatives, Committee on Appropriations, Subcommittee on Foreign Operations and Related Agencies, *Hearings on Foreign Assistance and Related Agencies Appropriations for 1969, Ryukyu Islands*, 1968, p. 25.

33 *Asahi*, 20 January 1967.

34 See Chūō Kōron Henshūbu (comp.), 'Okinawa o meguru samazama na shuchō', *Chūō Kōron*, December 1967, p. 176ff.

35 See chapter 1, note 1.

36 See, for the August 1968 survey, *Weekly Okinawa Times*, 31 August 1968; for the September 1967 survey, Asahi Shimbunsha, *Okinawa henkan*, p. 326.

37 *New York Times*, 23 November 1969, gives the text of the Nixon-Satō joint communiqué.

38 See, for example, an editorial of the *Jen-min jih-pao* (*People's Daily*), 28 November 1969 and an article which appeared in the *Pyongyang Times*, 1 December 1969. For the North Vietnamese response to the same event, see the *Vietnam Courier*, 1 December 1969.

39 A statement by the Japanese Defence Agency reported in *Asahi*, 26 November, 5 December 1969.

40 Ibid., 22 December 1969.

6 Government Departments and Policy

1 The special status of Okinawa is expressed by various agreements between Okinawa and Japan. On this point, see chapter 3, pp. 32-3.

2 The name of this agency, *Sōrifu*, may be better rendered as Prime Minister's Department to avoid creating the erroneous impression that it is in any way inferior to any other of the principal Ministries (*shō*). For convenience' sake, however, we shall follow its official English translation.

3 See Okinawa Zaidan (ed.), *Nijūnen no ayumi*, pp. 6-9, 45-7, 95-8.

4 See Yoshida Shigeru, *Kaisō jūnen*, vol. 3, pp. 25-6.

[5] Text of relevant documents in Nampō Dōhō Engokai (comp.), *Okinawa mondai kihon shiryōshū*, pp. 127-38.

[6] Ibid., pp. 149-50.

[7] This was originally set up on 15 November 1956 as a non-governmental association on the initiative of the Liberal Democratic Party. It developed into a semi-governmental body through an enactment of the Japanese Diet in 1957. In 1959 its functions were extended to include various matters related to the 'northern territories', i.e. Chishima, although the name of the Association remained unchanged.

[8] It publishes under the same title, *Minami to Kita* (formerly *Okinawa to Ogasawara*), two journals. One appears every ten days in an edition of 10,000 copies; the other appears quarterly in an edition of 2,000 copies. As of October 1965 it had also published forty-seven books and pamphlets.

[9] A summary of the activities of the Association is given in Nampō Dōhō Engokai, *Nampō Dōhō Engokai jigyō no aramashi*. It received the following government subsidies: 1958, yen 13.0 million; 1959, yen 14.0 million; 1960, yen 17.5 million; 1961, yen 45.8 million; 1962, yen 63.8 million; 1963, yen 178.8 million; 1964, yen 145.8 million; 1965, yen 123.0 million; 1966, yen 231.0 million; 1967, yen 165.7 million; 1968, yen 158.2 million; 1969, yen 127.2 million. See Ōkurashō Zaisei Chōsakai, *Kuni no yosan*.

[10] This step was taken in relation to various legislation accompanying the ratification of ILO conventions (*Asahi*, 18 August 1965).

[11] A brief account of the institutional development of the *Sōrifu* and its relations with Cabinet is available in Sōrifu, *Kanchō binran I: Naikaku Sōrifu*, pp. 37-9, 42-3.

[12] This was established by a decision of Cabinet on 27 August 1965 as one of the steps taken by the Prime Minister, Mr Satō, after his visit to Okinawa. It consists of the Ministers of Justice, Foreign Affairs, Finance, Education, Welfare, Agriculture and Forestry, Local Government and Postal Services. The *Sōmuchōkan* serves as its Secretary. In addition other Ministers and three principal officials of the Liberal Democratic Party (the Secretary-General, the chairman of the Executive Board and the chairman of the Policy Deliberation Council) may attend its meetings; Sōrifu, *Kaisetsu seifu no mado*, vol. 9, no. 19 (20 September 1965), pp. 33-4.

[13] U.S. Department of State, *Bulletin*, 11 May 1964, p. 755.

[14] The chart represents the state of affairs which existed in 1965 but which has remained almost unchanged. Two major changes that occurred thereafter were the enlargement of the functions of the Japanese Government Liaison Office at Naha in February 1968 (whereby the chief of that office was to be placed under the supervision both of the *Sōrifu* and the *Gaimushō*) and the establishment of a U.S.-Japan-Ryukyu Advisory Committee to the High Commissioner in Naha in January 1968. The new Committee's principal function was to 'advise and make mutually agreed recommendations to the High Commissioner on economic, social and related matters which are within the powers of the High Commissioner, in order to prepare for the smooth integration of the Ryukyuan socio-economic structure into that of Japan proper when administrative rights in the islands are reverted to Japan'. Ibid., 29 April 1968, pp. 570-1. The Advisory Committee was reorganized in March 1970 as the Committee for Preparation for the Return of Okinawa to Japan, composed of the U.S. High Commissioner, Japanese Ambassador and Okinawan Chief Executive (the last of which can attend as observer).

[15] *Asahi*, 19 (evening), 20 June 1956.

[16] Ambassador Allison's statement for the press on 27 June 1956 in Nampō Dōhō Engokai, *Okinawa kankei shiryō*, pp. 52-3.

[17] *Asahi*, 19 June 1956.

[18] Hōmushō, 'Okinawa no tochimondai ni tsuite', Nampō, op. cit., pp. 50-2.

[19] *Asahi*, 29 June 1956.

[20] Ibid., 29 (evening), 30 (evening) June, 3 July 1956.

[21] Ibid., 3 (evening) July 1956.

[22] Shūgiin, *Gaimu iinkaigiroku*, vol. 24, no. 58 (9 July 1956), p. 9.

[23] Shūgiin, *Gaimu-Naikaku-Hōmu iinkai rengōshinsakaigiroku*, vol. 24, no. 2 (13 July 1956), p. 6.

[24] For the debate on this point in academic circles see the articles by Professors Yokota Kisaburō and Taoka Ryōichi in *Asahi*, 30 June, 2 July 1956. For a review of this subject see Kotani Tsuruji, 'Gaikō hogoken', *Kokusaihō Gaikō Zasshi*, vol. 56, no. 4 & 5 (February 1958), pp. 101-19.

[25] For an elaboration of the theory that the Japanese government has rights of protection over Okinawans see the article by *Hōmushō* official, Hiraga Kenta, 'Okinawa oyobi Okinawa tōmin no chii', ibid., vol. 54, no. 6 (December 1955), pp. 1-26.

[26] USCAR, *Civil Affairs Activities in the Ryukyu Islands*, vol. 8, no. 2, pp. 43-4.

[27] *Okinawa Nenkan*, 1960, pp. 20-33. For the critical comments of the Japan Bar Association, see Nihon Bengoshi Rengōkai, *Okinawa shihōseido no kenkyū*, pp. 173-83.

[28] *Asahi*, 17 July 1959.

[29] Ibid., 3, 20 July, 5 August 1959.

[30] USCAR, op. cit., vol. 8, no. 1, pp. 21-2. For later developments see *Asahi*, 15 October 1964.

[31] *Asahi*, 27 July 1962.

[32] Ibid., 8, 13 September 1962.

[33] Ibid, 13 (evening) September 1962.

[34] Ibid., 2 (evening) November 1962.

[35] It is noteworthy that a high-ranking official of the *Sōrifu* attended when the Japanese proposal was put forward: *Okinawa Taimusu*, 31 March, 3 April 1963.

[36] Ibid., 13 August 1963.

[37] Ibid.

[38] U.S. Department of State, *Bulletin*, 11 May 1964, p. 755.

[39] *Asahi*, 26 April, 16 May 1963.

[40] *Okinawa Taimusu*, 17 October 1963.

[41] *Asahi*, 21 (evening) January, 13 (evening) February 1964.

[42] Ibid., 14 (evening) February 1964.

[43] The Owinawan press usually shows great interest in the appointment of the *Sōrifu*'s Director-General when the Japanese Cabinet is being formed. See also the editorial of the *Okinawa Taimusu*, 14 August 1963.

[44] According to the *Asahi*, 1 June 1969, this 'team' is composed of Shimoda Takezō (Amassador to the United States), Tanaka Hiroto (Special Ambassador for the Okinawa Problem), Mori Haruki (Deputy Undersecretary for Foreign Affairs), Tōgō Fumihiko (head of the United States Bureau) and Satō Shōji (head of the Treaty Bureau). They were all engaged in the negotiations for the revision of the Security Treaty in 1960, and now in those for Okinawa's return.

[45] Some of the government and Party leaders, including Vice-Chief Cabinet Secretary Kimura Toshio, are reportedly displeased with the position taken by the *Gaimushō* officials who emphasize the diplomatic considerations at the expense of the domestic ones. See, e.g. Kasumi Sekio, 'Henkan hōshiki o meguru kommei to kattō', *Asahi Jānaru*, 4 May 1969, pp. 14-18.

7   The Diet

[1] A Cabinet-Party Liaison Meeting is attended by the Prime Minister and several important Ministers on the Cabinet side and three principal officials on the Party side. Meetings are held sometimes regularly, say once a week,

and sometimes *ad hoc*. An example of the important role played by this informal institution in the field of foreign policies is provided by the vigorous participation of Party officials in making decisions for the revision of the U.S.-Japan Security Treaty in 1958-60 (*Asahi*, 18, 19 July, 5 December 1958).

[2] The name of this party at the time of the ratification of the treaties was the National Democratic Party (*Kokumin Minshutō*). Soon after it was renamed as Progressive Party (*Kaishintō*). For the sake of simplicity, we shall call both of them the Democrats.

[3] Of the total ten Members from Kagoshima, all Liberals except one Democrat, only two voted for the Peace Treaty and eight abstained; three voted for the Security Treaty and seven abstained.

[4] Shūgiin, *Heiwa jōyaku oyobi nichibei anzenhoshō jōyaku tokubetsu iinkaigiroku*, and its counterpart of the Sangiin (hereunder referred to, e.g., as Shūgiin, *Heiwa jōyaku iinkaigiroku*).

[5] Satake Haruki (Shakai Kakushintō): Shūgiin, *Heiwa jōyaku iinkaigiroku*, no. 8 (24 October 1951), pp. 5-7.

[6] Horiki Kenzō (Daiichi Kurabu): Sangiin, *Heiwa jōyaku iinkaigiroku*, no. 10 (5 November 1951), pp. 22-3; Nagai Junichirō (Daiichi Kurabu): ibid., pp. 20-2.

[7] Yoshida Shigeru (Prime Minister): Sangiin, *Honkaigiroku,* vol. 22, no. 3 (12 October 1951), p. 12.

[8] Nishimura Kumao (head of the Treaty Bureau): Sangiin, *Heiwa jōyaku iinkaigiroku*, no. 10 (5 November 1951), pp. 14-15.

[9] Kusaba Ryūen (Parliamentary Undersecretary for Foreign Affairs): ibid., p. 13.

[10] See, e.g., Nishimura Kumao: ibid., p. 17.

[11] Sone Eki (Socialist): ibid., no. 5 (22 October 1951), p. 6.

[12] Ashida Hitoshi (Democrat): Shūgiin, op. cit., no. 3 (18 October 1951), p. 14.

[13] Party affiliation of those who took part in the debate on Article 3 of the Japanese Peace Treaty in the Special Committee was as follows: three Liberals, four Democrats, one Socialist, two Communists and two others in the Lower House; one Liberal, one Democrat, three Socialists, one *Rōnōtō* man, one Communist and four *Daiichi Kurabu* men in the Upper House.

[14] Satake Haruki: Shūgiin, op. cit., no. 9 (25 October 1951), p. 12.

[15] Shūgiin and Sangiin, *Gikaiseido shichijūnen shi: kokkai gian kemmeiroku*, pp. 655-729.

[16] *Asahi*, 11, 13 (morning and evening), 14, 16, 17 February, 7, 9 (evening) March 1962.

[17] For a similar pattern of political manœuvring in local assemblies see [Jiyū Minshutō Soshiki Iinkai], 'Okinawa shiseiken kaifuku ni kansuru toriatsukai—hoppō ryōdo mondai to karamete', *Soshiki Jōhō*, no. 134 (10 August 1963), p. 1; [Nihon Shakaitō Kokuminundō Iinkai], 'Tōmen no Okinawa sokuji henkan yōkyū tōsō ni tsuite', *Shakai Tsūshin*, no. 360 (20 April 1962), p. 1.

[18] In the Japanese parliamentary system, each Standing Committee corresponds to a particular department of the government, e.g., Committee on the Cabinet *v.* Cabinet (including Prime Minister's Office), Committee on Judicial Affairs *v.* Ministry of Justice, Committee on Foreign Affairs *v.* Ministry of Foreign Affairs and so on. There are sixteen Standing Committees in each House, apart from several *ad hoc* committees.

[19] This is perhaps partly due to the overload of work on the Committee on the Cabinet which is in charge of, among other things, matters related to the Defence Agency and the Procurement Agency. This means that the Committee on the Cabinet is practically serving as a Committee on Defence.

[20] It is quite common for a Committee to hold meetings after the term of the House ends. Those meetings which were held after the term of the 24th session (i.e. 3 June 1956) and before the term of the 25th session (i.e. 12 November 1956) were counted in the 24th session. The same applies to the other sessions.

[21] The small share of the House of Councillors in the 24th session is mainly due to the fact that after the closing of that session the elections for half of the Members of that House took place and, therefore, only the Committees in the House of Representatives were in action in the subsequent period during which the Okinawa problem came up for discussion.

[22] An interesting account of the political process of the compilation of the budget for the fiscal year of 1966 is given in Nishida Makoto, 'Yosan kettei no uchimaku', *Chūō Kōron*, March 1966, pp. 140-51.

[23] For an early example of the Socialist proposal for this, see [Nihon Shakaitō], 'Shōwa sanjūsannendo dai ikkai chūōiinkai tōmu hōkokusho (mimeo), p. 102.

[24] See *Asahi*, 12 February, 10 (evening) March 1966.

[25] For a brief account of the background of the establishment of the Committee and its early activities, see *Okinawa Nenkan*, 1968, p. 93.

[26] Shūgiin and Sangiin, *Gikaiseido shichijūnen shi: shiryōhen*, pp. 281-2 and 285-7.

[27] The dates were as follows: 21 April 1961, 13 February 1962, 31 January 1964, 11 February 1966, 28 April 1967 and 2 February 1968.

[28] A public opinion survey conducted by a leading local newspaper in February-March 1968 shows that 75.4 per cent of those who were interviewed favoured Okinawan representation in the Japanese Diet while only 1.2 per cent opposed it; the remaining 23.4 per cent were undecided. As to the status of Okinawan representatives, 45.3 per cent insisted on full membership as against 23.8 per cent who viewed the matter with tolerance; the remaining 30.9 per cent were undecided. See Ryūkyū Shimpōsha *Owinawa no seron: dai sankai zenryū seron chōsa*, pp. 31-3.

[29] Japanese coined the words 'senzai giseki' (lit. latent seats) to refer to parliamentary seats promised to Okinawan representatives but not actually realized while the island remains under American rule. These words were formed on the analogy of the words *senzai shuken* or latent sovereignty of Japan over the Ryukyus.

[30] *Asahi*, 13 July 1967.

[31] See, e.g., an editorial comment on the agreement in *Asahi*, 11 October 1968.

[32] Ibid., 14 April, 6 August 1969.

8 Political Parties (1945-55)

[1] On the role of political parties in the making of policy in post-war Japanese politics, see: Oka Yoshitatsu, 'Seitō to seitōseiji' in Oka Yoshitake (ed.), *Gendai Nihon no seijikatei*, pp. 69-109; Masumi Junnosuke and R. A. Scalapino, *Parties and Politics in Contemporary Japan*; N. B. Thayer, *How the Conservatives Rule Japan*; Fukui Haruhiro, *Jiyū Minshutō to seisaku kettei*; Iwanaga Kenkichirō, 'Sengo Nihon no seitō to gaikō', *Tōkyō Daigaku Kyōyōgakubu Shakaikagaku Kiyō*, nos. 12-14 (May 1963-March 1965).

[2] For an analysis of the role taken by Yoshida in post-war diplomacy (especially in the conclusion of the Japanese Peace Treaty), see Kōsaka Masataka, 'Saishō Yoshida Shigeru ron', *Chūō Kōron*, February 1964, pp. 76-111.

[3] The term 'shirōto gaikō' (amateur diplomacy) was coined by some journalists in reference to foreign policy conducted under the leadership of a Minister of Foreign Affairs who is not a career diplomat. The appointment

of Kishi Nobusuke as Foreign Minister of the Ishibashi Cabinet provided the first post-war example of this.

[4] The Japan Liberal Party changed its name into the Democratic Liberal Party in March 1948 when it absorbed Shidehara Kijūrō and his group who seceded from the Democratic Party. In March 1950 another group led by Inukai Ken left the Democratic Party to join the DLP, which now renamed itself the Liberal Party. Despite the changes in name, leadership of the party rested constantly with Yoshida. This section will treat these parties *en masse* under the name of the Liberals.

[5] *Asahi*, 22 December 1949.

[6] Comment by a State Department official on the Diet's debate about the Yalta Agreement quoted in ibid., 28 December 1949.

[7] Ibid., 29 January 1950.

[8] Ibid., 27 June 1950.

[9] Ibid., 29 and 31 January 1951.

[10] Ibid., 2 February 1951. On the position of the Liberals on the territorial questions a writer said, 'So far as geographical questions were concerned, the Liberal Party advocated the reinstatement of island territories placed under Japanese jurisdiction after the Sino-Japanese war of 1894-95.' Cf. Baron Lewe Van Aduard, *Japan: From Surrender to Peace*, p. 174. This statement misrepresents the facts. If 'after' was replaced by 'before', it would become more plausible, although no evidence is available to show that the Liberals presented their policy in such a wording.

[11] *Asahi*, 2 February 1951.

[12] See Hatoyama Ichirō, *Kaikoroku*, pp. 85-92.

[13] In referring to the Democrats, not only *Kokumin Minshutō* (National Democratic Party) but also its predecessors, *Nihon Shimpotō* (Japan Progressive Party) and *Minshutō* (Democratic Party) and its successor, *Kaishintō* (Reform Party), will be discussed *en bloc*.

[14] Masumi and Scalapino, op. cit., take the former view. For the opposite view, see Noguchi Hachirō and Hirasawa Saburō, 'Shimpotō no kiso to seisaku', *Zenei* (JCP's organ), 15 March 1946, p. 16.

[15] See the National Democratic Party's Convention of January 1951 quoted in *Asahi*, 21 January 1951.

[16] For information on the work of the Committee, see ibid., 15, 16 June, 27 September 1950.

[17] Ibid., 6 October 1950.

[18] Ibid., 27 January 1951. According to an observer, the Democrats suggested a ten-year trusteeship; see, Mori Shōzō, *Sengo fūunroku*, p. 204.

[19] Ibid., 1 February 1951.

[20] For a description of the Kitamura group and its place in the Party, see Watanabe Tsuneo, *Habatsu: hoshutō no kaibō*, pp. 201-9.

[21] *Asahi*, 9 October 1951.

[22] See Table 6, p. 97.

[23] Miyamoto Yoshio, *Shin hoshutō shi*, p. 182. It is noteworthy that Karafuto was added to the list of areas the Party wanted to recover.

[24] *Asahi*, 5 (evening) December 1952.

[25] Ibid., 18 (evening) January 1954.

[26] The non-partisan *Asahi* expressed in its column, *tensei jingo*, strong support for the Democrats' position on this matter, saying that the Party's position on Okinawa reflected the feeling of most of the Japanese people (ibid., 21 July 1951).

[27] See the policy statement entitled 'Kōwamondai ni kansuru ippanteki taido', in *Shakai Shimbun* (organ of the JSP), 10 December 1949. For background, see J. A. A. Stockwin, *The Japanese Socialist Party and Neutralism*.

[28] What was meant by this was that having Okinawa and Ogasawara under Japanese rule would facilitate a solution for Japan's population problem (Suzuki's statement to reporters after his interview with Dulles: *Asahi*,

2 February 1951). This is one of the few attempts to justify Japan's desire for Okinawa and Ogasawara from the standpoint of economic necessity for Japan.

[29] 'Kōwajōyaku no naiyō ni taisuru wagatō no taido' (also referred to as 'Kōwajōyaku e no yōbō'), *Shakai Shimbun*, 25 September 1950.

[30] Ibid., 15 February 1951.

[31] A proposal put forward by Nomizo Masaru (a left-wing leader) included the most forthright statement on the territorial problem: 'The Party seems to have some hesitation in asserting Japan's rights to Karafuto and Chishima out of deference to the Soviet Union despite its endeavour to dissociate itself from the JCP . . . Japan should oppose any and all oppressive international treaties that have been concluded about Japan prior to the conclusion of a peace treaty with her. From this viewpoint, we should demand that those countries concerned should make restitution of such territories as Okinawa, Ogasawara, Chishima and the southern half of Karafuto to Japan' (Ōhara Shakaimondai Kenkyūjo, *Nihon Rōdō Nenkan* 1953, pp. 556-9). A left-wing member of the party, Mutō Unjūrō, wrote that in the circumstances which had emerged since the end of the war Japan could hope for modification of the Potsdam Declaration so that she could claim not only the southern half of Karafuto but also Taiwan (see Mutō Unjūrō, 'Zemmenkōwa no hōritsuteki kiso', *Jōhō Tsūshin*, 1 July 1950, pp. 22-3). These are examples of a strong nationalistic bent shown by some members of the left-wing Socialists despite the Party's official line.

[32] Sone Eki, 'Daresu-shi ni kaku yōseisuru; iwayuru Sone shian', ibid., 15 April 1951, pp. 3-10.

[33] See slogans for the October 1952 election (adopted at the August 1952 Convention of the right-wing Socialist Party) in *Nihon Rōdō Nenkan*, 1954, p. 673; also 'Gaikōmondai taisaku', *Jōhō Tsūshin*, 1 July 1952, p. 3; and 'MSA-enjo ni taisuru wagatō no taido', ibid., 25 May 1953, p. 6.

[34] 'Fubyōdōjōyaku gyōseikyōtei no kompontekikaisei no tassei kokuminundō ni kansuru enzetsushiryō', ibid., 5 June 1953, pp. 7-8. The April 1953 elections for both Houses of the Diet changed the balance of power between the right-wing and the left-wing Socialists in favour of the latter:

	right-wing	left-wing
Lower House before the election	60	56
after the election	66	72
Upper House before the election	31	31
after the election	26	40

[35] See, e.g., the debate at the January 1952 Party (left-wing) convention, described by Sasada Shigeru, *Nihon Shakaitō*, vol. 1, pp. 219-20.

[36] '1954-nendo undō hōshinsho sōan' (mimeo, January 1954), part 4, p. 4. The Party's Action Policy for 1953 advocated withdrawal of military facilities from the Soviet-occupied islands in the north as well as from the American-controlled islands in the south. See '1953-nendo undō hōshinsho', in *Tōkatsudō*, 10 February 1953, p. 7.

[37] See material prepared by the Unification Committee in *Jōhō Tsūshin*, 5 December 1953, p. 3.

[38] The left-wing Socialists took the position that their demand for the return of the Soviet-occupied islands of Japan was conditional on the American-held islands being returned first. See 'Dai jūyonkai teiki taikai gian' (mimeo, 19-20 September 1955), p. 5.

[39] *Jōhō Tsūshin*, 15 January 1955, p. 2.

[40] *Akahata*, 6 March 1946.

[41] Tokuda Kyūichi, Secretary-General of the JCP, in his interview for the magazine *Seinen Okinawa* (organ of the *Okinawa Seinen Dōmei*, a youth organization of the *Okinawajin Remmei*; see above), criticized Ashida's statement. Katō Kanjū, a Socialist Member of the House of Represen-

tatives, also accused Ashida of violating the Potsdam Declaration in a speech in the Diet (*Asahi*, 3 July 1947).

[42] It must be pointed out, however, that the Japanese Communists had not yet definitely committed themselves to support the Soviet claim for Chishima and Karafuto by that time. For example, the Party's policy concerning Peace Treaty issue (adopted by its central committee on 26 August 1948) demanded the return of 'those islands which ethnically and historically can be regarded as belonging to Japan' (*Akahata*, 1 September 1948). One can see no distinction between this and the position taken by the Democrats. For the criticism levelled later by a pro-Soviet faction at the 'nationalistic deviation' of the Party leadership, see Nihon Kyōsantō Chūōiinkai Gojūnenmondai Bunkenshiryō Hensaniinkai, *Nihon Kyōsantō gojūnenmondai shiryōshū*, vol. 3, pp. 218, 222.

[43] In connection with this, one may remember the Comintern's theses on the national and colonial question adopted by its second congress (28 July 1920) which said in reference to this point: 'For the bourgeoisie, the desire to re-establish national unity, to "re-unite with the ceded parts of the country", is nothing but an attempt of the defeated to assemble forces for new wars. The reunification of nations artificially torn apart is also in accordance with the interests of the proletariat; but the proletariat can attain genuine national freedom and unity only by means of revolutionary struggle and after the downfall of the bourgeoisie'. See J. Degras (ed.), *The Communist International: 1919-1943: Documents*, vol. 1, p. 140. A Japanese translation of these theses appeared in the June 1950 issue of *Zenei*. It is not unlikely that this influenced the Japanese Communists' thinking about Okinawa.

[44] Tokuda described the pre-war status of Okinawa as 'semi-colonial' and argued that Okinawa should now become an 'autonomous republic'. See his interview for the magazine *Seinen Okinawa*, cited above.

[45] For the social background of the Communist leader, see Rironsha (ed.), *Tokuda Kyūichi den*, pp. 39-87. Recently, a renowned Communist writer wrote an essay criticizing the style of leadership of the JCP; he said that, in effect, the leadership of Tokuda in the JCP's Okinawa policy in the early post-war period over-represented his personal views at the expense of the interests of the Party (or the working class) as a whole. See Nakano Shigeharu, 'Rōdōshateki to karayō', *Sekai*, May 1965, p. 215.

[46] Observer, 'Concerning the Situation in Japan', *For a Lasting Peace, For a People's Democracy*, 6 January 1950. This article also illustrated U.S. Okinawa policy as an 'aggressive policy', referring to MacArthur's interview with a correspondent of the London *Daily Mail*, 2 March 1949; MacArthur was quoted as having said, 'On Okinawa I have laid out 25 airfields, capable of ensuring 3,500 flights daily by our heaviest bombers . . . The Pacific is now an Anglo-Saxon lake'.

[47] See comment by Kamiyama Shigeo, Communist Member of the House of Representatives, on Hoshijima's speech at the Diet (*Asahi*, 29 January 1950).

[48] See, e.g., the Party's document entitled 'Tōmen no shōsū minzoku taisaku' (March 1951), quoted in Nikkan Rōdō Tsūshinsha (comp.), *Sengo Nihon kyōsanshugi undō*, p. 728. Also Takayasu Shigemasa, 'Okinawa Ogasawara henkan no kokumin undō ni tsuite', *Zenei*, February 1956, p. 23.

[49] See 'Tōmen no shōsū minzoku taisaku', cited above. Also Daidōji Shigeru 'Heiwa to dokuritsu no zemmen kōwa e', *Zenei*, January 1951, p. 4. The later argued that the political status of Okinawa and Ogasawara should be determined by the Four Powers (the United States, the Soviet Union, Great Britain and China) Foreign Ministers' Council, and that it would violate the Cairo Proclamation for one of the Allied powers to seize these islands under the pretext of a U.N. trusteeship.

[50] Takayasu, op. cit., p. 24.
[51] Ibid., p. 23. See also the same author's 'Okinawa kaihō to minzokumondai', *Zenei*, April 1957, p. 39.
[52] For German attitudes towards the territorial, particularly the Saar, question, see J. Freymond, *The Saar Conflict 1945-1955*, p. 238. For the Italian position on territorial and colonial questions after World War II, see N. Kogan, *Italy and the Allies*, pp. 132, 135, 163-8.

9   Political Parties (after 1955)

[1] For the process of formation of the new conservative party, see Miyamoto Yoshio, *Shin hoshutō shi*, chapter 9; Tamiya Eitarō, *Hatoyama būmu no butaiura*, chapters 6-7.
[2] [Nihon Minshutō], 'Seisaku taikō' (24 November 1954) cited in Miyamoto, op. cit., pp. 370-3. Among their slogans, two proposals deserve special attention: The establishment of a self-reliant defence force and revision of the Security Treaty on the basis of mutual co-operation.
[3] [Nihon Minshutō], 'Jishu heiwa gaikō seisaku' (4 January 1955), cited in *Asahi*, 5 January 1955. Incidentally, this document is significant because it made public for the first time the Party's positive attitude for diplomatic normalization with the Soviet Union and the People's Republic of China.
[4] See Miyamoto, op. cit., pp. 395-6.
[5] There were two intra-party groups which were opposed to Hatoyama's diplomacy *vis-à-vis* the Soviet Union. One was a group led by Ashida, chairman of the Research Council for Foreign Affairs of the LDP, widely believed to be behind the Foreign Minister Shigemitsu. Another was composed of those politicians who came from the former Liberal Party who were commonly called the Yoshida faction. In the last stage of the normalization of relations with the Soviet Union, these two groups, together with other groups led by Ishii Mitsujirō and Kishi Nobusuke, formed an association, called *Jikyoku kondankai*, opposing Hatoyama's visit to Moscow. (Kishi later withdrew from this association.) A list of the members of the *Jikyoku kondankai* is in Watanabe Tsuneo, *Habatsu*, pp. 24-6. See also Kawamura Kinji *et al.*, *Gaimushō*, pp. 38, 44; Yoshimoto Yuzuru, *Kishi Nobusuke den*, pp. 259-60.
[6] Shigemitsu at a press conference on 25 December 1953, cited in *Asahi*, 25 (evening) December 1953.
[7] Ibid., 20 (evening), 26 (evening) June 1956. Those attending these meetings included Kishi. The Permanent Undersecretary for Foreign Affairs, Kadowaki Suemitsu, attended one of these meetings to report on the Okinawa situation.
[8] Ishii Kanichi, 'Okinawa tochimondai ni tsuite', *Seisaku Geppō* (organ of the LDP), August 1956, pp. 88-9.
[9] *Asahi*, 18 July 1956; also Ishii, op cit.
[10] *Asahi*, 27 June 1956. According to the Party regulations (article 45), an *ad hoc* investigating committee *(tokubetsu chōsa iinkai)* is set up, when necessary, by the Policy Deliberation Council *(seimu chōsakai)* and works under the supervision of the chairman of the Council. The LDP Okinawa Committee was such a committee; it had three vice-chairmen: Fuchigami Fusatarō, Tokonami Tokuji and Itō Ryūji. The problem of recruitment of the Committee members will be discussed later.
[11] *Asahi*, 27 July 1956.
[12] Ibid., 1 (evening) August 1956. Also [Jiyū-Minshutō] 'Tōmen no Okinawa mondai ni kansuru taisaku', ibid., 3 August 1956. A slightly different version of this policy is given in Ishii, op. cit., p. 89.
[13] *Asahi*, 26 (evening) June and 28 (evening) October 1956.
[14] Ibid., 26 July 1958.

[15] See the so-called 'Takaoka Report' written by Takaoka Daisuke, a member of the LDP Okinawa Committee and head of the Diet delegation to Okinawa of March 1957, quoted in *Asahi*, 3 April 1957. It also appeared in *Kikan Okinawa to Ogasawara* (organ of the *Nampō Dōhō Engokai*), March 1957, pp. 6-10.

[16] Okada Tadao, *Seiji no uchimaku*, pp. 23-7.

[17] *Asahi*, 6 October 1958.

[18] For the decision made at a joint meeting of the JSP's Policy Deliberation Council and the International Affairs Bureau, see *Asahi*, 12 October 1958. See also the debates in the Lower House Cabinet Committee on 23 October 1958 and the Lower House Budget Committee on 30 October 1958.

[19] For the position taken by the Miki-Matsumura faction on this subject, see *Asahi*, 25 (evening) November 1958.

[20] Ibid., 3 (evening), 4 December 1958.

[21] Ibid. Ikeda Hayato and Satō Eisaku were believed to have supported Kōno on this point (*Nihon Keizai*, 5 December 1958).

[22] For opinions of the Kōno faction on this point, see *Asahi*, 6 September 1959.

[23] Text of the agreed minute on Okinawa in U.S. Department of State, *Bulletin*, 19 January 1960, p. 185.

[24] There were no regular political channels between Tokyo and Naha other than sporadic visits of GRI officials to Tokyo and of Japanese officials to Naha. (GRI's office in Tokyo and the office of the Japanese government at Naha deal only with non-political matters.) With the exception of Chief Executive Ōta Seisaku who frequently visited Tokyo, top-level contacts had been rare.

[25] *Asahi*, 5 July 1956.

[26] So the Action Policy of the JSP for the latter half of 1956 explained. See ibid., 25 (evening) July 1956.

[27] These figures show the relative strength of the right and the left in the JSP Okinawa Committee.

Date	Chairman	Vice-Chairmen	Right-Left Ratio
July 1956	Asanuma Inajirō (R)	Sata Tadataka (L)	9 *v.* 6
		Sone Eki (R)	
February 1957	Satake Haruki (R)	Shima Kiyoshi (R)	6 *v.* 6
		Furuya Sadao (L)	
June 1958	Nakamura Kōichi (R)	Morimoto Yasushi (L)	not available
September 1959	Akaji Yūzō (L)	Morinaka Moriyoshi (L)	not available

The criterion adopted here for determining whether a certain member is right or left is his membership *prior to* the unification of 1955. Some of those who are classified as 'right' (e.g. Asanuma and Nakamura) moved afterwards towards the left.

[28] *Asahi*, 12 April 1958.

[29] 'Heiwaundō no genjō to kadai—Tōitsugo no Nihon Shakaitō no kenkyū', *Shakaishugi*, January 1958, pp. 54-61. Also Ioka Daiji, 'Kokuminundō no tenkai no tameni!', *Gekkan Shakaitō*, July 1958, pp. 52-8.

Notes (Chapter 9)

[30] [Nihon Shakaitō], 'Dai jūrokkai teiki taikai gian' (mimeo, 12-15 September 1959), pp. 103-7.

[31] [Nihon Shakaitō], 'Shōwa sanjūsannendo dai nikai chūōiinkai tōmu hōkokusho' (mimeo, 19-20 January 1959), pp. 78-9.

[32] See, e.g., Nihon Shakaitō Seisaku Shingikai, *Nihon Shakaitō seisaku handobukku*, pp. 67-8.

[33] [Minshu Shakaitō], 'Okinawa shiseiken no sōki henkan o yōkyūsuru— Okinawa shiseiken henkan ni kansuru hōshin', *Seisaku to Tōron*, May 1961, p. 29. For the position of the JSP on this point, see Nihon Shakaitō Seisaku Shingikai, *1962 nendo no shinro—dai nijūikkai tōtaikai ketteishū*, pp. 54-5.

[34] The Socialists were fully aware of the increasing impact of the Communists. See Inamura Toshio, 'Korekara no Okinawa tōsō', *Gekkan Shakaitō*, October 1959, pp. 45-51.

[35] Perhaps for fear of a Russo-Japanese *rapprochement*, Mao Tse-tung expressed, in his interview with a Japanese Socialist Party delegation to Peking on 10 July 1964, China's support for the Japanese demand for the return of Chishima held by the Soviet Union. For Mao's statement and Khrushchev's comment on it, see Dennis J. Doolin, *Territorial Claims in the Sino-Soviet Conflict: Documents and Analysis*, pp. 42-4, 68-72.

[36] [Nihon Kyōsantō], 'Dai kyūkai taikai chūōiinkai hōkoku', *Zenei*, January 1965, p. 40. For the JCP's recent position on the subject, see *Akahata*, 6 March 1969.

[37] For a general account of the political parties in Okinawa, see Higa Mikio, *Politics and Parties in Postwar Okinawa*.

[38] *Asahi*, 2 (evening) August 1960.

[39] According to a newspaper report, the OLDP received some $U.S.30,000 from the *Nikkeiren*, Japan Federation of Employers Associations. Nomura Kichisaburō, former chairman of the LDP Okinawa Committee, exercised his good offices for this: *Okinawa Taimusu*, 26 October 1960.

[40] Ibid., 2 November 1962.

[41] For example, the OLDP sent its representatives to the LDP's national convention in September 1962: *Jijū Minshu*, 30 September 1962.

[42] USCAR, *Press Conference of High Commissioner Albert Watson II*, 17 September 1964, pp. 4-5.

[43] Ōta, graduate of Waseda University; Chief Officer for the Pescadores Islands (*Taiwan Sōtokufu*) at the time of Japan's surrender; legal practitioner 1951-7 at Yatsushiro, Kumamoto; Deputy Chief Executive of the GRI in 1957 and Chief Executive in 1959.

[44] Text of the resolution of 1 February of the Okinawan Legislature is in Nampō Dōhō Engokai, *Okinawa mondai kihon shiryōshū*, pp. 1081-2.

[45] *Asahi*, 4, 8 February 1962.

[46] See, e.g., the views expressed by Nagamine Akio, Speaker of the Okinawan Legislature and leader of the anti-Ōta group, in an interview with the editor of the magazine *Sekai*. Cf. 'Okinawa rippōin-giin ni kiku', *Sekai*, January 1965, p. 200.

[47] *Shakai Tsūshin*, 20 April 1957, pp. 11-14.

[48] Nihon Shakaitō, 'Dai jūyonkai teiki taikai tōmu hōkokusho' (mimeo, 24-26 February 1958), part 2, p. 51.

[49] For example, two representatives from Okinawa attended the national convention of the JSP in February 1964: *Okinawa Taimusu*, 23 February 1964.

[50] Chibana Hideo, chairman of the Policy Deliberation Council of the OSMP, expressed this opinion in an interview with the editor of the *Sekai*. 'Okinawa rippōin-giin ni kiku', *Sekai*, January 1965, pp. 203-4.

[51] For the American authorities' failure to establish the connection of the OPP with the JCP, see Higa, op. cit., p. 172.

[52] Furugen Sanekichi, an OPP Member of the Legislature, made this point clear in an interview with the editor of the *Sekai*. 'Okinawa rippōin-giin ni kiku', *Sekai*, January 1965, pp. 204-5.

[53] *Asahi*, 20 July 1965, 22 (evening) July 1969. The results of the Naha city assembly elections of 1969 were as follows (figures in brackets show the result of the 1965 elections): Liberal-Democrats 5 (15); Socialist Masses 6 (2); People's 5 (4); Kōmeitō 5 (4); Independent 9 (5). The Socialists gained no seats in either election.

[54] A 1967 opinion survey revealed that those who support a particular Okinawan party do not necessarily support its supposed counterpart in Japan proper.

	LDP	DSP	JSP	JCP	Kōmei	Others	No answer	(per cent)
OLDP	46.7	4.5	4.4	0	1.2	17.9	25.2	23.2
OSMP	5.0	8.6	41.6	0	2.2	10.8	31.6	20.7
OSP	0	4.2	54.2	12.5	4.2	4.2	16.7	2.3
OPP	2.4	9.8	29.3	7.3	4.9	22.0	24.4	3.9
Others	2.5	–	2.5	–	13.9	–	–	7.5
No answer	5.8	1.1	2.5	1.3	1.6	–	–	42.4
(per cent)	14.7	3.8	13.2	0.4	2.7	15.6	49.6	100.0

It is noteworthy that as many as 41.6 per cent of the OSMP supporters showed their preference for the JSP and that the OPP supporters gave a variety of answers on their liking for Japanese parties. Ryūkyū Shimpōsha, *Okinawa no seron: dai ikkai zenryū seron chōsa* (Naha, August 1967), pp. 50-9. Slightly different but basically similar results came from a later survey conducted jointly by the Ryūkyū Shimpōsha and the *Mainichi* (see *Mainichi*, 15 May 1969).

[55] See the Party's campaign pledges for the Upper House elections on July 1968, *Asahi*, 14 June 1968.

[56] Kaya Okinori, 'Okinawa shiseiken henkan ni taisuru shoken' (13 October 1967), cited in *Chūō Kōron*, December 1967, pp. 179-80.

[57] Quoted in *Asahi*, 5 September 1967.

[58] Miki's statement is in *Asahi*, 19 November 1968.

[59] *Asahi*, 10 April 1969.

[60] For the Socialist view, see Nihon Shakaitō Kyōsenkyoku and Kokuminundōkyoku, *Okinawa: sokuji zemmen henkan e no Shakaitō no shuchō*; for the Communist position see, e.g., Nihon Kyōsantō Chūōiinkai Shuppambu, *Okinawa Ogasawara mondai to Nihon Kyōsantō*.

[61] For the Democratic Socialist view, see Minshu Shakaitō 'Okinawa Ogasawara no shiseiken henkan hōshin' (23 August 1967); for the Kōmeitō's position, see Kōmeitō, 'Okinawa hondo fukki e no michi' (24 August 1967); both in *Chūō Kōron*, op. cit., pp. 182-3.

10 Individuals and Groups

[1] The breakdown was as follows: those who had been evacuated mainly to Kyūshū district during the war, 50,000; youth volunteer corps and drafted workers, 20,000; evacuees from the Mandated Islands in the Pacific and other areas, 30,000; permanent residents, 50,000. The permanent residents consisted only of those living in Kantō district. If those in the other

districts were included, the total obviously would have exceeded 150,000. *Asahi Nenkan,* 1946, p. 282.

[2] See the sixth instalment of the serial story of post-war Okinawa entitled 'Okinawa no shōgen', *Okinawa Taimusu,* 28 July 1968.

[3] Okinawa Asahi Shimbunsha, *Okinawa Taikan,* p. 290.

[4] Nakayoshi Yoshimitsu, b. 1888, Shuri, Okinawa; Waseda University (grad. 1912); journalist for the *Tōkyō Nichinichi Shimbun* 1912-40 (during which period two years in the United States); mayor of Shuri 1940-5; appointed as the mayor by the U.S. military government 1945, left Okinawa July 1946; chairman of the *Okinawashotō Nihon Fukki Kiseikai* (Tokyo) since 1946.

[5] Nakayoshi Yoshimitsu, *Okinawa sokokufukki undōki,* pp. 13-17.

[6] Ibid., p. 18. The original members of the *Kiseikai* included Baron Ie Chōsuke; Higashionna Kanjun, professor of history at the Takushoku University; Kamiyama Masayoshi, ex-civil servant for the *Ōkurashō.*

[7] Nakayoshi, op. cit., p. 19; also Kamiyama Masayoshi (comp.), *Nempyō: Okinawa mondai to zaikyō kenjin no ugoki (1868-1966),* p. 27.

[8] Isa Hideo, *Ozaki Yukio den,* pp. 1304-6.

[9] Nishime Junji, '[Nakayoshi-shi no] Fukkiundō kaisōki o yonde', in *Okinawa Taimusu,* 17 (evening) March 1964. The author, at present president of the Okinawa Liberal Democratic Party, was a leader of Okinawan students in Japan in the early post-war period.

[10] *Jiyū Okinawa* (organ of the Okinawan Federation), 25 August 1946, p. 2.

[11] Nakayoshi, op. cit., pp. 23-4.

[12] Kamiyama, op. cit., pp. 39-40.

[13] Nakayoshi, op. cit., p. 28.

[14] The resolution on Amami-Ōshima of November 1952, for instance, was sponsored by Representatives from Kagoshima. See *Asahi,* 1 (evening) November 1952. For a study of pressure activities of groups concerned with the 'northern islands', see Kuwabara Terumichi, 'Hoppō ryōdo no henkan yōkyū undō', *Kokusaihō Gaikō Zasshi,* March 1962, pp. 429-74.

[15] Kamiyama, op. cit., p. 42.

[16] The JCLU was founded in November 1947 with the assistance of Roger N. Baldwin who was a legal adviser on human rights problems to the Occupation authorities. It had Unno Shinkichi as chairman and some 3,000 members at the time of this event (*Asahi,* 13 January 1955, 22 August 1959).

[17] For a general description of the activities of the American Civil Liberties Union, see 'Private Attorneys-General: group action in the fight for civil liberties', *Yale Law Journal,* March 1949, pp. 574-81. See also H. Lasswell, *National Security and Individual Freedom,* p. 180.

[18] Baldwin's letter to Unno of 3 March 1954, cited in Okinawa Kaihō Sokoku Fukki Sokushin Kondankai, *Okinawa: sono kaihō wa Nihon no dokuritsu o kanseisuru,* p. 150.

[19] Text of the report in *Asahi,* 13 January 1955, as well as in *Hōritsu Jihō,* March 1955, pp. 60-3.

[20] Unno Shinkichi *et al.,* 'Okinawa o meguru hōritsu mondai', *Hōritsu Jihō,* March 1955, pp. 45-49.

[21] Ushiomi Toshitaka, professor of sociology of law at the University of Tokyo, made a report on the Okinawa problem at this conference (*Asahi,* 26 January 1955). See also Ushiomi, 'Indo to Chūgoku no tabi: Ajiya hōritsuka kaigi dayori', *Hōritsu Jihō,* April 1955, pp. 57-63.

[22] *Asahi,* 10 April 1955. The *Okinawa Sokoku Fukki Sokushin Kyōgikai* (Council for the Promotion of the Return of Okinawa to the Fatherland) was formed in Tokyo on 22 November 1953: Kamiyama, op. cit., p. 43.

[23] *Asahi,* 25 (evening) April 1955.

[24] These were Japan Council of Youth Organizations, National Federation of Parents and Teachers Associations, Federation of Regional Women's

Societies, All-Japan Buddhists' Association, and Central Agricultural Association. They were more or less under Socialist influence.

²⁵ Ishii Kanichi, 'Okinawa tochimondai ni tsuite', *Seisaku Geppō*, August 1956, pp. 88-9.

²⁶ *Asahi*, 3, 4 July 1956.

²⁷ For a brief account of its origins, see Okinawa Mondai Kaiketsu Kokumin Sōkekkitaikai Jikkōiinkai, 'Okinawa shiryō' (mimeo, 15 August 1956), series no. 3, pp. 20-6. Its official name was later changed to the Liaison Conference for the National Movement Demanding the Return of Okinawa (*Okinawa Henkan Yōkyū Kokuminundō Renraku Kaigi*).

²⁸ Takayasu Shigemasa, 'Okinawa kaihō to minzoku mondai', *Zenei*, April 1957, pp. 41-2; and 'Nihon no chūritsu to Okinawa dakkan no tatakai', ibid., May 1959, pp. 58-66.

²⁹ For the Senaga affair, see chapter 11.

³⁰ Tōkyō Okinawa Kenjinkai, 'Dai yonkai Tōkyō Okinawa Kenjinkai taikai gian narabini shiryō' (mimeo, 4 October 1959), pp. 73-5. See also Inamura Toshio, 'Korekara no Okinawa tōsō', *Gekkan Shakaitō*, October 1959, pp. 45-51.

³¹ *Okinawa Jijō* (organ of the *Okinawa Henkan Sokushin Jinkai*), 25 March 1962; 25 July 1964; and 5 August 1965. See also Takayasu, 'Shindankai ni kita Okinawa tōsō, *Zenei*, September 1959, pp. 11-16. After the return of Ogasawara to Japan, the word Ogasawara was omitted from the name of the League.

³² Apart from the various associations described in the text, there were some others of which the following two deserve mention. The first was the Association for the Promotion of Okinawa's Liberation and Its Return to the Fatherland (*Okinawa Kaihō Sokoku Fukki Sokushin Kondankai*), an *ad hoc* organization sponsored by Hoashi Kei (a Socialist Member of the Diet) and created for the specific purpose of advocating that the U.N. declaration on the liberation of colonial peoples be applied to Okinawa. The other was the Committee on Okinawa (*Okinawa o Kataru Kai*) which was headed by Ōhama Nobumoto (then president of the Waseda University and chairman of the *Nampō Dōhō Engokai*) and composed of about fifty prominent civic leaders, mostly men of moderate opinions. Ōhama also served as the chairman of the Council of Advisers on the Okinawa Problem (*Okinawa Mondai Kondankai*), an advisory body originally for the Director-General of the *Sōrifu* and then for the Prime Minister.

³³ This is not to say that these Opposition-oriented groups are entirely unconcerned with 'protective' functions. For example, the Society of People from Okinawa Prefecture (*Okinawa Kenjinkai*) is naturally and primarily concerned with the protection of its members' interests. In the given circumstances, however, it also promotes the cause of the return of the island to Japan (i.e. the restoration of the status of a prefecture in Japanese administration) and, in this latter respect, constitutes an important element of the *Okinawa-Ren*.

³⁴ Okinawa-Ken Sokoku Fukki Kyōgikai & Gensuibaku Kinshi Okinawa-Ken Kyōgikai, *Okinawa-Ken sokokufukki undōshi*, pp. 309-12.

³⁵ Their efforts seem to have been not so successful in this respect: a locally conducted opinion survey revealed that only one-quarter of the respondents knew and the remaining three-quarters did not know what day 28 April was. See Ryūkyū Shimpōsha, *Okinawa no seron: dai sankai zenryū seron chōsa*, p. 29.

³⁶ The choice of 15 August (V-J Day) was made perhaps for convenience' sake, although it was officially explained as having a positive significance (e.g. 'struggle against the resurgence of Japanese militarism'). *Okinawa Jijō*, 5 April 1964, pp. 1-4.

³⁷ The movement in Okinawa is not entirely immune from internal disagreements, because the *Fukkikyō* is a federation consisting of many organiza-

tions of different types and of different creeds except for their common concern with the return of Okinawa to Japan. For the difference of opinion among the members of the *Fukkikyō* over the means of presenting their case to the Prime Minister, Satō, during his visit to Okinawa, see *Asahi*, 21 August 1965.

³⁸ An abridged text of this report is in *Okinawa: sono kaihō*, pp. 238-50. The reporter, Miyagawa Hiroo, is a member of the Japan Bar Association.

³⁹ Sakamoto Tokumatsu, 'Dai sankai Ajiya Afurika rentai taikai ni shusseki shite', *Okinawa Jijō*, 25 February 1963, pp. 1-4.

⁴⁰ When a Socialist Member asked in the Diet what connection the U.N. declaration on colonialism had with Okinawa, the Japanese Foreign Minister Kosaka Zentarō denied any connection. In support of Kosaka's view, the acting head of the U.N. Bureau of the *Gaimushō* disclosed a report from the Japanese delegate to the United Nations that the delegate, although not a member of the Drafting Committee of the declaration, let Japan's position on the matter be known to some Committee members, namely that the declaration should be written so as not to convey the impression that it was applicable in such a case as Okinawa. Shūgiin, *Gaimu iinkaigiroku*, vol. 39, no. 9 (27 October 1962), p. 7.

⁴¹ Okinawa took a very prominent place in serious Japanese journalism in the last few years. For example the magazine *Sekai* devoted almost 10 per cent of its space to the problem in 1968. The number of articles (including letters to the editor, columns, etc.) appearing in it for that year was 37; the number of contributors was 75 (including 35 persons who wrote in reply to the editor's questionnaire).

⁴² Maruyama Masao, *Gendai seiji no shisō to kōdō*, vol. 1, p. 163.

⁴³ In the 1962 election for the House of Councillors (national constituency) one candidate from Okinawa won only 0.24 per cent of the total number of votes cast; in the 1965 election for the same House two Okinawan candidates won 0.78 per cent. None of these candidates was successful.

⁴⁴ This is a translation of 'kokuminundō' which has a specific connotation. It is defined by an expert as meaning a 'movement for the realization of the interests in which a highly political issue affecting various sections of the public or a matter of principle is involved as distinguished from sectional interests'. Ishida Takeshi, *Gendai soshiki ron*, p. 213.

11 The Press

¹ Daily circulation of Japanese newspapers in 1963 was 26,548,000 copies in all, of which the *Asahi Shimbun* accounted for 18.5 per cent (4,919,000 copies), the *Yomiuri Shimbun* for 14.6 per cent (3,875,000 copies) and the *Mainichi Shimbun* for 14.4 per cent (3,826,000 copies). The share of these big three came to 47.5 per cent of the total circulation (*Nihon Tōkei Nenkan*, 1963, p. 477; and data provided by the Japan Newspaper Publishers' Association cited in *Asahi Nenkan*, 1964, p. 577). For a brief discussion on some characteristics of Japanese newspapers, see W. Schram, *One Day in the World's Press—Fourteen great newspapers on a day of crisis, November 2, 1956*, pp. 105-6.

² In general, Japanese newspapers describe themselves as independent. Although it is often said that the *Asahi* is more critical of the government than the *Mainichi* and *Yomiuri* are, it is not easy to establish. In fact it is rare for these three newspapers to take a very different position on important political matters or, at any rate, on the Okinawa problem. In the following discussion, therefore, we will refer to the other papers only when they take significantly different attitudes from the *Asahi*.

³ For the purpose of the present study, any newspaper accounts which have bearings on the political status of Okinawa are counted. This means prac-

tically all accounts, because not only political matters in the strict sense but also economic, cultural, educational and any other kind of human activity assume 'political' significance once the relationship between Okinawa and the Japanese mainland is involved. Participation of an Okinawan team in a national athletic meeting is, for example, a subject about which 'patriotic' news stories are often written. When speaking of the increase of information in the press, one must remember that the papers' sizes increased substantially, from a small paper with few pages to a larger one of about sixteen pages supplemented (in the case of the biggest three) by evening editions. In fact, however, this does not make so big a difference as one would expect, because there has been an increase of so-called soft accounts (usually Okinawan news appears on the front or the second page).

⁴ The data contained in Fig. 3 are limited to the Japanese press activities until 1965. Although the comparable figures are not available for all of the more recent period, the tremendous increase of newspaper accounts on Okinawa is obvious. Take for instance July 1969; during that month 113 items (89 news stories, 16 instalments of a serial account, 4 editorials and columns, and 4 letters to the editor) appeared in the *Asahi*. They occupied 2.3 per cent of the total space available for news (i.e. except advertisements). The dominant theme of that month was lethal gas in Okinawa.

⁵ See Okinawa Asahi Shimbunsha, *Okinawa Taikan*, pp. 130-9, 291-6.

⁶ Ibid.

⁷ For example, Kohagura Yasuyoshi, a journalist of Okinawan origin working for *Mainichi Shimbun,* tried to enter Okinawa to report in 1950. He succeeded on the pretext of seeing his family there. Because of this event, however, he was not permitted to enter the island again until recently. Kohagura Yasuyoshi, 'Furusato: Kono mō hitotsu no Okinawa', *Sandei Mainichi* (published weekly by the Mainichi Shimbunsha), 6 February 1966, pp. 92-6.

⁸ See editorials in *Asahi*, 8 April, 17 August, 18 November 1951. Only the *'tensei jingo'* (a popular column in the *Asahi*) expressed its dissatisfaction with the territorial arrangement in the Peace Treaty (21 July 1951).

⁹ Ibid., 28 July 1951.

¹⁰ Ibid., 20 September 1951. Another 6 per cent answered that they were unhappy about the Soviet attitude towards Chishima. These two together with a third group who gave a vague answer that they regretted the loss of territories by Japan (11 per cent) ranked higher than the others.

¹¹ Ibid., 13 January 1955.

¹² One of these exceptions was an account which appeared in the *Akahata* (organ of the Japan Communist Party) immediately before the *Asahi* report (*Akahata*, 30 and 31 December 1954). Another example worthy of mention was 'Okinawa no kinkyō: gunyōchi ni oshidasareru tōmin', in the *Shūkan Asahi* (published weekly by the Asahi Shimbunsha), 12 July 1953.

¹³ *Asahi*, 20 January 1955.

¹⁴ Ibid., 3, 22 January 1955.

¹⁵ It must be pointed out that the reports were contradictory on this point. An Associated Press dispatch from Washington reported that two Congressmen interviewed by them admitted the existence of a serious issue in Okinawa and the necessity for some improvement in civil administration there: *Asahi*, 14 January 1955. Another dispatch from its own Washington correspondent furnished a completely different account of the responses of the same two Congressmen. They displayed, it said, a very strong dissatisfaction with the Union's view, describing it as being full of 'exaggerations and malevolence', and went further to say that 'the Japanese had no right to criticize us' about this matter: ibid., 15 January 1955.

¹⁶ The *New York World Telegram* gave a small space to that news, whereas

neither the *New York Times* nor the *New York Herald Tribune* referred to it: ibid., 15 January 1955.

[17] Ibid., 17 January 1955. They even suggested a possible connection between the Union's report and the account which appeared in the *Akahata* late in the previous year.

[18] These are among the findings revealed in a survey conducted by the Japan Mathematical Statistics Research Institute *(Nihon Sūritōkei Kenkyūjo)*. See Hayashi Chikio, 'Masukomi no eikyōryoku—tokuni shimbunkiji to dokusha no hannō', *Asahi*, 15, 16 November 1957.

[19] The first account written by the *Asahi*'s correspondent who visited Naha after World War II appeared on 31 July 1949. The reporter seems to be an *Asahi* correspondent usually resident at Naze (Amami Ōshima). It was only in August 1953 that the American authorities gave Japanese newspapermen permission to enter Okinawa. With these minor exceptions, there had been no first-hand reports on Okinawa until April 1955 when a group of Japanese journalists were invited to visit Okinawa by the American authorities. A Naha office of *Kyōdō* was established in 1957 and that of the *Asahi* in 1959. In addition to these the *Mainichi* and the *Yomiuri* as well as *NHK* maintain permanent offices at Naha.

[20] Survey data from the Newspaper Survey Institute study of July 1956 as cited in D. H. Mendel jun., *The Japanese People and Foreign Policy*, p. 130.

[21] See e.g., the column *'kyō no mondai'* in *Asahi*, 15 (evening) January 1955.

[22] An editorial of the *Asahi*, 21 June 1956, argued that the issue in Okinawa concerned not only the life of the inhabitants but also the fate of the Japanese people as a whole.

[23] One of the most candid expressions of this argument is provided by a pamphlet written by an important member of the LDP Okinawa Committee. See Fuchigami Fusatarō, *Korega Okinawa da*.

[24] The column *'tensei jingo'* in *Asahi*, 27 June 1956.

[25] This feeling was expressed by Kishi, the then Secretary-General of the Liberal Democratic Party, when he said to the foreign newspapermen that if the United States had taken a more reasonable view of Okinawa and Ogasawara in the preceding several months, she could have given Japan strong moral support in the territorial disputes with the Soviet Union: *Asahi*, 26 August 1956.

[26] 30 August 1956.

[27] 29 December 1956.

[28] See the fourteenth instalment of Tomihara Moriyasu (the then President of the Ryukyu Bank), 'Kaikoroku—kinyū no uramado jūgonen', *Okinawa Taimusu*, 22 July 1963.

[29] 26 November 1957, 14 January 1958.

[30] A British reporter described the Americans in Okinawa: 'the Americans justify their presence on Okinawa not only on military grounds . . . but also on the grounds of what they are doing for the welfare of the people—and without the least trace of cynicism. "A showcase for Asia", and "A real test for our methods and way of life" are phrases which spring continually to their lips': 'The Impact of America on Okinawa—Military Needs Paramount', *The Times*, 1 March 1957.

[31] *Asahi*, 29 June 1956.

[32] Ibid., 2 (evening) July 1956.

[33] Kishi's 'high posture' received favourable comments in the Japanese press. See, e.g., *Asahi*, 2 (evening) May 1958.

[34] *Yomiuri*, 16 September 1957; also Mendel, op. cit., p. 132.

[35] It was in 1959 that a Naha branch of the *Asahi Shimbun* staffed by reporters sent from Japan was established.

[36] 1 July 1959.

[37] *Asahi*, 1 (evening) July 1959.

[38] Ibid., 2 July 1959.
[39] Ibid., 20 May 1959.
[40] For instance Asato Tsumichiyo, head of the Okinawa Socialist Masses Party and speaker of the Ryukyuan Legislature, said that Japanese opinions on this issue were based upon some misunderstandings: *Asahi*, 5 June 1959.
[41] *Yomiuri*, 23 (evening) May 1959; *Tōkyō*, 26 May 1959.
[42] *Asahi*, 3 September 1959.
[43] Ibid., 24 October, 2 November 1958.
[44] *Yomiuri*, 12 October 1958, also expressed its objection to the Kishi proposal, while the *Mainichi*, 4 October 1958, supported Kishi.
[45] See, e.g., editorial in *Asahi*, 14 April 1963.
[46] The Japanese press displayed its irritation quite frequently, if not so pathetically as the Okinawan press, at the protracted negotiations for the establishment of consultative committees on Okinawa. For example, the *Asahi* took up this question six times in its editorial columns during the two years between the Kennedy statement on Okinawa and the final agreement about U.S.-Japan Consultative Committees on Okinawa.
[47] For the situation of 1951, see the survey conducted by *Asahi*, 20 September 1951.
[48] For the hostile feeling entertained by a Japanese Conservative leader against mass media, see Kishi Nobusuke, 'Political Movements in Japan', *Foreign Affairs*, vol. 44, no. 1 (October 1965), p. 91.

Conclusion

[1] A large part of the following discussion was originally presented in the present writer's article, 'The Okinawa Conflict and the U.S.-Japan Alliance', *Australian Outlook*, vol. 20, no. 1 (April 1966), pp. 36-42. For the study of alliances from a general perspective, see G. Liska, *Nations in Alliance: The Limit of Interdependence*; G. Modelski, 'The Study of Alliances: A Review', *The Journal of Conflict Resolution*, vol. 7, no. 4 (December 1963), pp. 769-76.
[2] For this, see an excellent study by J. Freymond, *The Saar Conflict 1945-1955*.
[3] A recent example of this was provided by the argument of President Park Chung-hee of the Republic of Korea that his government could not afford to let any decision by Japan or between Japan and the United States alone decide the future of the military bases in Okinawa (*Japan Times*, 26 April 1969). For opinions of other Korean politicians and newspapers, see *Asahi*, 19 March 1969.
[4] For the documents related to this subject, see Dennis J. Doolin (comp.), *Territorial Claims in the Sino-Soviet Conflict*, pp. 42-6.

Select Bibliography

BIBLIOGRAPHIES

Higa, S. and Kerr, G. H., *Ryūkyū bunken mokuroku* (*Bibliography of the Ryukyu*), Naha, 1962 (in Japanese and English).
Kinjō Chōei, 'Okinawa kankei tosho mokuroku', *Minzokugaku Kenkyū*, vol. 15, no. 2 (November 1950).
Okinawa Shiryō Sentā, *Shiryō mokuroku*. Tokyo, 1963 (mimeo).
Ryūkyū Daigaku Fuzoku Toshokan, *Ryūkyū kyōdo shiryō mokuroku*. Naha, 1957.
Ryūkyū Seifu Rippōin Jimukyoku Toshoshitsu, *Sengo Okinawa kankei zasshi kiji oyobi shiryō bunken kaidai*. Naha, 1960.
———, *Sengo Okinawa no bunken kaidai*. Naha, 1961.
Sakamaki, S. *Ryūkyū: A Bibliographical Guide to Okinawan Studies*. Honolulu, 1963.
———, *Ryukyuan Research Resources at the University of Hawaii*. Honolulu, 1965.

OFFICIAL PUBLICATIONS

Japan

Gaimushō, *Okinawa binran*, 1960.
———, *Okinawa no genjō ni kansuru kisoshiryō*, 1962 (mimeo).
Sōrifu, *Okinawa shisaku no taiyō*, 1963.
———, *Tokubetsu chiiki kankei hōreishū, sono ichi*, 1965 (mimeo).
———, *Okinawa sankō shiryō*, 1966 (mimeo).
Shūgiin, Gaimuiinkai Chōsashitsu. *Okinawa mondai shiryō*, 1964.
One should consult proceedings of both Houses of the Japanese parliament, especially those of Committees on Foreign Affairs and Budget and Special Committees on the Okinawa Problem. Unfortunately, no index is available for this material.

Ryukyu Islands

Secretariat of GRI Legislature, Administrative Section, *USCAR Legislation 1957.* A complete collection of outstanding pro-clamations, ordinances and directions with amendments thereto issued by the USCAR and its predecessors since 1945, effective 31 May 1957.

Ryūkyū Seifu, *Ryūkyū genkō hōki sōran,* 1961 to date.

———, *Ryūkyū shiryō, 1945-1955,* 10 vols., 1956-1964.

———, *Ryūkyū yōran,* yearly from 1955.

———, *Kōhō.* April 1952 to date. This is a successor to the following three items.

Okinawa Minseifu, *Okinawa Minseifu kōhō,* August 1948 to November 1950.

Okinawa Guntō Seifu, *Okinawa Guntō kōhō,* November 1950 to March 1952.

Ryūkyū Rinji Chūō Seifu, *Kōhō,* July 1951 to March 1952.

United States

U.S. Civil Administration of the Ryukyu Islands, *Civil Affairs Activities in the Ryukyu Islands.* Twice-yearly reports which started in March 1953. From vol. 9, no. 1 (1 October 1959 to 31 March 1960) under the title *Civil Administration of the Ryukyu Islands;* from vol. 11 (1 July 1962 to 30 June 1963) yearly.

———, *Press Release,* irregular (mimeo).

———, *Ryukyu Islands Fact Book.* November 1962 (mimeo).

U.S. Department of State, *Bulletin,* weekly.

———, *Conference for the Conclusion and Signature of the Treaty of Peace with Japan,* 1951.

———, *Foreign Relations of the United States: The Conferences at Cairo and Teheran 1943,* 1961.

U.S. House of Representatives, Committee on Armed Services. *Hearings, Military Public Works, on H.R. 5700, 4 May to 14 June 1955.*

———, Committee on Armed Services, Subcommittee. *Hearings on Okinawa Lands, held at Naha, Okinawa, 24 and 25 October 1955.*

———, Committee on Armed Services. *Report of a Special Sub-committee, Following an Inspection Tour, 14 October to 23 November 1955.*

———, Committee on Armed Services, Subcommittee No. 3. *Consideration of H.R. 1157 to Provide for Promotion of*

Economic and Social Development in the Ryukyu Islands, 31 March 1960.

——, Committee on Armed Services, Subcommittee No. 2. *Consideration of H.R. 10937 to Amend the Act Providing for the Economic and Social Development of the Ryukyu Islands, 9 and 10 May 1962.*

——, Committee on Armed Services. *Report to Accompany H.R. 10937, Amending the Act Providing for Promotion of Economic and Social Development in the Ryukyu Islands,* Report No. 1684, 16 March 1962.

——, Committee on Armed Services, Subcommittee No. 3. *Hearings on H.R. 12617 to Amend Act Providing for Economic and Social Development in the Ryukyu Islands, 23 March 1966.*

——, Committee on Armed Services, Subcommittee No. 3. *Hearings on H.R. 4903 to Amend Act Providing for Economic and Social Development in the Ryukyu Islands, 13 April 1967.*

——, Committee on Appropriations, Subcommittee on Foreign Operations and Related Agencies. *Hearings on Foreign Assistance and Related Agencies Appropriations for 1969, Ryukyu Islands, 25 March 1968.*

——, Committee on Foreign Affairs. *Report of Special Study Mission to Southeast Asia and the Pacific,* Committee Print, 29 January 1954.

U.S. Senate, Committee on Armed Services. *Report No. 2103, Amending The Act Providing for Promotion of Economic and Social Development in the Ryukyu Islands.* 18 September 1962.

——, Committee on Foreign Relations. *Hearings, Japanese Peace Treaty and Other Treaties Relating to Security in the Pacific, 21-25 January 1952.*

——, Committee on Foreign Relations. *Hearings, Treaty of Mutual Co-operation and Security with Japan, 7 June 1960.*

For further reference to Congressional papers on Okinawa see *Monthly Catalog of United States Government Publications.*

NEWSPAPERS AND PERIODICALS

In Japanese

Akahata (Japan Communist Party), Tokyo, daily.
Asahi Jānaru (Asahi Shimbunsha), Tokyo, weekly.
Asahi Nenkan (Asahi Shimbunsha), Tokyo, yearly.
Asahi Shimbun, Tokyo, daily.

Bungei Shunjū, Tokyo, monthly.
Chūō Kōron, Tokyo, monthly.
Gekkan Shakaitō (Japan Socialist Party), Tokyo, monthly.
Hōritsu Jihō, Tokyo, monthly.
Jimbun Shakaikagaku Kenkyū (Bulletin of Ryudai Institute of Humanities and Social Sciences, the University of the Ryukyus), Naha, irregular.
Jiyū Okinawa (Okinawan Federation). No. 1 (15 June 1946) to nos. 7-8 (25 August 1946). The author consulted its Kyushu edition.
Jōhō Tsūshin (Japan Socialist Party), Tokyo.
Kaizō, Tokyo, monthly (until 1954).
Keizai Kenkyū (the University of the Ryukyus), Naha, irregular.
Kokusaihō Gaikō Zasshi, Tokyo, bi-monthly.
Mainichi Shimbun, Tokyo, daily.
Minami to Kita, see *Okinawa to Ogasawara*.
Okinawa, see *Okinawa to Ogasawara*.
Okinawa Jijō (the *Okinawa Mondai Kondankai*), Tokyo, every ten days.
Okinawa Nenkan (*Okinawa Taimususha*), Naha, yearly from 1959.
Okinawa Taikan, published by the Okinawa Asahi Shimbunsha of Naha (which had no relationship to the Asahi Shimbunsha in Japan). The first edition (1953) only.
Okinawa Taimusu, Naha, daily.
Okinawa to Ogasawara (later *Minami to Kita* and then *Okinawa*), Tokyo. Two different kinds of publication are issued by the *Nampō Dōhō Engokai* under the same title; one is published every ten days, the other, quarterly.
Rōdō Nenkan (Ōhara Shakaimondai Kenkyūjo), Tokyo, yearly.
Ryūkyū Shimpō (formerly *Uruma Shimpō*), Naha, daily.
Seisaku Geppō (Liberal Democratic Party), Tokyo, monthly.
Seisaku to Tōron (Democratic Socialist Party), Tokyo, monthly.
Sekai, Tokyo, monthly.
Shakaishugi (Japan Socialist Party), Tokyo, monthly.
Shisō, Tokyo, monthly.
Tōkatsudō (Japan Socialist Party).
Uruma Shimpō (later *Ryūkyū Shimpō*), Naha, daily.
Yomiuri Shimbun, Tokyo, daily.
Zenei (Japan Communist Party), Tokyo, monthly.

In English
Asian Survey, Berkeley, monthly.

Far Eastern Quarterly (later *Journal of Asian Studies*).
Far Eastern Survey, New York.
Foreign Affairs, New York, quarterly.
Japan Times, Tokyo, daily.
Journal of Asian Studies, Michigan, quarterly.
New York Times.
Pacific Affairs, Richmond, quarterly.
The Times, London.
Weekly Okinawa Times, Naha, from December 1965.
World Today, London, monthly.

BOOKS, MONOGRAPHS AND PAMPHLETS

In Japanese

Asahi Shimbunsha, *Amerika senryakuka no Okinawa*. Tokyo, 1967.
——, *Okinawa henkan*, Tokyo, 1968.
——, *Okinawa hōkoku*. Tokyo, 1969.
Bōeichō Bōeikenshūjo Senshishitsu, *Okinawa hōmen rikugun sakusen*. Tokyo, 1968.
Fuchigami Fusatarō, *Korega Okinawa da*. Tokyo, 1957.
Fujishima Udai, *Nihon no minzokuundō*. Tokyo, 1960.
Fukki Mondai Kenkyūkai, *Zenryū kyōtsū seron chōsa*. Naha, 1968.
——, *Fukki modai kenkyū*, vol. 1. Naha, 1968.
Hatoyama Ichirō, *Kaikoroku*. Tokyo, 1957.
Higa Mikio, *Okinawa: seitō to seiji*. Tokyo, 1965.
Higa Shunchō *et al.*, *Okinawa*. Tokyo, 1963.
Higashionna Kanjun, *Ryūkyū no rekishi*. Tokyo, 1957.
Ikema Toshihide (ed.), *Ryūkyū kizokuron*. Naha, 1951.
Irie Keishirō, *Nihon kōwajōyaku no kenkyū*. Tokyo, 1951.
Kamiyama Masayoshi (comp.), *Nempyō: Okinawa mondai to zaikyō kenjin no ugoki, 1868-1966*. Tokyo, 1967.
Kinoshita Junji *et el.*, *Okinawa: hikisakareta minzoku no kadai*. Tokyo, 1968.
Kokusai Jōsei Kenkyūkai, *Okinawa o meguru shomondai*. Tokyo, 1962 (mimeo).
Kokusaihō Gakkai (ed.), *Okinawa no chii*. Tokyo, 1955.
—— (ed.), *Nampōshotō no hōtekichii*. Tokyo, 1958.
Mainichi Shimbunsha, *Tainichi heiwa jōyaku*. Tokyo, 1952.
Makise Tsuneji, *Nijū-shichido-sen no Okinawa*. Tokyo, 1963.
——, *Okinawa henkanundō*. Tokyo, 1967.
Matsukawa Kunio, *Okinawa no kichi keizai*. Tokyo, 1968.

Meiji Daigaku Hōgakubu, *Okinawa no sengosedai no shakaiishiki.* Tokyo, 1963.
Miyasato Seigen, *Amerika no Okinawa tōchi.* Tokyo, 1966.
Morita Toshio, *Amerika no Okinawa kyōiku seisaku.* Tokyo, 1966.
Nakano Yoshio et al., *Okinawa mondai nijūnen.* Tokyo, 1956.
Nakano Yoshio et al. (comp.), *Sengoshiryō: Okinawa.* Tokyo, 1969.
Nakayoshi Yoshimitsu, *Okinawa sokokufukki undōki.* Naha, 1964.
Nampō Dōhō Engokai (comp.), *Okinawa kankei shiryō.* Tokyo, 1957.
———, *Okinawa no gunyōtochi ni kansuru shiryō.* Tokyo, 1958.
———, *Tokubetsu chiiki kankei dantai meibo.* Tokyo, 1961.
———, *Beikoku no Okinawa kanri no hōkō*, series nos. 1-4. Tokyo, 1959-66.
———, *Okinawa mondai kihon shiryōshū.* Tokyo, 1968.
Nihon Bengoshi Rengōkai, *Okinawa shihōseido no kenkyū.* Tokyo, 1961.
Nihon Jiyū Jinken Kyōkai, *Jiyū Jinken Kyōkai Okinawa hōkokusho.* Tokyo, 1961 (mimeo).
Nihon Kyōsantō, *Okinawa Ogasawara mondai to Nihon Kyōsantō.* Tokyo, 1966.
Nihon Shakaitō, *Okinawa: sokuji zemmen henkan e no Shakaitō no shuchō.* Tokyo, 1967.
Nishimura Kumao, *Anzenhoshō jōyakuron.* Tokyo, 1960.
Ōhama Nobumoto, *Okinawa mondai no shōten.* Tokyo, 1967 (mimeo).
Okinawa Henkan Yōkyū Kokuminundō Renrakukaigi, *Shōwa 39-nendo undō hōshin.* Tokyo, 1964.
Okinawa Kaihō Sokoku Fukki Sokushin Kondankai, *Okinawa: sono kaihō wa Nihon no dokuritsu o kansei suru.* Tokyo, 1963.
Okinawa Mondai Chōsakai, *Mizuzeme no Okinawa.* Tokyo, 1957.
Okinawa Mondai Kaiketsu Kokumin Sōkekki-taikai Jikkōiinkai Jimukyoku, *Okinawa mondai shiryō*, series no. 1, no. 3. Tokyo, 1956 (mimeo).
Okinawa Ogasawara Henkandōmei, *Okinawa kokusho.* Tokyo, 1967.
Okinawa Shi-Chō-Son Chō-Kai, *Chihōjichi shichishūnen kinenshi.* Naha, 1955.
Okinawa Zaidan, *Nijūnen no ayumi.* Tokyo, 1967.
Okinawa-Ken Gakuseikai, *Sokoku-naki Okinawa.* Tokyo, 1956.
Okinawa-Ken Sokoku Fukki Kyōgikai, *Okinawa-Ken sokokufukki undōshi.* Naha, 1964.
Ōshiro Tatsuhiro, *Okinawa: genchi kara no hōkoku.* Tokyo, 1969.

Ōta Chōfu, *Okinawa kensei gojūnen.* Tokyo, 1932.
Ōta Masahide, *Okinawa no minshūishiki.* Tokyo, 1967.
———, *Minikui Nihonjin: Nihonjin no Okinawa ishiki.* Tokyo, 1969.
Ōta Masahide and Tsujimura Akira, *Okinawa no genron: shimbun to hōsō.* Tokyo, 1966.
Oyadomari Masahiro, *Okinawa keizai o ninau hitobito.* Naha, 1962.
Ryūkyū Daigaku Keizai Kenkyūjo, *Ryūkyū keizai no kenkyū.* Tokyo, 1964.
———, *Okinawa keizai kaihatsu no kihon to tembō.* Naha, 1968.
Ryūkyū Shimpōsha, *Okinawa no seron,* series nos. 1-3. Naha, 1967-8.
——— (ed.), *Kichi Okinawa.* Tokyo, 1968.
Sakihara Hisashi, *Ryūkyū jinji roku.* Naha, 1961.
Senaga Kamejirō, *Minzoku no higeki.* Kyoto, 1959.
———, *Okinawa kara no hōkoku.* Tokyo, 1959.
Taira Tatsuo, *Sengo no seikai rimenshi.* Naha, 1963.
Takano Yūichi, *Nihon no ryōdo.* Tokyo, 1962.
Tokonami Tokuji, *Okinawa no sokokufukki o meguru mondaiten.* Tokyo, 1964 (mimeo).
Tōkyō Okinawa Kenjinkai, *Dai-4-kai Tōkyō Okinawa Kenjinkai teiki taikai gian narabini shiryō.* Tokyo, 1959 (mimeo).
Ueda Kōichirō, *1970-nen to ampo-Okinawa mondai.* Tokyo, 1968.
Uenuma Hachirō, *Okinawa kyōikuron.* Tokyo, 1966.
Urazaki Jun, *Kieta Okinawa-Ken.* Naha, 1965.
Yara Chōbyō, *Watakushi no ayunda michi.* Naha, 1968.
Yoshida Shien, *Nampō shotō.* Tokyo, 1962.
Yoshida Shigeru, *Kaisō jūnen.* Tokyo, 1958.
Yoshino Toshihiko, *Ryūkyū ryokōki.* Tokyo, 1960.

In English

American Assembly, *The United States and the Far East.* New York, 1956.
Appleman, R. E. *et al., U.S. Army in World War II, The War in the Pacific, Okinawa: The Last Battle.* Washington, 1948.
Byrnes, J. F., *Speaking Frankly.* London, 1947.
Cary, J., *Japan Today: Reluctant Ally.* New York, 1962.
Conlon Associates Ltd., *United States Foreign Policy—Asia: Studies Prepared at the Request of the Committee on Foreign Relations, U.S. Senate.* November 1959.

Council on Foreign Relations, *Japan between East and West*. New York, 1957.

Dewey, T. E., *Journey to the Far East*. Washington, 1952.

Dunn, F. S., *Peace-Making and the Settlement with Japan*. Princeton, 1963.

Fairbank, J. K. (ed.), *The Chinese World Order*. Cambridge (Mass.), 1968.

Higa, M., *Politics and Parties in Postwar Okinawa*. Vancouver, 1963.

Japan Civil Liberties Union, *Report on the Human Rights Problem in Okinawa*. Tokyo, 1961 (mimeo).

Kerr, G. H., *Okinawa: The History of an Island People*. Tokyo, 1958.

Marion, G., *Bases and Empire: A Chart of American Expansion*. New York, 1948.

Mendel, D. H., jun., *The Japanese People and Foreign Policy: A study of public opinion in post-Treaty Japan*. Berkeley, 1961.

Murphy, R., *Diplomat Among Warriors*. London, 1964.

Nampō Dōhō Engokai, *Okinawa Problem: The most important problem pending between the United States and Japan*. Tokyo, 1967 (mimeo).

Olson, L., *Dimensions of Japan*. New York, 1963.

Packard, G. R., *Protest in Tokyo: The Security Treaty Crisis of 1960*. Princeton, 1966.

Passin, H. (ed.), *The United States and Japan*. Englewood Cliffs, N.Y., 1966.

Reischauer, E. O. et al., *Japan and America Today*. Stanford, 1953.

Reischauer, E. O., *The United States and Japan*. Cambridge (Mass.), 1957.

Syracuse University, Maxwell Graduate School of Citizenship and Public Affairs, *United States Foreign Policy: the operational aspects of U.S. foreign policy* (prepared at the request of the U.S. Senate Committee on Foreign Relations). 1959.

Tokonami Tokuji, *Review of the Okinawa Problem*. Tokyo, 1963.

Van Aduard, E. J. Lewe, *Japan: From Surrender to Peace*. The Hague, 1953.

PERIODICAL ARTICLES

In Japanese

One should remember that the following list represents only a very small portion of periodical literature written in Japanese on this subject. For further references, consult *Zasshi kiji sakuin* issued quarterly by the National Diet Library, Tokyo.

Abe Tomoji *et al.*, 'Satō gaikō no kyojitsu: Okinawa, Nicchū mondai o chushin ni', *Sekai*, 264 (November 1967).

Arasaki Moriteru, 'Tenki ni tatsu sokokufukki undō', *Sekai*, 211 (July 1963).

Baldwin, R. N. *et al.*, 'Okinawa jiyū, jinken', *Hōritsu Jihō*, vol. 30, no. 10 (October 1959).

Hidaka Rokurō *et al.*, 'Haisen 22-nen: Nihon no seiji to Okinawa no genjitsu', *Sekai*, 261 (August 1967).

Hiraga Kenta, 'Okinawa oyobi Okinawajin no chii', *Kokusaihō Gaikō Zasshi*, vol. 55, no. 6 (December 1955).

Ikema Hajime, 'Okinawa kichi hakusho', *Sekai*, 287 (October 1969).

Kawada Tadashi *et al.*, 'Nichibei ampo to 1970-nendai', *Sekai*, 290 (January 1970).

Kokuba Kōtarō, 'Okinawa to Amerika teikokushugi', *Keizai Hyōron*, vol. 11, no. 1 (January 1962).

———, 'Okinawa no Nihon fukkiundō to kakushin seitō', *Shisō*, 452 (February 1962).

Makise Tsuneiji, 'Okinawa ni okeru minzokuishiki no keisei to hatten', *Shisō*, 448 (October 1961).

———, 'Okinawa seitōron', *Shisō*, 458 (August 1962).

Miyasato Seigen, 'Okinawa shisei no genjitsu', *Chūō Kōron*, vol. 79, no. 12 (December 1964).

Nagamine Akio *et al.*, 'Okinawa rippōin-giin ni kiku', *Sekai*, 229 (January 1965).

Nakano Yoshio *et al.*, 'Okinawa wa shuchōsuru', *Sekai*, 275 (October 1968).

Nihon Bengoshi Rengōkai, 'Ryūkyū rettō keihō no kenkyū hōkokusho', *Hōritsu Jihō*, vol. 31, no. 11 (October 1959).

———, 'Okinawa hōkokusho', *Hōritsu Jihō*, special issue (March 1968).

Nihon Jiyū Jinken Kyōkai, 'Okinawa ni okeru jinken mondai', *Hōritsu Jihō*, vol. 27, no. 3 (March 1955).

Nishimura Kumao, 'Okinawa kizoku no kimaru made', *Asahi Jānaru*, vol. 1, no. 15 (21 June 1959).

———, 'Ampojōyaku kaitei no rekishi', *Kokusaihō Gaikō Zasshi*, vol. 59, nos. 1-2 (July 1960).

Obata Misao *et al.*, 'Okinawa henkan to 70-nen ampo', *Sekai*, 289 (December 1969).

Ōe Kenzaburō, 'Okinawa no sengo sedai', *Sekai*, 235 (June 1965).

Ōtsuka Akira, 'Wagakuni no Okinawaenjo no gaiyō', *Toki no Hōrei*, 454 (13 March 1963).

Sakamoto Yoshikazu, 'Fukkiundō no shisō to wa nanika, *Sekai*, 265 (December 1967).

Senaga Kamejirō, 'Sokoku ni uttaeru', *Sekai*, 145 (January 1958).

Shimabukuro Kuni *et al.*, 'Okinawa ni okeru hō to jiyū', *Hōritsu Jihō*, vol. 30, no. 10 (October 1959).

Shimota Seiji, 'Okinawa minzokuishiki no mondai', *Bungaku*, vol. 27, no. 8 (August 1959).

Shinsato Keiji *et al.*, 'Gendai Okinawa no rekishi', *Rekishi Hyōron*, 83 (January 1957).

Sugiyama Shigeo *et al.*, 'Jūhachinen-me no Okinawa', *Sekai*, 212 (August 1963).

Takahashi Minoru, 'Hembōsuru kichi Okinawa', *Sekai*, 258 (May 1967).

Unno Shinkichi *et al.*, 'Okinawa o meguru hōritsu mondai', *Hōritsu Jihō*, vol. 27, no. 3 (March 1955).

Watanabe Akio *et al.*, 'Satō shushō hōbei to Okinawa mondai', *Chūō Kōron*, vol. 82, no. 13 (December 1967).

In English

Ballantine, J. W., 'The future of the Ryukyus', *Foreign Affairs*, vol. 31, no. 4 (July 1953).

Barr, J., 'The Ryukyu Islands—A U.S. bastion in the Pacific', *World Today*, vol. 17, no. 5 (May 1961).

Braibanti, R., 'The outlook for the Ryukyus', *Far Eastern Survey*, 22 (June 1953).

———, 'The Ryukyu Islands: Pawn of the Pacific', *American Political Science Review*, vol. 48, no. 4 (December 1954).

Dulles, J. F., 'Policy for security and peace,' *Foreign Affairs*, vol. 32, no. 3 (April 1954).

Emmerson, J. K., 'Japan: Eye on 1970', *Foreign Affairs*, vol. 47, no. 2 (January 1969).

Fairbank, J. K. and Teng, S. Y., 'On the Ch'ing tributary system', *Harvard Journal of Asiatic Studies*, 6 (June 1941).

Ford, C. B., 'Occupation experience on Okinawa', *Annals of the American Academy of Political and Social Sciences*, 267 (January 1950).

Haring, D. G., 'Amami-Gunto: Forgotten islands', *Far Eastern Survey*, vol. 21, no. 16 (November 1952).

Harper, N. D., 'Australia and the peace settlement with Japan', in Australian Institute of International Affairs, *Australian Papers for Eleventh Conference of Institute of Pacific Relations* (Lucknow, 1950).

Higa, M., 'Okinawa: Recent political development', *Asian Survey*, vol. 3, no. 9 (September 1963).

———, 'The Reversion theme in current Okinawan politics', *Asian Survey*, vol. 7, no. 3 (March 1967).

Karasik, D. D., 'Okinawa: A problem of administration and reconstruction', *Far Eastern Quarterly*, vol. 7, no. 3 (May 1948).

Kerr, G. H., 'Sovereignty of Liuch'iu Islands', *Far Eastern Survey*, vol. 14, no. 8 (April 1945).

Kublin, H., 'The Attitude of China during the Liu-ch'iu controversy, 1871-1881,' *Pacific Historical Review*, vol. 18, no. 2 (May 1949).

Lattimore, E., 'Pacific ocean or American lake?', *Far Eastern Survey*, vol. 14, no. 22 (November 1945).

Lineberger, P. M. A., 'America's Okinawa policy', *World Affairs*, vol. 126, no. 2 (Summer 1963).

McGuire, F. G., 'Mace-B bases readied on Okinawa', *Missiles and Rockets*, 13 March 1961.

Miyasato, S., 'Hopes and realities in Okinawa', *Japan Quarterly*, vol. 12, no. 2 (April-June 1965).

Quigg, P. W., 'Japan in neutral', *Foreign Affairs*, vol. 44, no. 2 (January 1966).

Reischauer, E. O., 'Our dialogue with Japan', *Foreign Affairs*, vol. 45, no. 2 (January 1967).

Sakai, R. K., 'The Satsuma-Ryukyu trade and the Tokugawa seclusion policy', *Journal of Asian Studies*, vol. 23, no. 3 (May 1964).

Sakamaki, S., 'Ryukyu and Southeast Asia', *Journal of Asian Studies*, vol. 23, no. 3 (May 1964).

Smirov, I., 'Okinawa: U.S. military base', *International Affairs* (Moscow), December 1962.

Smith, H., 'Economy of the Ryukyu Islands', *Far Eastern Survey*, vol. 20, no. 10 (May 1951).

Stires, F. H. 'Ryukyus: An American dependency—An analysis of the military and civil administrations of the Ryukyu Islands, 1945-1958'. Unpublished dissertation, Department of Government, Georgetown University, September 1960.

Wakaizumi, K., 'Japan beyond 1970', *Foreign Affairs*, vol. 47, no. 3 (April 1969).

Walker, G., 'Peace: Japanese style—"Treaty Bureau" lets out "secret" version of what would be acceptable', *Christian Science Monitor* (Weekly Magazine Section), 24 January 1948.

Warner, D., 'Our fire brigade on Okinawa', *The Reporter*, 23 (13 October 1960).

Watanabe, A., 'Okinawa in United States strategy, *Australia's Neighbours* (Melbourne), 4th series, nos 8-9 (September-October 1963).

———, 'The Okinawa conflict and the U.S.-Japan alliance', *Australian Outlook*, vol. 20, no. 1 (April 1966).

Weiss, L., 'U.S. military government on Okinawa', *Far Eastern Survey*, vol. 15, no. 15 (July 1946).

Wurfel, D., 'Okinawa: Irredenta on the Pacific', *Pacific Affairs*, vol. 35, no. 4 (Winter 1962-3).

Index

Acheson, Dean, 21, 138
Afro-Asian Solidarity Organization, 146
Aichi Kiichi, 76
Allied Council for Japan, 21, 174
Allison, J. M., 87
Amami Agreement (1953): conclusion, 33-4; discussed at Diet, 34; significance in America's Okinawa policy, 34-5, 40; criticized by Shigemitsu, 122
Amami-Ōshima, Is., 62, 98, 101, 112, 113, 127, 139, 152, 153
American Civil Liberties Union (ACLU), 140, 160, 196
Ampo kōgai, see kichi kōgai
Asahi Shimbun: on revision of Security Treaty, 125, 160; on human rights problem in Okinawa, 140; reports on Okinawa, 150-62; circulation, 198
Asanuma Inajirō, 115, 193
Asato Tsumichiyo, 201
Ashida Hitoshi, 23, 27, 99-100, 112, 116, 137, 192
Asian Lawyers' Conference, 140
Atlantic Charter, 97, 112
Australia, 28, 184

B-52 strategic bombers, 15, 60, 64, 66-7, 77, 182
Baldwin, Roger N., 140, 160; *see also* American Civil Liberties Union
Bonin, Is., *see* Ogasawara
Booth, Gen. D. P., 46, 89
Byrnes, James F., 173

Cairo Proclamation, 18, 114
Caraway, Gen. Paul W., 46, 47-8, 51-3, 57, 58, 180

Chiang Kai-shek, 18, 171
China, 34, 215; historical relations with Okinawa, 4-7; dispute with Japan over Okinawa, 7-8; claim to Okinawa at Cairo, 18; *see also* People's Republic of China; Republic of China.
Chishima (Kurile), Is., 19-20, 23, 84, 101, 111, 112, 113, 114, 115, 116, 118, 129, 156-7, 167.
Chūō Kōron, 146
Collins, Gen. W. R., 63
Colonialism: United States accused of, 40, 157-8; *see also* United Nations
Cominform, 117
Comintern, 191
Currency conversion (in Okinawa), 45
Cyprus: compared to Okinawa, 157, 158.

Democratic Party, 23, 104-5, 107, 111-13, 118, 120; its attitude on Peace Treaty, 97, 98; *see also* Japan Democratic Party
Democratic People's Republic of Korea, 78; *see also* Republic of Korea
Democratic Socialist Party (DSP), 101, 106, 129, 134; its relations with Okinawan parties, 131-2, 195
Diet (Japanese parliament), 88, 137, 139, 153; Okinawan representation in it, x, 8, 47, 92, 106-7; on Amami Agreement, 23; and foreign-policy making, 96, 103, 105, 107-8; on territorial problems, 100-3, 122; Budget Committee, 103-4; Foreign Affairs

215

L